Revolution in Judaea

Revolution in Judaea

Jesus and
the Jewish Resistance

by Hyam Maccoby

Taplinger Publishing Company / New York

Second Printing
First published in the United States in 1980 by
TAPLINGER PUBLISHING CO., INC.
New York, New York

Designed by Marjorie Reed

Library of Congress Cataloging in Publication Data

Maccoby, Hyam, 1924–
  Revolution in Judaea.

  Originally published by Orbach and Chambers Ltd., London.
  Bibliography: p.
  Includes indexes.
  1. Jesus Christ—Jewish interpretations. 2. Judaism—
History—Greco-Roman period, 332 B.C.–210 A.D.
3. Palestine—History—To 70 A. D.   I.   Title.
          BM620.M3 1980   232.9'01   80-16752
          ISBN 0–8008–6784–X

To Cynthia

Contents

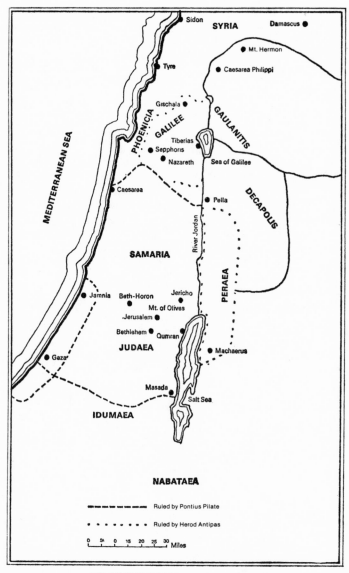

Map labels:
Sidon
SYRIA
Damascus
Mt. Hermon
Tyre
Caesarea Philippi
Gischala
PHOENICIA
GALILEE
GAULANITIS
Tiberias
Sepphoris
Nazareth
Sea of Galilee
MEDITERRANEAN SEA
Caesarea
Pella
DECAPOLIS
River Jordan
SAMARIA
PERAEA
Jamnia
Beth-Horon
Jericho
Mt. of Olives
Jerusalem
Bethlehem
Qumran
JUDAEA
Machaerus
Gaza
Masada
Salt Sea
IDUMAEA

NABATAEA

‒ ‒ ‒ ‒ ‒ Ruled by Pontius Pilate

• • • • • • • Ruled by Herod Antipas

0 5A 0 15 20 25 30 Miles

PALESTINE IN THE TIME OF JESUS

9

Introduction

There are certain advantages in being Jewish when attempting to understand the Gospels, especially if one has been brought up in close contact with the Jewish liturgy, the ceremonials of the Jewish religious year, the rabbinical literature and the general Jewish moral and cultural outlook. Many aspects of the Gospels which, for the non-Jew, are matters for scholarly enquiry, are for the Jew as familiar as the air he breathes.

When Jesus drank wine and broke bread at the Last Supper he was doing what a Jew does every time he performs the Kiddush ceremony before a Festival or Sabbath meal. When Jesus began his prayer with "Our Father that art in heaven . . ." he was following the pattern of Pharisee prayers which still form part of the Jewish Daily Prayer Book. When he spoke in parables and used startling phrases (such as "swallow a camel" or "the beam in thine own eye") he was using methods of expression familiar to any student of the Talmudic writings.

At the same time a Jew reading the Gospels is immediately aware of aspects which do not seem authentic, for example, the accounts of the Pharisees wanting to kill Jesus because he healed on the Sabbath. The Pharisees never included healing in their list of activities forbidden on the Sabbath; and Jesus's methods of healing did not involve any of the activities that *were* forbidden. It is unlikely, therefore, that they would have disapproved, even mildly, of Jesus's Sabbath-healing.

Moreover, the picture of bloodthirsty, murderous Pharisees given in the Gospels contradicts everything known about them from Josephus, from their own writings, and from the Judaism, still living today, which they created.

So here we have a contradiction in the Gospels between those passages which seem authentic and those which do not. To a Jew studying the Gospels the contradiction is manifest, and he wants to know how it arose. And the issue widens as he considers the religion based upon the Gospels, Christianity itself, with its curious mixture of Jewish, non-Jewish and anti-Jewish elements.

How does it come about that a religion which borrows so heavily from Judaism has, for the major part of its history, regarded the Jews as pariahs and outcasts? In a civilization based on the Hebrew Scriptures, a civilization whose languages are permeated with Hebrew idioms, the Jews have been treated with extraordinary hate, culminating in the Holocaust of 6,000,000 European Jews during the second world war.

A study of Jesus with the emphasis on his Jewish background and with the kind of approach that comes most naturally from a Jew may throw some light on these questions which are of importance to both Jews and Gentiles.

I should like to acknowledge the great help and inspiration I have received from long discussions on a wide variety of topics with George Frankl. I wish to thank my wife, Cynthia, without whose unfailing encouragement, keen criticism and constant help the book could not have been started or completed. Finally I wish to thank Michael Chambers for many very valuable suggestions, which I have adopted, on the organization of the book.

1

The Problem of Barabbas

The story of Barabbas makes an excellent introduction to the problems posed by the Gospels. In this episode all the *dramatis personae* come together, as in a focal crowd-scene of a play. The Romans are represented by Pilate (a rare appearance, this, for in general the Romans are surprisingly unobtrusive in the Gospels). All the Jewish groups are represented: the High Priest with his Sadducean followers, the Pharisees, the revolutionary Zealots, the Herodians, and the Jewish masses—all shown united in their hatred of Jesus. If we could really understand the Barabbas episode we would understand the Gospels as a whole; for this episode contains in miniature not only the elements that go to make the Gospel story but also the Gospel orientation and attitude towards the life and death of Jesus.

Let us recall the story, pieced together from all four Gospels. Jesus has been captured and handed over to Pilate. In the same prison where Jesus is lying there is another prisoner called Barabbas, a rebel or bandit. The time is the Passover-festival, and at this time the Jewish crowd of Jerusalem has the right to demand the release of one prisoner. Pilate, the Roman Governor, has been favourably impressed by the personality of Jesus and is also convinced of Jesus's innocence of the charges against him. The crowd begin to shout for the customary release of a prisoner. Pilate seizes the opportunity to offer to release Jesus, the "king of the Jews." But the Jewish priests have been moving among the crowd, persuading them not to accept this offer. The crowd accept the Priests' persuasions and refuse Pilate's offer to release Jesus. Instead, they shout for the release of Barabbas, the man of violence. Pilate, sorrowfully realising that he will have to comply, asks what he should do with Jesus. "Crucify him! Crucify him!" shout the crowd. Pilate is horrified by this bloodthirsty request, which he also cannot refuse. However, he wishes to absolve himself from guilt in the matter, so he publicly washes his hands in token of his innocence. The Jewish crowd, on the other hand, insist on their own responsibility, calling a curse on their own heads and on the heads of their children. And so Barabbas is released, and Jesus is led away to be crucified.

Certain questions present themselves at once. Why, after all, did Pilate have to crucify Jesus? If the Jews had the right to release the prisoner of their choice, that did not give them the right to dictate to the Governor what penalty he should inflict on other prisoners who were not released. One of the Gospels, that of John, gives an answer to this question: the Jews blackmailed Pilate by threatening to report him to Caesar if he did not execute Jesus, for "whosoever maketh himself a king speaketh against Caesar." But why should Pilate have to be reminded of this, especially by the Jews who were not remarkable for their subservience to Roman power? Why is Pilate, the Roman Governor, oblivious of the fact that a claim to be "king of the Jews" amounted to sedition against Rome? So oblivious is he of this that he actually endorses Jesus's kingship, presenting him to the people with the words, "Behold your King!" and asking the crowd, "Will ye that I release unto you the King of the Jews?"

These questions are puzzling enough, but even more perplexing questions arise when we consider the events leading up to the Barabbas incident. Only a few days earlier, Jesus had entered Jerusalem to huge popular acclaim. His Triumphal Entry, as it is called, is described in all the Gospels as an event of national importance. The people hailed him as the Son of

David, and also as a Prophet. As Jesus rode by on an ass's foal the crowd greeted him enthusiastically by waving palm-branches and spreading their cloaks in the road before him. Then came the Cleansing of the Temple. Jesus entered the Temple and in defiance of the Temple police overturned the tables of the money-changers and traders and drove them out of the Temple grounds with a whip. He was able to do this, say the Gospels, because the authorities were cowed by Jesus's strong popular support. "They were afraid of the people, who looked on Jesus as a prophet" (Matthew).

Jesus's Triumphal Entry, according to the Gospel accounts, was on Sunday. On Thursday night he was arrested. On Friday he was dead. And the Barabbas story describes how the final word lay with the Jewish masses, the Jerusalem crowd. They called eagerly for Jesus's death, and insisted that he should die by one of the cruellest punishments known to man.

The crucial question posed by the Barabbas story, then is: Why did a crowd that acclaimed Jesus as a hero on Sunday howl for his blood on Friday?[1] The explanation most commonly given is that the crowd were disappointed in Jesus. They had had great hopes that he was the promised Messiah who would defeat the Romans and restore Jewish independence. Instead, he had been easily overcome and had accepted his defeat and arrest with passive meekness and silence. Barabbas, on the other hand, was a man of violence. He too had been overcome and arrested; but no doubt he had shown great qualities of violent resistance which had endeared him to the crowd. Consequently, with the fickleness of crowds, they switched their allegiance to Barabbas. Their previous enthusiastic love for Jesus turned to hatred and contempt, and in this mood they were easily persuaded by the high priests and elders to demand Jesus's death.

This is no doubt the impression that the story is intended to convey. Jesus stands for a lofty pacifism, while Barabbas stands for the materialism of violence. The unspiritual crowd do not understand that Jesus is not the grossly successful Messiah whom they had been expecting. His kingdom is not of this world; he is the Son of God who must suffer defeat and death in order to atone for the sins of mankind. The choice of Barabbas was a choice of this world, and a rejection of the Kingdom of the spirit.

However, the difficulties of the crowd's change of attitude remain. Jesus had entered Jerusalem on Palm Sunday in the style of a monarch, and had accepted without demur the kind of welcome reserved for a claimant to the throne. His action in expelling the money-changers from the Temple certainly showed no pacifism or general principle against violent action. He had issued swords to his disciples (Lk. xxii. 38), and there had been some resistance at the time of his arrest. The Jewish populace had no reason to suppose that Jesus was a pacifist. His intention to endure crucifixion without a struggle had been confided only to his closest intimates, and even they did not quite believe it. The crowd, who knew of Jesus's miracle-cures, would not despair of his eventual success just because he had been arrested. They would be waiting expectantly for some miracle on his part, such as the crumbling of the walls of his prison. Such a miracle would be part of their picture of the Messiah. The fact that Jesus disdained the support of a regular army, that he was silent for the most part to the charges made against him, would have argued his quiet confidence in supernatural support on which he would surely call when the time was ripe. And when the Roman Governor came forward, obviously impressed and awed by Jesus, and offered to release him, this would have been regarded by the crowd as the very miracle for which they had been waiting. Roman Governors were not usually disposed to favour a pretender to the throne; one, moreover, who had entered Jerusalem with a high hand in the style of a conqueror. Clearly, God had made the Roman Governor mad in order to destroy him.

Instead of seeing Pilate's offer as the confirmation of their hopes in Jesus, the crowd turned against him and with extraordinary spite called for his death. Popularity is liable to wane and crowds are notoriously fickle, but such fickleness would ordinarily lead to neglect, not to active persecution. One could understand the crowd forgetting Jesus if a glamorous new hero came along. Barabbas, as it happens, was no more successful than Jesus. He too had been arrested and put in prison. And it was not as if Barabbas was Jesus's enemy, so that support for Barabbas necessarily implied antagonism for Jesus. Both men lay in the prison of the Roman Governor for what must have seemed to the crowd very similar reasons. Both had become objects of suspicion to the occupying authorities because of their popularity among the native population who were becoming restive with hopes of liberation from Roman rule. The situation was not at all like that of the fickle Roman crowd depicted in Shakespeare's "Julius Caesar," switching their allegiance from Pompey to Caesar, from Caesar to Brutus, and then from Brutus to Antony. All these switches were from one leader to his deadly enemy. The analogy often drawn between this Roman crowd and the Jewish crowd depicted in the Gospels is false. The Jewish crowd is not just fickle; it is inexplicably treacherous and malicious; it shows a motiveless hatred which clearly serves some purpose of the narrator, but has no probable basis in reality.

It should be noted that only the latest account, that of John, describes Barabbas as a "bandit." The earlier three accounts describe him as a rebel. Evidently John wishes to emphasize the senseless malice of the Jews even more, by representing them as preferring a mere robber to Jesus. The words "robber" and "bandit" have been used throughout history to denigrate freedom-fighters. The Greek word for "bandit" (lestes) was frequently used to describe the Jewish freedom-fighters by those who were unsympathetic to them. Even actual bandits never gain popular esteem unless they have some social aims; at the very least a propensity to rob the rich and help the poor. In John's account, the Jews favoured Barabbas just because he was a bandit. They are left without any excuse for their choice.

The historical use to which the story of Barabbas was put is plain enough. It was used, time and again, as a weapon against the Jews; as proof that responsibility for the death of Jesus lay not with a minority of priests or elders, but with *the whole Jewish people*. It was vital to the Christian Church to establish itself as the true Israel, to prove that the Jews had forfeited their position as the people of God by their betrayal of Jesus, and that all the Old Testament "promises" now applied not to the Jews but to the Christian Church. This story, then, was of the greatest importance, for it showed the Jews rejecting Jesus and taking upon themselves the responsibility for his crucifixion. The cry of the Jewish crowd, "Crucify him! Crucify him!" was the basis of the Christian treatment of the Jews as a guilty nation.

Was this the purpose of the Barabbas story itself, or was this just an interpretation put on it by the Christian Church? Was the Barabbas incident simply an invention inserted into the record in order to discredit the Jews and saddle them with the corporate responsibility for Jesus's death? If so, how did the story develop? Surely there must have been some kernel of truth, however many distortions it may subsequently have undergone? How can we account for the crowd-scene outside Pilate's residence, the calling of the crowd for the release of a prisoner, the name "Barabbas" itself? Even if we reject the story as the literal truth, we must give some explanation of it as an element in the Gospels.

Another difficulty in the Barabbas story, just as puzzling as the contradictory and malicious behaviour of the crowd, is the part played by the Roman Governor, Pilate. Unlike Barabbas, Pilate is mentioned in writings outside the New Testament. It is possible, therefore, to obtain an independent assessment of his character. In the Gospels he is shown as being mild and good natured. The picture that emerges from the accounts of Philo and Josephus is entirely different: he is cruel, rapacious and corrupt. He was responsible for many unjust executions and was finally dismissed from office for carrying out a senseless massacre. The New Testament itself contains a hint of this in its reference to "the Galileans whose blood Pilate had mixed with their sacrifices" (Lk. xiii.1). Yet the picture given in the Barabbas incident is of a man who, at the worst, can be accused of weakness; a well-meaning person, anxious to avoid injustice, reluctant to shed blood, but easily intimidated by a hostile mob.[2]

But even if Pilate had been an honest, conscientious official, the role given to him in the Barabbas story does not make sense. Why is he so unaware of the political implications of the title "King of the Jews" that he actually presents Jesus to the crowd as their king? Why is he helpless in face of the crowd's determination to bring about Jesus's death? If he is really convinced of Jesus's innocence there is nothing to stop him from setting him free.

The "Passover privilege" itself is another dubious element in the story. There is no evidence in any other source that such a privilege existed, and it is inherently unlikely that the Jews of all the peoples of the Empire had been granted the unique privilege of freeing a prisoner accused of sedition. It would hardly be possible for a Roman Governor to keep an unruly province in order if trouble-makers could be released three times a year[3] at the whim of the very crowd from which sedition could be most expected. Scholars nowadays are almost unanimous in regarding the "Passover privilege" as fictional.[4]

The general *aim* of the story, so far as it concerns Pilate, is to increase the guilt of the Jews by exonerating the Romans. Although the final decision to execute Jesus was Pilate's, and the actual sentence and method of execution were Roman, the authors of the Gospels manage to show that the Romans were not really responsible! The Governor's hand was forced, both by the "Passover privilege" and by the attitude of the Jewish crowd. All that Pilate could do was to wash his hands and bow to the inevitable. However, when one examines the mechanics of the story, one becomes aware of a kind of optical illusion. There is no real reason given for Pilate's helplessness.

We may widen our enquiry at this point and ask the question, "What is the role of the Romans in the Gospels?" Or rather, *"Where are the Romans in the Gospels?"* The answer is that they are scarcely mentioned. Anyone familiar with Jewish history around the time of Jesus must find this very puzzling. The overriding political fact of the period was the Roman occupation of Judaea where the last remnant of political independence had ceased only very recently, (6 A.D., when Jesus was about 12 years old). Yet in the Gospels the Roman Occupation is treated as a matter of no interest or importance. It is as if someone were to write about France in the years 1940–45 without mentioning that it was under the occupation of Nazi Germany. And to the Jews (as to the French) national liberty was not just a matter of politics; it was also of great spiritual significance.

In the whole of the four Gospels the word "Romans" occurs only once (in John xi. 48). This is an extraordinary fact which requires explanation. Like the dog which did not bark in the Sherlock Holmes story, the *absence* of the Romans is of the utmost significance.

Twice, only, is some role assigned to Roman characters. The first occasion concerns Pilate in the story we have been considering. The other occasion concerns the Roman centurion who observes Jesus on the cross and says, "Truly this man was the Son of God"; his conduct being contrasted with that of the Jews who are represented as reviling Jesus on the cross. Both occasions are strongly favourable to the Romans. Pilate and the centurion are represented as sensitive to Jesus's divine status and as pitying his sufferings, in contrast with the Jews who are represented as blind to his divinity and as hounding him to death.[5]

It seems, then, that the Gospels are not only anti-Jewish but also pro-Roman, both in the sense of ignoring and omitting everything which might put the Romans in an unfavourable light (e.g. their domination of Judaea, their idolatry, their rapacity, their cruelty), and also in the sense of representing them as spiritually superior to the Jews.

Why are the Gospels hostile to the Jews and favourable to the Romans? In order to answer this question we must investigate the historical background of the Gospels: the history of the period in which Jesus lived, and *also* of the period (a later one) in which the Gospels were written. It will be necessary to go into the political history of the Jews, and particularly to bring into the foreground the shadowy figures of the Romans who, in the Gospels, scarcely have walking-on parts to play. It will be necessary to bring to life the various Jewish sects and factions whose labels are hardly differentiated in the Gospels, all being united in their malevolence against Jesus. And then it will be necessary to look closely at the people who *wrote* the Gospels to determine why they wrote as they did; why their standpoint was so anti-Jewish and pro-Roman.

Once we have done this we can approach the whole story with more understanding and hope to appreciate the true significance of Jesus and his movement. In particular, we shall be able to offer a solution to the problems of the Barabbas episode in which all the focal difficulties of the Gospel story are encapsulated.

2

How the Romans Came

The Roman Occupation, to the Jews, was a desecration of the Holy Land of the One true God by a nation of cruel and evil idolators. It was a mockery of two thousand years of Jewish history dedicated to the celebration of liberty and the refusal to accept enslavement. That the people of God should be deprived of their autonomy was a horror and a mystery which could be understood only as the preliminary to a new drama of liberation greater even than the Exodus from the slavery of Egypt, the return from Babylon, or the expulsion of the Greek imperialists two hundred years before.

Jesus, however, is portrayed in the Gospels as oblivious to the Occupation. He never appears to question the right of the Romans to dominate Palestine with their troops, to bleed the country for their exorbitant tribute, and to massacre and crucify whenever their power was challenged. On only one occasion, according to the Gospels, did Jesus deign to consider the problem posed by the Occupation. This was when the Pharisees and the Herodians (a strange combination, as we shall see) asked him, "Is it lawful to give tribute unto Caesar, or not?" Jesus's reply, "Render unto Caesar the things which are Caesar's and unto God the things which are God's" has been variously interpreted. For the present, we simply note that this single incident is a very inadequate representation of the enormous fact of the Roman Occupation.

The reasons for the suppression in the Gospels of reference to the Romans will be discussed later, in the context of the political situation at the time of the composition of the Gospels. It is important, at this stage, to make the effort to visualize the situation as it really was; to realise that in Jesus's lifetime Palestine was not a settled Roman province such as Gaul or Greece, that the Jews were far from reconciled to Roman rule, and that there were several serious risings aimed at throwing the Romans out.

How did the Romans come to be in Palestine? How did they first enter the country? What were the stages by which they tightened their hold on the Jewish nation and incorporated it into their Empire?

The Jews were able to trace back their history further than any other nation in the Roman world except the Egyptians. They had lost their independence many times before, but had always managed to recover it. Despite their desperate position as a small nation in a world of warring empires, the Jews saw themselves as essentially a free, self-governing people, not as a client-state compelled to submit to one or other of the power-blocs. Yet in fact it had been a long time since they were a powerful sovereign state secure within its own boundaries—not indeed since the days of David and Solomon (about 1000 B.C.). Ever since then the Jews had been ground between the millstones of great powers whose armies passed to and fro across their land. In 722 B.C., Assyria came and took away into exile a large portion of their people—the lost ten tribes of Israel. Those who were left became known as the Jews after the tribe of Judah, the largest remaining tribe. Later even these were exiled from their land and taken away to Babylon; but when the mild rule of the Persian Empire supervened they were allowed to go back and set up their state again, (516 B.C.). Here, under Ezra and his successors, a republican theocracy was set up, governed by the Law of Moses as administered by Scribes and Priests.

The Persian Empire was overthrown by the Greeks, under Alexander the Great. Alexander conquered Palestine in 332 B.C., but treated the Jews with some respect, careful not to disturb their constitution. After Alexander's death the empire was divided between his successors who were frequently at war with each other. At first the Jews were under the Ptolemies who ruled from Egypt and were a tolerant dynasty; but later they came under the more oppressive rule of the Seleucids, who ruled from Syria. It was one of these, the mad Antiochus Epiphanes, who goaded the Jews into rebellion by trying to force them to give up Judaism and adopt the Hellenistic way of life, including the worship of himself as a god. The Jews found a leader, Judas Maccabaeus, who in a series of battles drove the armies of the Syrian-Greek dynasty out of Palestine in 160 B.C., and set up the beginnings of an independent Jewish state. The degree of independence achieved was greater than the Jews had enjoyed for the previous 500 years.

This independence, however, could not last. It was a result of the chaos and "power-vacuum" that followed the death of Alexander, and which was finally resolved by the rise to supreme power of the Romans. For a while, even after the Romans achieved mastery over every other power in the area, the Jews were able to maintain a limited, uneasy independence. The Romans were still engaged in fighting each other for control of their conquests. But once these internal disputes were settled by the establishment of the Imperial dynasty of Augustus, Jewish independence was doomed.

Ironically, the first appearance of the Romans on the scene of Jewish history was in the guise of friends. Judas Maccabaeus, after expelling the Syrian-Greeks, made a treaty of friendship with Rome, (160 B.C.). Rome at this time was already greatly feared by the Seleucid rulers of Syria, and the effect of the treaty was to protect the Jews from further invasion by the Greeks. However, it is a commonplace of history that a small power invokes the protection of a larger power at its peril. The Jews escaped from the Greeks only to enter the sphere of influence of the Romans. This did not become apparent for quite a long time, however, and a useful interlude was gained in which Jewish morale had an opportunity to revive.

It was an outbreak of dissension within the Jewish royal family that was the immediate cause of direct Roman intervention in Jewish affairs. This royal dynasty, the Hasmoneans, were the descendants of the Maccabaean brothers, led by Judas, who had expelled the Syrian-Greeks, (the name "Hasmoneans" being derived from Judas's great-grandfather Hasmon). The early Hasmoneans had been actuated by religious ideals, and were supported by the religious party of the Hasidim (later called Pharisees) who had first put them in power. However, when they adopted secular aims and assumed the title of "king" the Pharisees denounced them, and relations between them became bitterly antagonistic.

There was a brief period between 76 B.C. and 67 B.C. during which Queen Alexandra returned to the early Hasmonean ideal, and ruled in harmony with the Pharisees. But after her death, her two sons Aristobulus and Hyrcanus engaged in a squabble for the succession, and it was this that led to Roman intervention, in the shape of the army of Pompey the Great.

Pompey at this time was fighting against Mithridates, King of Pontus (Asia Minor). One of his officers called Scaurus was stationed at Damascus and heard about the civil war in Palestine between the two Hasmonean brothers, Aristobulus and Hyrcanus. Scaurus scented profit and offered to intervene. Both brothers were prepared to pay him the sum of 400 talents (about $1,600,000) for his support. Scaurus decided that he was more likely to get his money from Aristobulus, whom he then helped by sending a threatening message to Hyrcanus's ally, the Arab king, Harith, who decamped at once. Another officer of Pompey's, Gabinius, also extracted huge bribes from Aristobulus. The Roman vulture had arrived, and this was the end of Jewish independence. From now on, the Romans were aware that there were rich pickings to be had in Palestine.

The other Hasmonean brother, Hyrcanus, had an extraordinarily intelligent minister named Antipater, who understood the art of doing business with the Romans. Antipater was an Arab (Edomite) by birth, but practised Judaism because he came from a region which had been conquered and forcibly converted. When Pompey himself came south to Syria, after defeating Mithridates, the cunning diplomacy of Antipater won him over to the support of Hyrcanus. Aristobulus's bribes had been spent for nothing; and Aristobulus now made the mistake of showing fight to Pompey. Aristobulus shut himself into Jerusalem and defied the Romans. Pompey had a well-trained army of ten legions (50,000 men), one of the most formidable armies ever seen in the region. With typical Roman methodical skill he besieged and took Jerusalem. To the horror of the Jews, the Roman soldiers entered the Temple where only priests were allowed to set foot. The priests were actually performing sacrifices at the time and refused to interrupt the service, whereupon the Roman soldiers cut them down. Then Pompey himself, full of curiosity, entered the Holy of Holies, that most sacred place where only the High Priest could go, and then only once a year on the Day of Atonement. He found no image there, and so confirmed the Jewish claim that they worshipped an Invisible God, (rumours spread by the Alexandrian Greeks were to the effect that the Holy of Holies contained the image of an ass). Pompey did not rob the Temple of its treasures, but the very fact that a Gentile could enter the Holy of Holies with impunity was a terrible blow to the Jews. The Hasmonean dream of independence had now ended. The whole incident was a kind of rehearsal in miniature for the tragic drama of the Jewish War against Rome 133 years later when the Temple was razed to the ground. The massacres of that war were to make the 12,000 Jews killed by Pompey's army seem a mere handful in comparison.

The upshot of Pompey's defeat of Aristobulus, ironically enough, was not the installation of Hyrcanus as king, but the appointment of the subtle Antipater as Governor, with Hyrcanus relegated to the position of High Priest. Thus Pompey inaugurated the Roman policy of ruling Palestine through native quislings who were made responsible for collecting the "tribute," in money and corn, which was the ultimate motive for Rome's policy of conquest.

Antipater now became the Romans' chief ally in Palestine. He helped the rapacious officers Scaurus and Gabinius to extort huge sums as protection-money from Harith, king of Nabataea, and Ptolemy, king of Egypt. Whenever the Jews attempted to rebel against Roman rule, Antipater acted on the side of Rome. When the Jews of Galilee, for example, encouraged by a heavy Roman defeat in Parthia, rose up in revolt, Antipater helped Cassius (the friend of Brutus) to crush them. He also made many influential friends among the Romans, including a young man called Mark Antony, at that time beginning his career as a campaigner in the Middle East.

After the death of Pompey, Antipater attached himself to the new star, Julius Caesar, and was of immense help to him in his campaigns in Egypt. In gratitude Caesar gave Antipater the Roman title of Procurator as well as making him a full Roman citizen, with exemption from taxes. Julius Caesar, unlike most Roman commanders, had a certain liking and respect for the Jews (in this he resembled his Greek counterpart, Alexander the Great); but even Caesar did not forget the purpose of Roman imperialism in Palestine. He enacted that one quarter of the crop every year (except the seventh, which was a fallow year by Jewish law) should be paid to Rome as tribute. This may seem a heavy enough tribute, but it was regarded as a relief by the Jews after the years of depredation since Pompey's conquest. Corrupt officers like Scaurus had enriched themselves, the Temple (whose treasures were spared by Pompey) was robbed in 53 B.C. by Crassus of 10,000 talents of gold (about $40,000,000), and taxes of irregular extent were levied and farmed out for collection to tax-farmers or "publicans" who, backed by the power of the Roman legions, used every cruelty to ensure payment. Caesar forbade tax-farming and safeguarded the contributions to the Temple which were sent regularly by Jewish communities from Spain to Babylonia. He also gave his protection to Jewish citizen-rights and freedom of worship throughout the Roman world. When Julius Caesar was assassinated, he was mourned by all the Jews of the Empire.* If subsequent Roman rulers had been like him there would have been no Jewish War.

It should be emphasized at this point that the Jews of Palestine formed only part of the Jewish people. There were about 3,000,000 in Palestine and rather more than 3,000,000 outside.[2] The Jews had belonged to so many Empires that the centrifugal forces of empire-building had flung them across the whole known world. There was even a Jewish settlement in India dating from 175 B.C. when Alexander's Indian conquests were still attached to Hellenism. Jewish settlements in North Africa and Spain had followed in the wake of the Carthaginian Empire. The Jews were adventurous traders, and were also used by successive empires as soldiers. In Alexandria, the great Hellenistic city of Egypt, the Jewish community numbered about 500,000. The large and prosperous community of Babylonia, which enjoyed virtual self-government under the Parthians, dated from the Babylonian and Persian Empires. But the Jews of the Diaspora, or Dispersion, as it was called, retained their identity because of their distinctive religion. Moreover, frequent pilgrimages to Jerusalem for the major festivals meant that contact with the homeland was preserved.

After the death of Caesar in 44 B.C. the Jews of Palestine soon had good reason to mourn, for Cassius who, unlike Brutus, was not reluctant "to wring/From the hard hands of peasants their vile trash/By any in direction" immediately demanded tribute of 700 talents (about $2,800,000). Antipater was ordered to collect this sum. When some of the Jews showed reluctance to

---

*Incidentally, one of the marks of favour shown by Caesar to the Jews was that Hyrcanus, the High Priest, and all Jewish ambassadors were granted free seats at Roman gladiatorial combats and wild beast shows. The comments of Hyrcanus and the Jewish ambassadors on this favour are not recorded.[1]

pay, Cassius sold the entire population of four towns into slavery. Probably as a result of this, Antipater was assassinated by poison and his role passed to his son Herod, afterwards called "the Great."

Herod was as cunning and resolute as his father. His extraordinary talents, throughout his career, were directed towards making the Jewish kingdom into an integral part of the Roman Empire. He was intelligent enough to realise that this aim could not be achieved by suppressing Judaism or by destroying the distinctive Jewish culture. He therefore played up for all he was worth the Jewish claims for special consideration as the bearers of a faith of awesome antiquity and purity. He rebuilt the Jewish Temple at such lavish expense that it was admired even by the Greeks as one of the wonders of the world. Herod was an efficient administrator, and his astute manipulation of trade relations with Arabia brought great profit to his country.[3]

Despite all this, however, Herod failed completely to reconcile the Jewish people to membership of the Roman Empire. Although outwardly successful, his personal life became more and more gloomy, he became isolated from his people, and he died a friendless tyrant. The moment his death was announced, the Jews rose in rebellion against their Roman overlords.

The main reason for Herod's failure to accomplish his aim was that, as a foreigner, he did not understand the Jewish temper and self-image. Herod, like his father Antipater, was very ambitious; but his horizon was limited by the Roman Empire. The height of his ambition was to cut a great figure on the imperial scene; to hobnob with men like Antony and Augustus on equal, or almost equal, terms. He had no real conception of the Jewish ambition. With their hopes fixed on the coming of the Messiah the Jews were unimpressed by all Herod's glory and were not inspired by his vision of the Jewish role within the Roman Empire. Herod's way was certainly the way of common-sense. The other way led to head-on conflict with Rome, to disestablishment and exile; but the protest against the "peace" of Rome was part of the Jewish mission.

They had not crossed the Red Sea, spent forty years in the desert, survived the empires of Assyria, Babylonia, Persia and Greece, just to finish up as contented contributors to Roman culture.

Herod's position was that of a "client-king." This carried certain privileges, for client-kingdoms, unlike subject provinces, did not have to pay taxes direct to Rome or to undergo military service in the Roman army. Nevertheless, Palestine, like the other client-kingdoms of the Middle East (Armenia, Cappadocia, Galatia and Commagene), was very thoroughly part of the Roman Empire. The main tasks of a client-king were to keep his kingdom in good order and loyal to Rome, and to repulse any attacks from Rome's enemies on the borders of the Empire. Herod could not make any important decision, even involving his own family, without permission from the Emperor. He was liable to be summoned to Rome to give an account of his actions or answer charges made against him. He could be deposed at any time, if he proved incompetent or unreliable.

However, under Herod's regime the Jews of Palestine were spared the more obvious humiliations of Roman rule. No Roman armies overran the country, as in the days of Pompey or Cassius, demanding tribute and selling off defaulters into slavery. Herod had his own army, officered by Jews. When the Roman statesman, Agrippa, came to Palestine in 15 B.C. he came not with an army but as a visitor, Herod's friend, and showed his appreciation of Herod's welcome by generous banquets and a munificent offering to the Temple. It was, on the surface at any rate, a regime of co-existence. While Herod ruthlessly suppressed any manifestations of Jewish nationalism which had an anti-Roman tendency, he encouraged non-political manifestations of the Jewish spirit, such as the legal studies of the Pharisees and the monastic asceticism of the Essenes. Yet at the same time, the process of Romanization was going quietly on. Herod rebuilt the Jewish Temple; but he also built a temple to the "divine" Augustus. He sent his sons to Rome to be educated. And he introduced "the Actian Games"

in the Greco-Roman style, with chariot-races, theatrical performances, athletic events and gladiatorial contests to the
death.

The Pharisees, after initial opposition to Herod (for his illegal
execution of the Galilean patriot Ezekias, in the days when
Herod's father Antipater was still alive), and after suffering
martyrdoms at his hands when he first seized the throne, were
won over for a time by his astute policies. But they began to
realise the direction in which Palestine was heading, and
Herod's reign ended, as it began, with the Pharisees opposed to
his Romanizing policies. The Sadducees, on the other hand,
who had originally been Herod's bitterest opponents (because
of their loyalty to the Priest-Kings of the Hasmonean house),
ceased to oppose him. There were no Hasmoneans left; Herod
had exterminated them all. The High Priest was now always a
creature of Herod's, who appointed and dismissed High Priests
at will. And since the High Priest was always the centre of the
Sadducees' religious life, whoever managed to control him
would also control the Sadducees. They became docile collaborators with Herod and with the Romans.

When Herod died, after a pitiable old age disfigured by
madness and murder, the Jews began to face the realities of
Roman power. No longer sheltered by Herod's formidable
influence with the Roman leaders, they learnt how far Herod
had delivered them into Roman hands. It was in the bitter
conditions of this awakening that Jesus spent his childhood.

3

The Roman Administration

After the death of Herod in 4 B.C. there was no-one to continue his role of client-king, a role which had depended entirely on his personal qualities and his ability to form friendships with the Roman overlords. In the insane suspicions of his last days, Herod had murdered his abler sons and nominated as his successor his son Archelaus, a man who inherited his father's cruelty but not his cunning. This appointment, however, had to be ratified by the Emperor Augustus, for no client-king could automatically choose his successor. Before Archelaus could travel to Rome to receive Augustus's approval he was faced by a rebellion of the Pharisees or "teachers of the Law" who had been in conflict with Herod just before his death. He dealt with the matter summarily by massacring about 3000 of their followers. Archelaus then set off for Rome, followed by his brother Herod Antipas, who hoped to persuade Augustus to make him King of the Jews instead.

The Romans now closed in. While Archelaus and Antipas were sailing to Italy, Roman troops under Sabinus were taking possession of Jerusalem. Sabinus was under the authority of Varus, the Roman Legate of Syria, who had assured Archelaus that the Romans would hold their hand until his return from

Rome. But Sabinus, in the disorder following the death of Herod, sensed that there were pickings to be had. He knew there were treasures in Herod's palace in Jerusalem and even greater treasures in the Temple. The Empire at this time was not yet as tightly controlled as it later became. The corruption and oppression of Roman officials had reached such proportions during the Republic that there was a real danger of killing the goose that laid the golden eggs; even the richest provinces of the Empire, Syria and Egypt, were nearing bankruptcy. Augustus had no intention of allowing anyone to make a personal fortune except himself. But his campaign against corruption had not reached Palestine, which throughout the lifetime of Jesus was ruled by rapacious officials who regarded their position as a heaven-sent opportunity to line their pockets by every kind of extortion.

Sabinus entered Herod's palace and settled there with his 5000 heavily armed Roman soldiers and about 5000 auxiliary troops of other nations. Jerusalem at the time was crowded with Jewish pilgrims who had come to celebrate the festival of Pentecost. Their dismay and horror can be imagined. For 37 years, during the reign of Herod, the Holy City, and indeed the whole of Palestine, had been free from Roman troops. Now these iron-clad monsters were back, defiling the City with their idolatrous standards, ready to rob and slaughter as in the days of Pompey and Scaurus. The palace of Herod adjoined the Temple itself, and it was clear that Sabinus, after completing his survey of Herod's treasures, would turn his attention to robbing the Temple. Memories were stirred of the time (53 B.C.) when the infamous Crassus had robbed the Temple treasury in order to pay for his campaign against Parthia. The people of Jerusalem, augmented by the pilgrims, rose in a body against Sabinus. The battle was won by the Romans with some difficulty and, in the fighting, part of the Temple was set alight. Sabinus took the opportunity to do just what was feared; he plundered the Temple. The Roman soldiers carried off huge sums, Sabinus himself appropriating 400 talents, ($1,600,000).

The Jews however continued to press Sabinus hard, and he

was besieged in Herod's palace. News of what was happening in Jerusalem spread throughout the country and the Jews began to take to arms in various regions, including Galilee, the birthplace of Jesus. This was the first appearance of the famous anti-Roman guerrilla fighter, Judas of Galilee, the son of the patriot Ezekias (Hezekiah) whose execution at the hands of Herod incurred the indignation of the Pharisees.

Sabinus was now in some danger, and wrote to his superior officer, Varus, for help. Varus, though he may have been annoyed at Sabinus's buccaneering exploits, could not let a Roman legion be overwhelmed. He set off with two more legions, together with a large number of auxiliaries, to the relief of the Roman forces in Jerusalem. Having accomplished this, he also subdued the armed bands in the countryside. Now the Jews began to learn what it meant to rebel against Rome. Varus introduced into Palestine a form of punishment which was to become a familiar feature of the landscape; he crucified 2000 of the captured rebels. Jesus, at this time, was about two years old.

Crucifixion is the most barbarous form of punishment ever invented. The exquisite cruelty lay in the long-drawn accumulative agonies. Some victims lasted for as long as three days. The cross was usually T-shaped, and the victim's feet did not touch the ground. It was considered a less cruel method if the victim's hands and feet were pierced with nails as this led to a quicker death. When cords were used the feet were not fastened at all so that the weight of the body was borne by the outstretched arms. This position, which soon produced complete immobility and helplessness, led to gradually increasing constriction and agonising pain. The victim was always naked, and his suffering was increased by the scourging which preceded crucifixion. This was so severe that his flesh would hang in strips.

Crucifixion was originally not a punishment but a form of human sacrifice used in fertility cults because a slow-dying victim was held to produce more beneficial effects on the crop. It was used particularly in the cult of Tammuz, the dying-and-resurrected god of the Lebanon and Phoenicia. Later, crucifixion was used merely as a form of execution, especially when the criminal was considered deserving of the utmost contempt and humiliation. The Carthaginians (who were Phoenician in origin) used crucifixion extensively, and it was from them that the Romans derived this form of execution. According to Roman law crucifixion was confined to slaves or to those who had committed abominable crimes. In Palestine the Romans used crucifixion as a deterrent against rebelliousness. They crucified thousands, perhaps hundreds of thousands, of Jews during the period of their occupation. The cross became as much a symbol of Roman oppression as nowadays the gas-chamber is a symbol of German Nazi oppression. It is necessary to stress this because of the determined effort in the Gospels to associate the guilt of the cross with the Jews rather than with the Romans—which is comparable to branding the Jewish victims of the German gas-chambers with the guilt of *using* gas-chambers instead of suffering from them.

To the Jews, crucifixion was a particularly loathsome and horrifying form of inhumanity. It was outlawed in Jewish law to such an extent that it was forbidden even to crucify a dead body (see Deuteronomy xxi. 23). The fact that the Romans were crucifiers was sufficient to condemn them as savages. The Gospels, however, which condemn the Pharisees, the chief victims of the Roman policy of crucifixion, for various alleged crimes of hypocrisy and complacency, nowhere condemn the Romans for the time of crucifixion, or, indeed, for anything else.

Varus's crucifixion of 2000 Jews in the very year of Herod's death showed the Jews, with sickening plainness, the kind of brutal treatment to which they were now exposed. In one year they had seen their holy places defiled and robbed and the best men of their nation who had risen to defend the shrine, contemptuously tortured to death. It is no wonder that these events, with their attendant despair, gave a great impetus to apocalyptic dreams of God's salvation. Such things could only happen, many devout Jews reasoned, in the throes of the Last

Days. From this time Messianic movements of every kind flourished. One of these was the movement of John the Baptist. Another was that of Jesus of Nazareth.

The immediate outcome of the events of the year of Herod's death was a return to something like the conditions prevailing during Herod's lifetime. Augustus decided, after long deliberations in Rome, to confirm Herod's will and make Archelaus ruler of Judea and Samaria (comprising about half of Herod's realm). The rest of Palestine was shared between Herod's other two surviving sons, Herod Antipas and Philip. Galilee, where Jesus was living, came under the rule of Herod Antipas. Archelaus was not given the title of King, however, as his father had wished; he was put on probation. If he proved a good ruler he would eventually become king. Meanwhile, he had to be content with the title "ethnarch." Augustus had thus decided not to subject Palestine to *direct* Roman rule, but to continue with the system of client-princedoms. However, the dependence of the Jews on Rome, which had been disguised by the flamboyance of Herod's personality, was now plain for everyone to see. The Jewish princes had attended on Augustus, cap in hand, to supplicate for confirmation in their rule; and in their absence Roman troops had given the Jewish people a bitter foretaste of what direct Roman rule would be like.

Direct rule was not long in coming. Archelaus did not pass his probation, and never became king. After ten years Augustus became dissatisfied with him and dismissed him to banishment in Vienna, (Vindobona). His princedom now came under direct Roman rule for the first time since the days of Pompey. Judaea and Samaria were declared to be part of the Roman province of Syria, and a second-class Roman official called a Procurator was appointed to be the ruler of the land of David and Solomon. The humiliation of the People of God was now complete. In Galilee, where Herod Antipas still retained his client-princedom, some shreds of sovereignty remained; but Herod Antipas was a very minor figure compared with his father and was clearly nothing more than a Roman official himself. In his style of life, too, he was more of a Roman than a

Jew. It is his entourage which is called in the Gospels "the
Herodians." The Jews of Galilee disliked and despised him.
They were famous for their fierce Jewish patriotism, and the
events in Judaea affected them deeply. Jerusalem was for them
their capital and Holy City, and that it was now under direct
Roman rule was as much a blow to them as to the Jews of
Judaea. It is quite understandable that the leader of the
anti-Roman movement which now gathered strength was a
Galilean, Judas of Galilee. Even though Galilee itself was not
under direct rule, Jesus grew up in an atmosphere more
patriotic and anti-Roman than if he had been born in Jerusalem
itself.

The title "Procurator" was that of a fiscal rather than a
military or political official; the title means something like
"Chief Tax-inspector."[1] The chief task of the Procurator, then,
was to collect taxes from Judaea. The Jews, of course, had been
forced to pay taxes under their own kings, but the situation was
now very different. Herod, despite his huge expenditure, had
improved the country's agriculture and through his astute
policy of cornering the rich trade in spices from Arabia, had
doubled the revenue of his kingdom and was even able, in some
years, to remit his subjects' taxes altogether. The Arabian trade
now went straight to Rome and did nothing to ease the Jewish
tax-payers' burden. The Procurators had little interest in
schemes of economic betterment for the country. They knew
that their term of office was likely to be short and that they
would probably never again have such an opportunity to enrich
themselves by dipping their hands into the Imperial till. The
next Emperor, Tiberius, had a policy of keeping such officials
in office for longer periods, on the principle, as he said, that
gorged horse-flies suck less blood than fresh ones. This saying,
which is usually quoted to show Tiberius's humanitarian
concern for the subjects of Rome, also shows his cynical
acceptance of the fact that Roman governors were out for their
own enrichment.

The first years of direct rule in Judaea are unfortunately
poorly documented. We do know, however, that there were

four Procurators in the space of 20 years (6 A.D. to 26 A.D.). Their names were Coponius (6-9), Marcus Ambibulus (9-12), Annius Rufus (12-15) and Valerius Gratus (15-26). On Tiberius's principle, such frequently-changing officials must have been horse-flies of continually ungorged appetite. We know from the Roman historian Tacitus that the Jews sent a delegation to Rome during this period to protest about their sufferings from over-taxation (17 A.D.). We know also that the infamous system of tax-farming which had been abolished by Julius Caesar was re-instituted as soon as the Romans moved in. This amounted to handing over the collection of taxes to private contractors (who were little better than gangsters) whose profit on the deal depended on collecting as much as possible over and above the face-value of the taxes. Details of the activities of these tax-farmers (called in the New Testament "publicans") can be found in the writings of Philo. They hired gangs of ruffians who demanded such huge sums that their victims often fled in despair. When this happened, the tax-collectors tortured the fugitive's family on racks, wheels and other appliances of torture in order to make them either disclose the whereabouts of the fugitive or make payment in his stead. Suicides were common in order to avoid this torture. If all else failed, the victim or his family were sold into slavery. The tax-collectors could always call on the Roman army for support, if necessary. The tax-farming contracts were usually given to Roman citizens whose underlings were recruited from the worst elements of the country on whom they battened. These wretches who were prepared to join in the organized robbery of their own countrymen for the sake of a percentage of the loot were regarded as criminals by their compatriots. These are the "publicans" with whom Jesus consorted in order to reclaim them from sin. If they were social outcasts, it was for good reason. It was the measure of Jesus's optimism and faith that he hoped to reclaim even these most abandoned of torturers and extortionists.

It is not surprising that the appearance of the "publicans" was a signal for revolt. The first act of the new government was to institute a census of the inhabitants of Judaea and Samaria. The Prefect of Syria himself, whose name was Quirinius, came to Judaea to conduct this census, together with the newly-appointed Procurator, or Chief Tax-inspector, Coponius. This took place in 6 A.D., after the banishment of Archelaus, when Jesus was about 12 years old. (The Gospel of Luke gets this wrong, antedating the census of "Cyrenius" by twelve years to the time of Herod; no Roman census ever took place in a client-kingdom, and in any case the census did not include Galilee which remained a client-princedom.) The Jews understood well enough that the census was the preliminary to taxation. It was the resistance to this census that led to the founding of the Zealot party by Judas of Galilee, a Pharisee rabbi. Of the Zealots Josephus says, "These men agree in all other things with the Pharisaic notions; but they have an inviolable attachment to liberty and say that God is to be their only Ruler and Lord." The Romans crushed the rebellion and Judas of Galilee was killed, (Acts v. 37). But his movement, the Zealots, lived on and they were eventually the chief architects of the Jewish War of 66 A.D.

The census of Cyrenius was a very thorough one, consisting of a valuation of all property and incomes as well as a listing of the inhabitants. The taxes levied were a land-tax, an income-tax and a poll-tax, a water tax, city tax, taxes on meat and salt, a road tax, house tax, boundary taxes, a market tax, as well as various burdensome customs-duties, bridge-tolls, etc.[2] The Jews also paid a voluntary tax for the upkeep of the Temple, and the Romans generously agreed not to confiscate this tax for their own use. (After the Jewish War this concession was rescinded and the Romans collected the Temple-tax for themselves, making it compulsory.) There was no pretence that the taxes collected by the Romans were to be used for the benefit of Palestine. Certain sums were indeed earmarked for public works, but the bulk of the money and goods collected was sent to Rome and paid into Augustus's personal account, the "fiscus." The Romans at this time frankly regarded their Empire as a vehicle for exploitation. The furthest they went in the direction of "trusteeship" was to have a concern not to over-tax to the point of destitution, as when Tiberius reproved a zealous Governor of Egypt for sending to Rome an extravagantly large sum in taxes, saying that it was a Governor's job to fleece the sheep not to flay them.[3] The Roman thinker Cicero gives two explanations of the Roman "right" to exact tribute from conquered regions.[4] One is that the tribute is a fine or indemnity for having had the temerity to resist Roman power. The other is that the Romans own the conquered territory by right of conquest and are therefore entitled to demand rent from the inhabitants. It was not until about 80 A.D. that some bright Roman apologist[5] thought of an explanation more in line with the edifying self-justifications of modern empires: that the Romans were entitled to payment for the boon of the "pax Romana."

In addition to the depredations of the "publicans," the Jews had to endure the exactions of the Governors or Procurators themselves. In the larger provinces Augustus's programme of reform was beginning to have some effect, but in the minor subject areas like Judaea there was as yet little curb on the rapacity of Roman officials. By the time a Roman in public life had succeeded in obtaining a provincial governorship he was usually heavily in debt because of the huge bribes, both to individuals and to the public (in the way of entertainment), that it was necessary to pay for public advancement. The governorship was the reward for these expenditures; here was the point of the exercise, the opportunity to repay one's debts and build up a personal fortune as well. Not only the Governor but the subordinate members of his staff were out to exploit the opportunities for enrichment. Their ingenuity in extracting money from their unfortunate subjects was notorious. For every service, "baksheesh" was required; before a man could see the Governor on a matter of elementary justice he had to pay a host of officials, ending with the Governor himself. For suitable sums of money one could buy "protection" from orders to billet troops, or to supply free grain and means of transport for the army. The Governors were not even above setting up funds for "voluntary" donations to the Governor in gratitude for his services.

At the same time the setting up of Roman rule in a new area was the signal for the entry of various sinister characters from Rome whose business was to profit from the distress of the natives. They advanced loans to those who were hard-pressed to pay the new taxes at up to 50% interest, and sold their debtors into slavery when they had squeezed out the last possible penny. They used their ample funds to corner the wheat harvest and then sold the wheat in areas of shortage at hugely inflated prices. To be taken over by Rome, at this time, was like being taken over by a swarm of locusts. Judaea was not the only sufferer, or even the worst; the peasants of Egypt, for example, where the pickings were richer, suffered even more.

In the Gospels, criticism of Roman rule is carefully avoided. However, some faint echoes of the conditions described above do occasionally creep in. For example, in the Gospel of Luke (iii. 12), John the Baptist is represented as advising the tax-gatherers, "Exact no more than the assessment." Then follows: "Soldiers on service also asked him, 'And what of us?' To them he said, 'No bullying; no blackmail; make do with your pay.' "

In order to enforce their rule the Romans had troops stationed in Judaea. The quarters of these troops were at Caesarea, a coastal town which had been built by Herod in the Greco-Roman style. There was a permanent body of 3000 soldiers at Caesarea and smaller garrisons in the other main towns. In Jerusalem the Roman garrison consisted of 500 soldiers. It is probable that a large proportion of these soldiers consisted of Samaritans, i.e. men from the Palestinian district of Samaria where a variant of Judaism was practised with a dissident Temple on Mount Gerizim. The occupying forces were thus not large, but they could be quickly reinforced in time of trouble from the large Roman force in Syria (15,000 Roman heavily-armed troops, together with about the same number of light-armed auxiliaries). The Samaritans were much disliked by the Judeans, not only because they belonged to a heretical sect, but also because they habitually robbed and killed Jews who entered their territory. It must have been very galling to the Jews to be under the authority of a Roman occupying force in which the traditionally hostile Samaritans were given a prominent place.[6]

Though the usual headquarters of the Procurator were in Caesarea, about 60 miles from Jerusalem, he came up to Jerusalem with a large armed escort at festival times, three times every year, when the large crowds of pilgrims needed to be policed. This accounts for the presence of Pilate in Jerusalem at the time of the arrest of Jesus.

Even more important to the Jews than loss of liberty and physical and economic oppression was the humiliation they now suffered in connection with their religion. Officially, the Romans continued the policy of Alexander the Great and Julius Caesar of respect towards the Jewish religion; but the period with which we are concerned, the lifetime of Jesus, was one in which this official policy was very inadequately realised in practice. The Romans were aware that nothing goaded the Jews to fury so much as an insult to their religious practices or beliefs; so the instructions of the Emperors Augustus and Tiberius (who suceeded Augustus in 14 A.D.) were to avoid any such provocation. In particular, it was agreed that no idolatrous images, including the military standards of the Roman troops, were to be displayed in the Holy City, Jerusalem. However, the Procurators were brutal, narrowminded men, who had no appreciation of Jewish monotheism and saw it merely as an affront to their pride as Romans. The Jews were in continual anxiety that the Temple would be polluted by some deliberate act of idolatry. They had not forgotten the desecrations perpetrated by the Syrian-Greek tyrant, Antiochus Epiphanes, who turned the Jewish Temple into a shrine of Zeus and offered swine's flesh there in his honour. The continuance of the worship of the One God in the Holy City now depended on the whim of the Roman Emperor who might change his mind at any moment and decide to instal the statue of a pagan god or even a statue of his own "divine" self in the Holy of Holies.

That this anxiety was not groundless was shown not many
years later (in 39 A.D.) when the Emperor Caligula did indeed
issue an order that a statue of himself should be set up in the
Temple and worshipped as a god. A general rising of the Jews at
this time was only prevented by Caligula's opportune death.

The Roman Procurators, observing that the Jews were a
people of unusually strong religious feeling, attempted to use
this feeling to their own advantage by exercising control over
the Jewish religious Establishment. It was natural that the
Romans should think that the Temple was the centre of Jewish
worship and that the chief official of the Temple, the High
Priest, was the chief object of veneration and religious loyalty.
In this the Romans were mistaken. Under the influence of the
Pharisees the Temple, despite its imposing rites, had ceased to
be of primary spiritual importance to the Jews, and the
priesthood had long ago lost their spiritual and moral authority
to the Pharisee lay-leaders (or "Hakamim") centred in that
extraordinary institution, the Synagogue. Nevertheless, the
Roman measures to take over control of the Temple were
deeply resented. For example, the vestments of the High
Priest, which were used in the New Year and Day of Atonement
ceremonies, were taken in charge by the Roman Procurator
with the implied threat that in case of insubordination they
would not be made available for the atoning ceremonies. No
doubt the Romans exaggerated the importance of these vestments in the Jewish mind; they thought that the Jews regarded
the garments as having a kind of "mana," like the veil of the
goddess Tanit in the Carthaginian religion the loss of which led
to the disintegration of military morale. This was not the case;
yet the Jews were indeed irritated and resentful to think that
these much-loved vestments were in Gentile hands.

More important was the fact that the Romans now actually
appointed and dismissed High Priests at will. Valerius Gratus,
the Procurator immediately before Pontius Pilate, deposed and
appointed four High Priests. His last appointment was
Caiaphas, the High Priest who was concerned in the arrest of
Jesus. Again, the Romans did not achieve what they expected

by these tactics; the result was not a deeper submission to Roman rule but an increased contempt for the occupant of the High Priesthood. The ceremonial rites at which the High Priest officiated were not invalidated by the fact that he was personally contemptible as a creature of the Romans; but there was no question of such a High Priest having any teaching authority in matters of morals or religion. It had been a long time, in any case, since the High Priest had held such authority. Herod the Great had used the High Priests as lackeys. Before his time, the Hasmonean policy of combining the High Priesthood with the royal throne had destroyed the religious authority of the High Priest in the eyes of the Pharisees and the masses who followed their teaching. Nevertheless, the High Priesthood itself was still an institution of historic importance, and the cynical way in which the Romans manipulated it and reduced it to a mockery was much resented. It was bad enough that Herod the Great had manipulated the High Priesthood. Herod, though an unpopular king of foreign extraction, was at least a Jew, and in his reign the Jews could entertain the illusion that they were a free people. But that the High Priest was appointed to office by an idolator of a foreign nation was a mark of the slavery into which the Jewish people had now sunk.

In 26 A.D. the fifth Procurator, Pontius Pilate, began his term of office. As we have seen, the Gospels portray him as a well-meaning, humane man. From other sources, however, it appears that he was the worst Procurator so far. Philo of Alexandria, the great Jewish philosopher, quotes this judgment of Pilate: "He was cruel by nature and hard-hearted and entirely lacking in remorse." Philo also gives the following account of Pilate's rule in Judaea: ". . . bribes, vainglorious and insolent conduct, robbery, oppression, humiliations, men often sent to death untried, and incessant and unmitigated cruelty."[7] Josephus portrays Pilate as deliberately seeking to outrage the religious feelings of the Jews. He took the unprecedented step of marching his army of occupation from its usual quarters in Caesarea to the Holy City, "in order," says Josephus, "to abolish the Jewish laws." The standards of the

Roman troops contained images of Tiberius Caesar pictured as
a god. To the Jews the presence of these idolatrous images in
Jerusalem was an affront to the One God. Previous Procurators
had all understood that the Jews were prepared to suffer mass
slaughter rather than allow this blasphemy, and whenever they
brought troops into Jerusalem, therefore, they would leave the
offending standards behind. Why then did Pilate depart so
conspicuously from the policy of his predecessors and deliberately carry out this act of provocation? It has been suggested
that he was given secret orders by his patron Sejanus, the
powerful minister of Tiberius.[8] It is thought that Pilate received
his appointment in Judaea through the influence of Sejanus, a
bitter anti-Semite who had helped to foment anti-Jewish
pogroms in Alexandria.

In the event, Pilate's move failed. He had hoped that once the
standards were established in Jerusalem, the Jews would accept
the *fait accompli*. Evidently, his orders were not to push the
matter to the point where the Jews would break out into
rebellion. When he found that the solidarity of the Jews was
complete, he withdrew the offending standards. Sejanus
wished to humiliate the Jews, but not if it would cause
embarrassment with his master Tiberius.

Though Pilate failed in this affair his general conduct of the
Roman administration was brutal and corrupt. It was during
the period of this man's rule that Jesus's public career took
place. It was a time when distress, despair, apocalyptic yearn-
ings and helpless resentment of the Roman tyranny were at
their height. It was a time when no Jew could avoid sharing the
deep unhappiness caused by the Roman presence, when the
Jewish people and especially the poorest among them were
being driven to despair by exorbitant taxes, and when the Jews
were compelled to compare the reality of constant humiliation
with their soaring aspirations as a people. Yet the Gospels
portray Jesus as an unpolitical figure to whom the independence of his people from the yoke of idolatrous, cruel, and
exploiting invaders was a matter of no importance.

4

Romans and Jews

How did the Jews appear to the Romans? And how did the Romans appear to the Jews? It is important to investigate these questions in order to understand the phenomenon of the Jewish Resistance.

From the standpoint of Greco-Roman society the Jews were "barbarians." That is to say, the Jews of Palestine did not form part of the general culture nowadays called "Hellenistic" which dates from the conquests of Alexander the Great and derives ultimately from the great cultural advances of Athens. Hellenistic culture had the same self-confidence and belief in its civilizing mission as could be found, until very recently, in the Western industrial civilization of modern times. Even in centres of ancient civilization, such as Egypt, the Hellenistic culture established itself and proved irresistible. Alexandria, in Egypt, was a great Hellenistic city; so was Antioch in Syria. The fascination of Hellenistic culture came from a compound of many things: the new military science which was copied by all the militaristic powers including the Carthaginians and the Romans; the brilliant life of the Hellenistic city with its citizen assemblies, its theatre, with its repertory of tragedy and comedy, its amphitheatre or stadium for athletic performances and contests, its libraries and universities; its literature, with its tremendous range—poetry in various metres and styles, drama, philosophy, history; and its wonderful discoveries in science and mathematics, an ever-growing fountain of achievement. Even barbarian kings whose lands lay outside the Hellenistic zone were over-awed by the Hellenistic culture and were proud to call themselves, on inscriptions and medals, "Phil-Hellene."

The Romans were originally a barbarian nation but they adopted the Hellenistic culture and eventually, by their conquests, became the dominant power in the whole Hellenistic region. This region was not identical with that comprised by the conquests of Alexander the Great, which had extended as far as India. Areas in the West of Europe and Africa were added by the Romans; areas in the East were lost to the Parthians and other non-Hellenic peoples before the Romans became dominant. The Romans became whole-hearted Hellenists. They abandoned their own crude culture and remodelled their literature on the Greek pattern. They even altered their legends in order to give themselves an Hellenic background; they gave currency to a legend that they were descended from Aeneas, one of the Trojan heroes celebrated by Homer. Yet it is true to say that all this Hellenism did not go very deep. Underneath the Hellenistic veneer, even despite the brilliant Hellenistic literature which they produced, the Romans were still Romans, a nation with war and violence in its soul. Behind the graceful legend of Aeneas, the son of the goddess of love, lay another legend, that of Romulus and Remus, twin sons of the god of War, suckled by a she-wolf. In this legend the city of Rome was founded in blood, for Romulus quarrelled with Remus and murdered him as they worked on the foundations—a Cain-and-Abel story in which Cain is the hero. And the good omen which Romulus saw while working on the foundations was a flight of twelve vultures, showing that Rome would be a warlike and powerful nation, since the vulture is "fond of prey and slaughter." In Rome, Cicero might make speeches in the accents of Demosthenes, or Virgil sing in golden hexameters of the civilizing mission of Rome, but in Judaea the meaning of Rome was the vulture and the wolf. The institutions of crucifixion, of the gladiatorial combat and the wild beast show were the distinctively Roman contributions to Hellenistic civilizations.

Yet as the representatives of Hellenism the Romans felt themselves entitled to feel superior to the Jews, a "barbarian" nation who had actually refused to conform to the Hellenistic mould. Not that the Jews were untouched by Hellenism; but they had the audacity to approach it in a critical spirit, to assess it in the light of their own cultural tradition, to approve part of it and to reject part of it. In Alexandria the Jews (who comprised a large proportion of the population) became very Hellenized. They spoke Greek and adopted Greek names; they studied and even wrote Greek literature. But their main intellectual effort was to incorporate the Hellenic insights into their own Judaic tradition. Philo, the Alexandrian Jewish philosopher, whose life overlapped that of Jesus, created a synthesis of Judaism and Hellenism which later became a model to the Christian Church in its struggle to create a theology. In Palestine itself Hellenism was actively rejected because Hellenistic rulers, about 200 years before the birth of Jesus, had made strenuous efforts to eradicate Judaism and introduce Hellenism by force. Yet even here Hellenism was allowed some value. The rabbis studied Greek science and mathematics and admired the beauty of the Greek language. (A rabbinical interpretation of the verse in Genesis, "God shall give beauty to Japheth, and he shall dwell in the tents of Shem" was "This refers to the Greek translation of the Bible.")[1]

But the Jews had no reason to succumb wholly to Hellenism as the Romans and other nations tried to do, because the Jews had an intellectual and cultural tradition beside which that of Hellenism seemed brilliantly parvenu. The Hebrew Bible is not a book but a whole literature comprising history, myth, lyric poetry and impassioned ideology. Though Hebrew literature lacks the range of artistry to be found in Greek literature it contains qualities that Greek literature cannot parallel: a

majesty and universality, a seriousness of purpose and a sense
of social justice. Other ancient cultures (the Egyptian, for
example) resisted Hellenism, but none resisted it so success-
fully. The Jewish culture was not a fossil, it was still very much
alive.

As for the Romans, they were newcomers even in the field of
Hellenism. The literary works which have raised the name of
Rome above that of mere conquerors were, in the time of Jesus,
achievements of the very recent past (Virgil died in 19 B.C.).
The average Roman, even of the ruling patrician class, would
know very little about them; while among the Jews the Bible
was the subject of elementary education even among artisans
and agricultural labourers. Thus the situation of the Roman
occupation of Palestine was rather like that in China in the 19th
century, at the period of the infiltration of the Western powers
who regarded themselves as representatives of the world's most
advanced civilization, while the Chinese regarded them as
uncouth Johnny-come-latelies.

It was not only the Jews who despised the cultural preten-
sions of the Romans. The Greeks too regarded their Roman
masters as uncouth; but unlike the Jews, the Greeks accepted
their military defeat as final. It was the Greeks who, unprompt-
ed, were the first to offer divine worship to the Roman
Emperor and the goddess Roma. The attitude of the Greeks to
the Romans was sycophantic to their faces and sneering behind
their backs. A symbolic incident was the visit of Nero to Greece
about 30 years after the death of Jesus. Nero, the Roman
Emperor, fancied himself as a musician, singer and poet. He
entered for the various artistic competitions in Greece, taking
the matter with the utmost seriousness and waiting nervously
for the judges' verdict. In every competition he was unanim-
ously adjudged the winner and acclaimed as a genius; while at
the same time the Greeks were laughing among themselves at
the amateurishness of his performances. This incident sym-
bolizes the relationship between Greece and Rome: the pathetic
yearning of the Romans to share in Hellenistic culture and the

complete submission of the Greeks to Roman military power combined with a tongue-in-cheek sense of superiority.

The Jews never adopted this attitude to Rome because they never wholly submitted. Greek culture, despite its magnificence, did not contain the stuff of martyrdom or the will to fight to the end for freedom (though the creed of Stoicism did have its individual heroic martyrs). This is perhaps the reason why the Greeks of the Roman Empire so hated the Jews. The historical origin of anti-Semitism is among these very Greeks who resented the fact that the Jews never lost their innermost freedom to Rome. In Alexandria, where Greek hatred of the Jews was most bitter, the Greeks continually denounced the Jews to Rome as disloyal and were particularly resentful because the Jews had been granted the privilege of not having to give divine worship to the Roman Emperor.

The Jews respected Hellenism, though they had strong reservations about it. They had no respect for Rome which they regarded as a purely militaristic power. They identified Rome with Esau, the warlike brother of Jacob. Perhaps the most distinctive thing about the Jewish cultural tradition, a characteristic which made it unique in the ancient world, was that it contained no glorification of war. The Romans (like the Nazis) really thought that war was the nurse of all the virtues. The Jews fought bravely on many occasions for their liberty; but they regarded war as an unmitigated evil. Their heroes were lawgivers and prophets, not men of war. The exception was King David; but he was not allowed to build the Temple, being a man of blood; and his son, Solomon, who symbolized the ideal king, the Messiah, had a name which means "peace," and reigned in Jerusalem, which means "the city of peace." It was a shocking thing, therefore, that the Romans glorified war.

There was no reason for the Jews to think that the Romans were bringing them the benefits of civilization for which they ought to be grateful. In so far as the Romans were the bearers of Hellenistic civilization the Jews had already had experience of this, since the time of Alexander the Great three hundred years before, and had assimilated as much of it as they wanted. In so far as the Romans were political organisers, able to impose a system of law and order, the Jews had no need of this either. They had a long tradition of self-government; they had been civilised when the Romans were still a band of outlaws. They had their own time-honoured institutions and their own code of law which in humanity and true civilization was superior to that of Rome. Roman culture was disfigured by degrading slavery, infanticide, human sacrifice, judicial torture, cruelty to animals—features which had been banished from Jewish culture.

Those historians, therefore, who complain that the Jews were awkwardly "restless" under Roman rule and ought to have settled down like other nations to enjoy the "pax Romana" are wide of the mark. It was not gratitude for the "pax Romana" which made the other nations settle down under Roman rule; it was fear of Roman might and (even more important) worship of Roman success. The Jews were not success-worshippers, and valued their own culture too highly to wish to see it enslaved.

Moreover, it is important to realise that in the time of Jesus the Roman Empire was only just emerging from its free-booting stage. Though Augustus had begun to make the first movements towards the establishment of respectability, many more years were to pass before the concept of trusteeship became of practical importance. Augustus (Octavian) himself, after his victory over Antony and Cleopatra, had carried off the entire contents of the Egyptian royal treasury. In successive conquests, vast hoards of treasure in the form of gold, silver, jewels, and works of art, were looted by the Romans from Greece, Pontus, Syria and Egypt. Later, under the Flavian and Antonine emperors, when the available accumulations of trea-sure had all been transferred to Rome, the Roman Empire became a single administrative unit and a feeling of responsibil-ity developed; but in the time of Jesus the Romans were still hungrily exploiting their military success. It should be em-phasised, too, that the richest parts of the Roman Empire were in the East, where lay the greatest accumulations of wealth. To the Romans of this time the East was the Eldorado in which fortunes could be made if only one was resolute and ruthless enough. We should think of the Romans of this time not in the image of Marcus Aurelius but in the image of the Spanish conquistadores who looted South America.[2]

Even if one abandons the idea of the superiority of Roman culture, it could be argued that the Jews were unrealistic to dream of freeing themselves from the all-powerful Roman war-machine. There is much more reason in this charge. Palestine was a small land, and the Jews a comparatively weak people. How could they possibly hope to resist the most formidable professional army the world had yet seen, hardened by a continuous tradition of battle for the past four hundred years? Moreover, Palestine, though in itself not a rich land, was strategically important to the Romans since it was a corridor leading to the rich corn-land of Egypt, the granary of Rome. It was important that Palestine should not fall into the hands of Rome's chief enemies in the East, the Parthians, who did in fact occupy Palestine for a brief period 40 years before the birth of Jesus, and who often threatened to occupy it again. Yet despite all this the Jews continued to hope that they could expel the Romans and resume their existence as an independent kingdom.

Why did the Jews alone, of all the nations conquered by Rome, develop a Resistance which continued to struggle for political independence for about 200 years? Why did the Jews hurl themselves against Rome in two bloody wars marked by extraordinary successes as well as by tragic defeat? This phenomenon, dismissed by historians as ingratitude for the benefit of Roman civilization, or as mere restlessness or "turbulence," has never had the attention it deserves.

5

Religion and Revolt: The Pharisees

The motive force behind the Jewish Resistance was the Jewish religion. This is a difficult point for the modern reader to grasp because we are not used to thinking of religion as a political, activist, revolutionary force. Also, the picture of Jewish religion given in the New Testament is that of a rigid Establishment clinging to the status quo, allied to the Romans in opposing any innovation. There is no indication in the New Testament of any conflict between Jewish religion and Roman power. In fact the whole issue of Roman power is played down to such an extent that there is hardly a hint of *any* opposition to Rome. The aim of the Gospels is to present the revolutionary issue of the day as between Jesus and the *Jewish* Establishment. The fact that there was a Roman Establishment against which revolutionary forces existed is veiled so that the Establishment against which Jesus rebelled can be represented as entirely Jewish.

There was one small religious party, the Sadducees, who were collaborationists, supported the status quo, and accepted official posts under the Romans and their hangers-on, the Herodians. The Sadducees were the party of the wealthier

55

land-owners and priestly families. The High Priest himself was a Sadducee, and it is one of the most important points to grasp in New Testament studies that the High Priest was appointed by the Romans. As a member of a quisling minority group he was regarded with contempt by the great mass of the nation. Religious authority lay not with the priests but with an entirely different body of people called the Rabbis, who were the leaders of the Pharisees.

Thus the picture given in the Gospels of a Jewish religious Establishment which supported the status quo is true in so far as it relates to the Sadducees, who were an Establishment only in the sense that they were established by the Romans. As far as the mass of the Jewish people were concerned the true Establishment was the dispossessed party of the Pharisees who held no positions of political power and whose leaders neither sought nor received recognition from the Romans.

There were two great wars waged by the Jews against the Romans (quite apart from many minor revolts and insurrections): the Jewish War of 66–70 A.D. and the Bar Kochba revolt of 132–135 A.D. The first of these is sometimes called the Zealot War, as it stemmed from the activity of the Zealot party founded by Judas of Galilee during Jesus's lifetime.[1] The Zealots were Pharisees. Judas of Galilee himself, and his partner Zadok, were Pharisee rabbis. The Zealots were the militant activist wing of the Pharisee party, sharing all religious view points with their fellow-Pharisees and differing from the majority of the party only on the question of the timing of active resistance against the Romans. The second great war, the Bar Kochba revolt, was entirely Pharisee in direction and inspiration. Bar Kochba himself was a Pharisee (as has been strikingly confirmed from letters of his that were recently discovered)[2] and his chief supporter was Rabbi Akiva, the most influential Pharisee rabbi of the time. So from first to last, the Resistance against Rome came from the Pharisee party.

This statement will come as a surprise to those whose knowledge of the Pharisees depends on New Testament accounts. The Pharisees there are represented as being concerned only to safeguard their own official positions. The idea that such people could take part in subversive activities, that they could risk their lives for freedom, that they could die, as so many of them did, heroically and in agony on the cross, seems quite remote from the New Testament portrayal.

Who were the Pharisees? What were the religious points at issue between them and the Sadducees? Why did the Pharisees adopt an anti-Roman standpoint, while the Sadducees were collaborators? In the Gospels, the Pharisees are portrayed as allied to the Sadducees and the Herodians in opposing Jesus and in supporting the status quo. The Pharisees are not exactly shown as collaborators with the Romans, but this is only because the Romans are such shadowy figures in the Gospels that the question whether to resist them or collaborate with them hardly arises. The Powers-that-be are the Jews; Pilate the Roman appears only as a background figure on whom the Jews call in their vendetta against Jesus and whom they have to manipulate and mislead in various ways in order to wreak their vengeance.

Fortunately, there exists a wealth of source-material from which it is possible to obtain a more truthful picture of the Pharisees. Josephus gives much valuable information about the history and attitudes of the Pharisees, and there is also a huge literature written by the Pharisees themselves.[3] Perhaps the best way to correct the stereotype of the Pharisees as dry-as-dust hypocritical legalists is to read the beautiful liturgy, composed by the Pharisees, which still forms the main part of the Jewish Daily Prayer-book and which was the main influence on the formation of the Christian liturgy.

The central religious distinction between the Pharisees and the Sadducees was on the question of the "Oral Law." The Pharisees held that in addition to the revealed word of God in Scripture (i.e. the "Old Testament," as Christians later called it, and especially the five books of Moses known as the Torah or "Teaching") there was an oral tradition consisting of interpretations and enactments supplementing and developing the Written Law. The Sadducees, on the other hand, held that the

whole of Judaism lay in the Written Law in the Bible which was
a closed and final revelation standing in no need of interpretation or development.

The Sadducees, it may be said, wanted to keep Judaism
simple. They wanted it to be centred round three great
institutions, the Scripture, the Priesthood and the Temple.
Judaism, to them, was mainly a matter of fulfilling the cultic
requirements of the Temple worship as laid down in the
Priestly code. As for contemporary economics or politics,
nothing could be found about them in Scripture and consequently such matters lay outside the sphere of religion and
could be decided purely on grounds of convenience. Such a
doctrine appealed particularly to rich landowners and practical
politicians who wanted to avoid interference from religious
idealists and reformers. The Sadducees would not have denied
that Scripture contains rules of moral conduct as well as ritual
prescriptions, but they had no desire to adapt the moral rules or
complicate them in any way to make them more relevant to the
circumstances of their own day.

To the Pharisees, however, this policy was, in their own
graphic phrase, "to put the Torah into a corner."[4] The Torah
was, to them, a living thing which must continually encounter
and grapple with new circumstances, thus giving rise to new
decisions which became part of the developing Oral Law. This
does not mean the Pharisees regarded the Bible as imperfect. It
was the Word of God, revealed to Moses and the Prophets. But
new circumstances were continually drawing out of it new
depths of meaning; its content was inexhaustible. This growing
knowledge of the possibilities of the Torah, revealed through
time in the processes of history, was the Oral Law. In other
words, the place of the Torah was "not in heaven, but in the
hands of men,"[5] and the Oral Law was thus the working,
human reality of the divine revelation.

Since they could not "put the Torah in a corner" the
Pharisees could not compartmentalize life or narrow down the
scope of religion. To them, there was no such thing as a
"religious sphere," or a neutral sphere to which religion did not

apply. The Torah was not limited or circumscribed in its subject-matter. It was meant to be applied to the whole of life; and if there was no explicit text which could be shown to be relevant it was necessary to apply the principles and spirit of Judaism to arrive at a judgment. The Pharisees, consequently, far from being Establishment figures were usually critical of the Establishment. Originally called "Hasidim," they fought against the Syrian-Greek Emperors and their quisling Jewish High Priests. Soon, however, they were at odds with the new Jewish royal dynasty, the Hasmoneans. When this dynasty was supplanted by Herod, the Pharisees were eventually his chief opponents. And when, after Herod's death, the Establishment became the Roman occupying force backed once more by a quisling High Priesthood it was the Pharisees who were the backbone of the opposition.

Since the Sadducees were the conservatives who opposed innovations and reform it has been assumed by most writers that they came first. The Pharisees, however, always claimed that the Oral Law, of which they were the supporters and champions, went back to the origins of Judaism and that the Sadducees, in denying the Oral Law, were heretics who were attempting to abolish a fundamental religious principle. Both Josephus and Philo attest that the Pharisees were the guardians of very ancient traditions.[6] It is possible that the Sadducees began as a protest movement against the accumulation of extra-Scriptural traditions and the growth to authority of the "Scribes" or "rabbis" who were the experts on these traditions.

Just as the Sadducees were the religious party of the rich and powerful, the Pharisees were the religious party of the poor and powerless. Again, this is a fact that can be ascertained easily enough from Josephus and the Talmud but which is entirely obscured in the New Testament. Josephus's testimony is as follows: ". . . the Pharisees have delivered to the people a great many observances by succession from their fathers, which are not written in the laws of Moses; and it is for this reason that the Sadducees reject them, and say that we are to esteem those observances to be obligatory which are in the written word, but are not to observe what are derived from the tradition of our forefathers. And concerning these things it is that great disputes and differences have arisen among them, while the Saducees are able to persuade none but the rich, and have not the populace obsequious to them, but the Pharisees have the multitude on their side."[7] Josephus says also about the Pharisees: "These have so great power over the multitude that when they say anything against the king, or against the high priest, they are immediately believed."[8] From the Talmud we learn that the leading Pharisees such as Hillel, Shammai, Hanina ben Dosa and Akiva, came from the working class, and even at the height of their fame worked as woodcutters, shepherds, carpenters, shoemakers, etc.

The Pharisees numbered in the time of Jesus about 6000, according to Josephus. These were the members of the body of "Comrades" (Haverim) as they called themselves. Their leaders were called "Wise Men" (Hakamim), and were later given the title "Master" (Rabbi) before their names. These leaders were also sometimes known as the "Scribes," after the title of Ezra and his followers in late Biblical times.[9] The Pharisees, in fact, regarded Ezra as the founder of their movement, and they regarded themselves as the heirs of the Prophetic tradition.

The Priests and the Rabbis were two distinct groups with quite different functions. The Priests (Kohanim) were a hereditary caste, the descendants of Moses' brother Aaron. Their main function was to perform the service of the Temple, assisted by the Levites who performed the Temple music, carried the water for the ablutions, etc. The whole priestly tribe of Levi (of which the Kohanim formed one family) was forbidden to own land and lived on voluntary tithes contributed by the devout. When the Temple was destroyed the role of the Priests and Levites ended and they ceased to be of importance in Judaism; though as a memento of their previous role they were given certain privileges in the service of the synagogue, (being called up first to the Reading of the Law, and blessing the congregation with the Priests' Blessing which has been incorporated into the Christian liturgy).

The Priests, as such, had no teaching role and had no power to pronounce on matters of religious doctrine or practice. This was the province of the Wise Men, or Rabbis, who, for their part, had no role in the service of the Temple. In order to become a Priest one had to be born into the House of Aaron, but to become a Rabbi no qualifications of birth were required. The position was open to anyone who had the necessary ability. The Rabbi was essentially a lay leader who followed his own trade but gave his knowledge and advice as a teacher and judge when required. This tradition of unprofessionalism in the rabbinate lingered for a long time. As late as the Middle Ages great rabbis like Maimonides and Nachmanides refused to accept payment for their services and made their living in some other profession, often as doctors.

While there was conflict between Pharisees and Sadducees, there was no antagonism between the Rabbis and the Priests. The division of function between them was too well understood for that. The Priests not only lacked teaching authority; they never even claimed it. Most of the Priests were themselves Pharisees, or supporters of the Pharisees. It was only the rich High Priestly families who were Sadducees. The Priests were accorded a more lofty status among the Sadducees, but this was more in theory than in practice. As Josephus points out, even the Sadducees followed the rulings of the Pharisees in most cases.

The division of function between Priest and Teacher did not begin with the Pharisees. It was one of the oldest features of Judaism. Moses, the prototype of the Teacher, was not a Priest; he gave this function to his brother Aaron. The Prophets who succeeded Moses were rarely Priests, though there was no *bar* against a Priest becoming a Prophet, like anyone else, if he discovered that he had the gift. (Ezekiel, for example, was a Priest.) The distinction between Priest and Teacher enabled the Jews to preserve the heart of Judaism from corruption. (This

remains true even though there were certain periods when the
roles of Priest and Teacher did coalesce.) But it was very hard
for Gentiles, such as the Greeks and the Romans, to understand
that the religious official who wore the gorgeous robes and
presided at religious ceremonies with pomp and circumstance
was ultimately of no religious significance, and that the religious authority whom the Jews most revered might be some
penurious village shoe-maker who was the chief repository of
the Law.

The Pharisees, then, were a movement which presents many
paradoxes to the modern enquirer who is used to making a
dichotomy between reform and tradition, or between revolt
and conservatism. The Pharisees were both traditionalist and
reformist; they were both centres of authority and centres of
dissent. They were a lay brotherhood whose function was to act
as the critics of society and the guardians of authentic Judaism.
They stood aside from positions of power in the institutional
sense, but were willing to act as advisers when called upon.
When the ruling power, whether royal or sacerdotal, became
corrupt, they opposed it implacably but never with the sense of
overturning established authority—rather with the sense of
protecting it from parvenu claimants to an inauthentic kind of
authority. They regarded the Scripture as divinely revealed,
but they claimed the right to add to its teaching in the sense of
developing its inner riches and allowing it to grow like a living
thing; to worship it as a closed oracle, as the Sadducees did, was
for them a kind of idolatry and also a kind of contempt.

It is interesting to see how Josephus regards the Pharisees.
He is, on the whole, against them, but whereas the Gospels
attack the Pharisees as hidebound reactionaries, bound to "the
traditions of the fathers," and as supporters of the powers-
that-be, Josephus attacks them as wild men and trouble-
makers. Josephus is on the side of the Romans, and he also takes
pride in his connections with the High Priesthood. He admires
the Pharisees in many ways, and at one point in his career he
even joined them. But in the end he condemns them. He calls
them "people with the greatest capacity for acting against

kings."[10] The Pharisees were not against kings as such, any more than they were against High Priests. But nearly all the kings and High Priests found the Pharisees a thorn in their flesh because of their demand that they should be true kings and true High Priests according to the standards of the Torah and the Oral Law. Again and again the king and the High Priest must have felt like echoing Ahab's bitter cry to Elijah the prophet: "Art thou he that troubleth Israel?"

Since so many writers have denied that the Pharisees were reformers and have tried to substantiate the New Testament picture of them as ultra-conservatives, there are set out in Appendix 5 some of the actual reforms and developments in Jewish Law and religion for which the Pharisees were responsible. However, the Pharisee attitude towards the Sabbath deserves special mention since it is so severely criticized in the New Testament. Here too the Pharisees introduced important reforms. They stipulated that any danger to life overrode the Sabbath law; for example, in the case of a conflagration or the subsidence of a building, all Sabbath prohibitions concerning digging, quenching fires, etc., were suspended for the duration of the crisis. Indeed, anyone who attempted to observe the Sabbath at the risk of his own or another's life was denounced by the Pharisees as a sinner; it became a positive duty to disobey the Sabbath law in such a situation. When Jesus said, "The Sabbath was made for man, not man for the Sabbath" he was quoting a familiar Pharisee maxim which is found in almost the same words in Pharisee writings.

The question of healing receives much prominence in the Gospels where the Pharisees are represented as objecting violently to Jesus's practice of carrying out faith-cures on the Sabbath. Yet the truth is that the Pharisees would have had no objection to such cures. Healing was not one of the activities which they forbade on the Sabbath; the most they said was that if the complaint being treated was *trivial*, and the *method* of treatment involved some breach of the Sabbath laws (e.g. pounding herbs to make a medicine), treatment should be postponed until after the Sabbath or another method of treat-

ment used.[11] Since Jesus's method of healing involved no
breach of the Sabbath law[12] the Pharisees would not have had
the slightest objection to it, even in the case of trivial com-
plaints. It is puzzling, therefore, that the Gospels ascribe such
views to the Pharisees; and the most likely explanation is that
the dispute was orginally (i.e. in the first version of the Gospel
story) between Jesus and the *Sadducees*.[13] The fact that the
Gospels were re-worked in order to put the Pharisees in a bad
light will be shown in some detail later in this book.

The Pharisee movement, then, was the authentic expression
of Judaism in Jesus's day. It was a movement with a long and
honourable history of courageous defence of Judaism against
tyranny and usurped authority. It was a movement which
stood for a living, developing Judaism; which, in its hard
thinking and sustained activity, sought to make Judaism ap-
proximate more and more to high standards of decency,
humanity and compassion. It was a movement in which the
common man, the layman, was of increasing importance, and
in which the hereditary aristocracy of Priests and landowners
was given little respect. Accordingly, it was the movement
which had the support of the common people.

It is hardly surprising that it was this movement rather than
that of the Sadducees which provided the opposition to Rome.
Sadducaism had turned Judaism into a holy, dead relic. For the
Pharisees, Judaism was a living reality.

6

The Jewish Sects

It would be wrong, in reaction against the Gospel portrayal, to represent the Pharisees as wild fanatics ready to take up arms at the drop of a hat. This description would be fairly accurate in relation to one small section of the Pharisees, namely the Zealots. The majority of the Pharisees, however, regarded the Zealots as lacking in common-sense and realism.

The Zealots were in a state of open warfare with the Romans from the time that the Roman occupation began in 6 A.D. They had indeed fought against the Romans even earlier, during the confused period after the death of Herod (4 B.C.) when Archelaus, Herod's son, was away in Rome seeking to have his succession confirmed and Roman troops were over-running Palestine looking for loot. At this time Judas the Galilean, the leader of the Zealots, captured the capital of Galilee, Sepphoris, and held it against the Romans. Eventually, Varus, the Governor of Syria, took and burned Sepphoris, but Judas escaped and continued to organise resistance for some years.

The Zealots took their name from Phinehas the Zealot, the son of Aaron, who "was zealous for his God" (Numbers xxv. 13) with sword in hand. It was believed that Phinehas, as a reward for his violent zeal, had never died and was identical

with the prophet Elijah who would come back one day to act as
the fore-runner of the Messiah (Malachi iv. 5). The choice of
this name as the watchword of the movement had, therefore,
Messianic overtones.

The Zealots did not believe in assessing the relative military
strength of Jews and Romans. They believed that God would
come to their aid if they launched themselves against the
Romans just as He had come to the aid of Judas Maccabaeus, of
Samson, of Gideon and of Joshua, who had all fought against
apparently hopeless odds. On the other hand, the Zealots did
not believe that God would help the Jews if they merely waited
passively for God's deliverance; God would only help those
who showed "zeal" and who were prepared to risk their lives.

The Zealots were not completely unrealistic. They did not
expect immediate miracles; they expected a long, hard guerrilla
campaign in which many of their number would be killed; but
they did believe that victory would be theirs in the end despite
the overwhelming military superiority of the Romans. The
moderate Pharisees, on the other hand, while just as anti-
Roman as the Zealots did not believe that the time had yet come
for open resistance. They did not rule out the possibility that a
deliverer would arise, as had happened so often before in Jewish
history, who would defeat the enemy; but they were inclined to
be cautious and sceptical when someone claimed to be such a
deliverer because they also knew of many disappointments in
Jewish history, of deliverances which had failed to materialise.
Meanwhile, they accepted the hard realities of the Roman
occupation, with one proviso: that the Romans must not flout
the basic Jewish sanctities. If these were threatened (as by
Caligula's plan to set up his statue for worship in the Jewish
Temple) even the most moderate Pharisees were prepared to
fight, for on such matters it was a Pharisee doctrine that death
was preferable to compromise.

The moderate Pharisees, then, bided their time waiting for a
favourable opportunity to revolt. Meanwhile, they paid their
taxes to the Romans and refrained from open revolt; but they

did not accept any official post in the Roman Occupation and they refused to co-operate in the Roman police actions to track down and kill the Zealots. Eventually, the Zealots instituted a full-scale war in which all the Jewish parties were involved (even the Sadducees). In this war (66–73 A.D.) the Zealots fought to the last man. The heroic last-ditch defence of Massada is well-known. Here, the last of the Zealots under the leadership of Eleazar ben Jair, a descendant of the first Zealot, Judas of Galilee, after a stubborn defence died by their own hands rather than fall captive to the Romans. The Zealots disappeared from history and the survival of the Jews and of Judaism remained in the hands of the more moderate Pharisees.

There is a good description of the attitude of the Pharisees in the New Testament (Acts v). When Peter (some time after the death of Jesus) was arrested by the Sadducean party of the High Priest and brought before the Sanhedrin, the Pharisee leader Gamaliel defended Peter as follows: "But a member of the Council rose to his feet, a Pharisee called Gamaliel, a teacher of the law held in high regard by all the people. He moved that the men be put outside for a while. Then he said, 'Men of Israel, be cautious in deciding what to do with these men. Some time ago Theudas came forward, claiming to be somebody, and a number of men, about four hundred, joined him. But he was killed and his whole following was broken up and disappeared. After him came Judas the Galilean at the time of the census; he induced some people to revolt under his leadership, but he too perished and his whole following was scattered. And so now: keep clear of these men, I tell you; leave them alone. For if this idea of theirs or its execution is of human origin, it will collapse; but if it is from God, you will never be able to put them down, and you risk finding yourselves at war with God.' "

This passage shows the wait-and-see attitude of the moderate Pharisees. Note that there is no hint of condemnation of the "subversive" activities of Theudas and Judas. He acknowledges their aims (i.e. the defeat of the Romans) but is only doubtful whether their inspiration was truly from God. It is especially

interesting to see what a different picture we have here from the
picture of the Pharisees given elsewhere in the Gospels and in
Acts. What has happened to the persecuting Pharisees who
allegedly hounded Jesus to death? This very Pharisee leader
Gamaliel, it is claimed later (Acts xxii, 3), was the teacher of
Paul who, in his allegedly Pharisee days, hunted the followers
of Jesus to their deaths. Gamaliel was not just a Pharisee leader;
he was the head of the whole Pharisee party, the son, or
possibly grandson, of the great Hillel. No view could be more
characteristic of the Pharisees than his; yet here he is urging
toleration towards the early followers of Jesus. If Paul really
was a pupil of Gamaliel where did he learn his intolerance
from? This incident, which has somehow escaped the anti-
Pharisee re-working of the *Acts of the Apostles*, should be borne in
mind as an indication (and there are others, as we shall see) of
the true character of the Pharisees as evidenced even in
anti-Pharisee documents.

Cautious as they were in assessing the chances of would-be
deliverers, the moderate Pharisees were capable of breaking out
into full-scale rebellion if they once became convinced that the
right leader had arrived. In the second great war against the
Romans (132–135 A.D.) the Jewish leader Bar Kochba had the
support of the highly influential Pharisee leader, Rabbi Akiva,
who declared Bar Kochba to be the Messiah. This war was
better planned and more successful than the Zealots' revolt.
The Romans were actually hurled out of Palestine and an
independent Jewish state set up which lasted for over two
years. Unfortunately, our knowledge of this period is scanty as
this war did not have its Josephus to record it in detail and the
Talmudic records are sparse; but some information can be
obtained from Roman historians, and recent archaeological
finds have thrown some light on the period. Eventually, Bar
Kochba was defeated and killed by the Roman general Julius
Severus, recalled from Britain to deal with the Jews. In the
cruel aftermath of the war Rabbi Akiva was flayed alive. Other
rabbis were burnt to death with damp wool laid over their

hearts to make their sufferings last longer.[1] Even crucifixion, on this occasion, was considered inadequate. The Jewish state was abolished and almost the entire remaining population deported. This was the end of 200 years of Pharisee opposition to Rome.

The Bar Kochba revolt shows that even the moderate Pharisees were capable of open rebellion, though it is probable that the reason for their desperate action was not only the desire for political independence but the decision of the Emperor Hadrian that circumcision was to be forbidden and that a pagan temple was to be built on the ruined site of the Jewish Temple. In general, the moderate Pharisees unlike the Zealots were prepared to endure foreign rule provided that their sanctities were not outraged. Yet this patience never amounted to acceptance. It never occurred to them that the Romans were there to stay. They assumed that God would eventually send a redeemer who would save the Jews from the Romans, as they had been saved from other invaders.

It would be wrong, too, to represent the Sadducees as mere traitors and quislings. Unlike the Pharisees, they collaborated with the Romans, but like the Pétainists in Occupied France they felt that by accepting posts of authority they were preserving some kind of native independence and shielding their fellow-countrymen from the horrors of direct military rule. In acting against the Resistance they believed that they were acting in the best interests of the Jewish people who, they thought, were being endangered by such intransigence. Their attitude is well expressed in the Gospel of John: "If we leave him alone like this the whole populace will believe in him. Then the Romans will come and sweep away our temple and our nation." (xi. 48). Such people, of course, are adept at deceiving themselves; they exaggerate their own power and hide from their own consciousness the extent to which they are swayed by love of office and position. Nevertheless, the Sadducees were still Jews. In the days of Aristobulus and Hyrcanus they had fought bravely against the Romans; and when the die was cast for war in 66 A.D. they too joined in the fight. Only the

Herodians, who were not a religious but a purely political party, supported the Romans in the War.

Even the Pharisees did not withdraw entirely from public life during the Roman Occupation. They continued to be represented strongly in the Sanhedrin, the supreme legal court of the Jews. Judaism was a religion of Law and one of the most important functions of the Pharisee leaders, the Rabbis, was to act as judges. The Romans were chiefly interested in collecting their taxes, and took no interest in purely religious offences. The Sanhedrin, therefore, continued to function, as did the minor courts in every town, in all of which the Pharisees were dominant. Ever since the time of Queen Alexandra, the Pharisees had held the majority in the Sanhedrin. The High Priest, by virtue of his office, acted as President of the Sanhedrin. This does not mean that his opinion on legal matters was important, much less decisive. The number of judges in the Sanhedrin was seventy, and any disputed matters were settled by majority vote.[2]

Though the High Priest was powerless in the Sanhedrin he dominated his own Court, which met to consider matters which came under his jurisdiction as an officer of the Romans. The High Priest was, in effect, a police official whose job, as a Roman appointee, was to look out for signs of sedition against the occupying authority. He had powers of arrest and examination and if satisfied of seditious behaviour he would send the arrested man to the Roman procurator for trial and punishment.[3] According to the New Testament, Jesus was tried before the Sanhedrin on a religious charge of blasphemy. It will be argued later in this book that he never came before the Sanhedrin, but was examined on charge of sedition in the High Priest's police court.

The Sanhedrin, it should be noted, was not in any way an instrument of the Romans. It was concerned with religious law, and whenever a case had a bearing on the power of interests of Rome it was outside the Sanhedrin's jurisdiction and had to be referred to the Procurator. Even such referral was not the responsibility of the Sanhedrin; but it is likely that the High

Priest used his position as President of the Sanhedrin to become aware of cases that had an aspect of interest to the Romans.

Even more pro-Roman than the High Priest's party, the Sadducees, were the Herodians. These were the remnants of the royal court of Herod the Great and of his son Archelaus who had been banished by Augustus to exile in Vienna. The Herodians hoped that their banished master, or some relative of his, might one day be restored to power. In Galilee, of course, the Herodians were still in power in the client-princedom of Herod Antipas, another son of Herod the Great. In Judaea, the Herodians tried to ingratiate themselves as much as possible with the Romans and some of them served as officers in the Roman military forces. The Herodians were the only important group among the Jews which was not religious in motivation. Their style of life was Greco-Roman and their chief interest was in money and political power. They had nothing whatever in common with the Pharisees. Yet so remote is the New Testament from the facts of the period that the Gospels sometimes represent the Pharisees and the Herodians as allies!

At the opposite extreme of the religio-political spectrum to the Herodians were certain movements which were even more fervently unrealistic than the Zealots. These were the short-lived movements which arose from time to time round some inspired prophet or messiah-figure. In the despair aroused by the Roman Occupation these movements became fairly frequent. Two of these movements are mentioned in the New Testament: that of Theudas (Acts v. 36), and that of the "Egyptian" (Acts xxi. 38). We learn more about these risings from Josephus. Theudas (whose rising is dated ten years too early in Acts) promised the people that he would enable them to cross the Jordan on dry land, as in the days of Joshua (whose name, of which "Jesus" is a variant, means "Saviour"). He attracted a following, but was captured and beheaded by the Roman Procurator of the time, Fadus. The "Egyptian" (i.e. Alexandrian Jew) assembled the people on the Mount of Olives (a favourite place for would-be messiahs because of the prophecy of Zechariah) and promised that he would cause the

walls of Jerusalem to fall down by a miracle (again there is here
an allusion to Joshua who caused the walls of Jericho to fall
down). The Procurator Felix sent his soldiers against the crowd
and in the ensuing slaughter the Egyptian escaped and did not
appear again. Mention of several other such movements can be
found in the writings of Josephus who treats them all unsym-
pathetically. The essence of such movements was the expectation of a miracle in fulfilment of some Biblical prophecy. They
were hardly military in character. An undisciplined, ecstatic
mob, stirred by the charismatic figure of the prophet, would
move forward only to be mown down by Roman soldiers. They
might carry a few weapons but would not expect to have to face
a serious military engagement since they were convinced that
God would intervene on their behalf. These were the
"apocalyptic" movements, so called because they arose out of
the hopes of salvation contained in the "apocalyptic" (revela-
tory) literature such as the Book of Daniel, Joel, Zechariah,
Enoch and the Assumption of Moses. The Zealot movement
had its apocalyptic aspects, though it differed from the other
movements in being more realistic in tone; it was not centred
round some inspired prophet-figure but round a military leader
who organised armed bands on guerrilla lines. The moderate
Pharisees also believed in the prophecies of some at least of the
apocalyptic writings; but they were very wary about accepting
anyone who came forward claiming to be the promised saviour
or messiah. Not that they considered there was anything wrong
or blasphemous about making such a claim; they preferred to
wait and see. In the words of Gamaliel quoted above, "If this
idea of theirs is of human origin, it will collapse; but if it is from
God, you will never be able to put them down, and you risk
finding yourselves at war with God."

There was one apocalyptic movement which is of special
interest, namely the Essenes. These were known from the
writings of Josephus and Philo, but the discovery of the Dead
Sea scrolls has increased our knowledge about them enor-
mously. The significance of these discoveries for the study of
Christian origins was at first greatly exaggerated; for example,

the Teacher of Righteousness of the Dead Sea scroll sect was identified with Jesus by one scholar on the basis of a text which was misread as referring to the Teacher's crucifixion. Certain features of the Dead Sea sect made it seem similar to the early Christian community; e.g. their belief in a "New Covenant," their community of goods, their religious community meals, and their negative attitude towards sex. However, these features were already known from descriptions of the Essenes by Josephus and Philo; and the new knowledge about the Essenes provided by the Scrolls made them seem rather less like the early Christians.[4]

The Essene or Dead Sea sect (if they were indeed identical) most probably belongs to the history of the Sadducees. They may have broken off from the main body of the Sadducees in Hasmonean times in protest at the growing worldliness and corruption of the Sadducee High Priesthood and the consequent defilement of the Temple. It is noteworthy that they called themselves not Essenes but Zadokites or Sons of Zadok, a name which is identical with "Sadducees" (the name is derived from Zadok who was High Priest during the reign of King David). This would explain the sect's extreme reverence for the priesthood, combined with a loathing for the official Temple priesthood of Jerusalem. It is quite likely that the Sadducee movement, despite its later worldliness, was originally a movement of true religious fervour, which the Dead Sea sect alone preserved.

This, however, is speculation; and there is a great deal more to be learnt about the Dead Sea sect. What is certain is that they were anti-Roman. So far were they from collaboration that they withdrew almost entirely from the general community and lived in monastic settlements where they dreamed of ultimate victory both against the Romans and against the rival Jewish sects.

We have now surveyed the whole spectrum of religious sects of the Jews in the time of Jesus. In most of them we have noted that anti-Roman feeling was bound up with the hope for the Messiah. Even the Sadducees, the only religious group to collaborate with the Romans, had not given up this hope, though they relegated it to the very distant future and did not allow it to interfere with practical affairs. It is now time to examine more closely this idea of the Messiah which played such an important part in the Jewish Resistance against Rome.

7

The Messiah

The title "Messiah" (Greek—"Christos") was not a divine title among the Jews. It simply means "anointed." It was given to two Jewish officials, the King and the High Priest, who were both anointed with oil at their inauguration ceremony. When David was anointed by Samuel he became a Messiah, or Christ. Every Jewish king of the House of David was known as Messiah, or Christ, and a regular way of referring to the High Priest was "the Priest Messiah," i.e. the Priest Christ; even the corrupt Roman appointees of Jesus's day had this title. It is necessary to labour this point because the word "Christ" has become so imbued with the idea of deity that it is very hard for a non-Jew to appreciate what these words meant to the average Jew in the time of Jesus.

This is not to deny that the word "Messiah" had acquired a strong aura of romance and glamour. It had come to mean not just "King" but the deliverer who would rescue the Jews from their subjection to the cruel and humiliating power of Rome. It meant the unknown descendant of the House of David who, with the miraculous aid of God, would one day restore Israel's independence under the rule of its own much-loved Davidic dynasty. We can see something similar in English history in the

charisma of the exiled Stuart dynasty in the minds of those who
yearned for a restoration after 1688. One difference, however,
is that the House of David had ceased to rule about 600 years
before. There had been other royal dynasties since; the Hasmoneans and the Herodians. The former had been a disappointment, and the latter were actually hated as foreign
interlopers and agents of Rome. There were well known
prophecies in Scripture that the line of David would never die
out and that eventually his dynasty would be restored. It could
not actually be proved with any certainty who the descendants
of David were. Some families claimed this descent but there
might well have been others who were descendants of David
without even knowing it. The field was wide open. Any leaders
who succeeded in driving out the Romans and setting up an
independent Jewish state would have little difficulty in being
recognised as the Messiah. His very success would prove his
claim. Thus Bar Kochba was recognised as the Messiah by
Rabbi Akiva even though there was no evidence of his descent
from David.

There was also a belief that there would be a *precursor* to the
Messiah: none other than the prophet Elijah who had never
died. The return of Elijah was a necessary preliminary for
several reasons. Firstly, this had been directly prophesied by
the prophet Malachi: "Behold, I will send you Elijah the
prophet before the coming of the great and dreadful day of the
Lord." (Mal. iv. 5). Then, a true Messiah would have to be
anointed by a true Prophet, as David had been anointed by
Samuel. Even more important, the return of Elijah would
signify the return of God to his people, for ever since Malachi
(about 400 B.C.) the Jews had been without a prophet. By
sending them a prophet God would re-establish the link of
communication which had been broken by their sins; and this
would be the natural signal for their reestablishment as a
sovereign people under their king, the Messiah. Thus, several
Messianic movements took the form of a prophetic campaign
preparing the way for the Messiah. John the Baptist, for
example, never claimed to be the Messiah but his movement

was messianic nonetheless, and therefore political in intention, as Herod Antipas realised when he executed him.

These beliefs about the Messiah and Elijah the prophet were widespread, especially among the Pharisees and consequently among the mass of the people. However, many other doctrines were also current. Some believed in a Messiah son of Joseph, others in a Messiah son of Aaron, others in various combinations of these with the Messiah, Son of David. Some believed that the deliverance of Israel would come at the hands of God Himself without the intervention of a Messiah figure; others that God would send an angel, called the Son of Man, to accomplish the deliverance (see particularly the Book of Enoch). The Son of Man was *not* a Messiah. He was an angel identified with the Guardian Angel of Israel, with Metatron, with the angel who guided the Children of Israel in the wilderness,[1] and with Enoch himself who, like Elijah, never died. (It was only after the advent of Christianity that the figure of the Messiah and the figure of the Son of Man were fused into one, with the additional ingredient of the Son of God derived from Gnosticism and from the mystery cults.) The prophecies of Scripture about the Last Days were extremely vague and could be reconciled with any or all of the beliefs current at the time.

In Jesus's day, the idea of a *divine* Messiah was unknown. Those who believed that deliverance would come through a Messiah, "the King of the Jews," thought of him as a human being, the next occupant of the Jewish throne. Those who believed that deliverance would come by entirely supernatural means thought of the deliverer as God Himself, or as an angel. The idea of a human being who was also divine was unthinkable. The whole of Jewish history cried out against such a concept. The first of the Ten Commandments forbade the worship of a human being. It was precisely because of their refusal to worship the human-divine figures which filled the Ancient World, from Pharaoh to Caligula, that the Jews had undergone their long history of suffering. Other nations deified their great national heroes; the Jews refused to do so. If they had not deified Moses who delivered them from Egypt they were not going to deify the Son of David who would deliver them from the Romans.[2]

Even among the Pharisees, there were many differences of opinion about the form deliverance would take. Some believed that the Messiah would inaugurate a new era for the whole world; that the nations of the world would acknowledge the One God and his Temple in Jerusalem; that the Jews would be revered as the chosen priests of the One God; and that an era of world peace would begin when, in the words of Isaiah's wonderful internationalist vision, the swords would be beaten into ploughshares and the wolf would lie down with the lamb. Some, however, did not believe that the coming of the Messiah would necessarily bring about an era of international peace. There might be many Messiahs—many more sorrows and comfortings, defeats and victories—for the Jewish people before that happened. After all, there had been Messiahs before and none had brought everlasting peace. The vision of Isaiah was acknowledged by every Pharisee as the word of God but it was not necessarily attached to the expectation of the coming Messiah who would defeat the Romans. Like the Assyrians, the Babylonians, the Persians and the Greeks, the Romans might be just an incident in the long history of the Jewish mission and the Last Days might still be far ahead.

One group among the Pharisees, namely the Zealots, were opposed to the idea of the Messiah. A group among them, at least, were republicans and wished to abolish the Jewish monarchy altogether. Their slogan was "God is our only Ruler and Lord." When Menachem, the son of Judas of Galilee, assumed royal power at the time of the Jewish War (66 A.D.). thus claiming to be the Messiah, he was killed by members of his own party who argued, according to Josephus, "It was not right when they had revolted from the Romans out of desire for liberty to betray that liberty to any of their own people."[3] Again, the Zealots' wish to abolish the monarchy, and thus the Messiahship, was not heretical. It could easily be justified from Scripture, which is on the whole anti-monarchical—see, for example, Samuel's criticism of monarchy, (I Samuel. viii). The Zealots were certainly not lukewarm in their desire for independence from Rome or in their religious sense of the Jewish mission; but they had jettisoned the belief in the Messiah. No doubt they wished to see an independent Israel ruled by a republican Council or Sanhedrin as in the days of Ezra and his successors, the "men of the Great Synagogue," and as in the days of the judges.

Despite this wide variety of belief or opinion about the Messiah and about eschatology (the doctrine of the Last Things), the most popular belief among the Pharisees and among the people was undoubtedly that salvation would come through the Son of David who would be heralded by the return of the prophet Elijah. The Son of David would claim his right to the Jewish throne and, at the head of an army, put the Romans to flight. He would be helped by God and by his own valour like Jewish heroes of the past such as Joshua, Gideon and David. He would be more than an ordinary king; he might have prophetic power like King Solomon, and be able to work miracles like Moses or Elisha. Like Moses, he would perhaps be able to feed the people in a wilderness, and like Elisha (and Elijah) he would perhaps be able to raise people from the dead. Such miracles would not prove him to be divine but only that he was the equal of the prophets and miracleworkers of old.

The idea of the Messiah was certainly an inspiring one, especially in its internationalist form based on the prophecies of Isaiah, Joel and Zechariah, in which the era of the Messiah became significant for the evolution of humanity as a whole. Even in this form, however, Jewish Messianic ideas were very different from those which developed later in the Christian Church. There was no concept of a Suffering Messiah who would die on the cross to purge mankind of sin. About a hundred years after the death of Jesus the idea of a Suffering Messiah did enter Judaism, in a sporadic, nondogmatic way;[4] but this only arose in the despondency that followed the bitter defeat of Bar Kochba in 135 A.D. In some Jewish sects it was thought that the Messiah son of Joseph would die in battle and

that victory would then be achieved by the Messiah son of
David. This was an attempt to reconcile the conflicting traditions about the Son of Joseph (derived from the Northern
Kingdom) and the Son of David (derived from the Southern
Kingdom). Death in battle is very different, anyway, from
death on the cross. The Jewish idea of the Messiah is more
"down to earth" than the Christian one. To the Jews salvation
was a physical not a purely spiritual concept. The Messianic
age, to the Jews, was to be the culmination of human history on
earth. Even the World to Come was to take place on earth, and
the rebirth of the righteous was to be a Resurrection of the Body
in an Earthly Paradise—not a bodiless Heaven. Behind this
difference lay a difference in attitude towards the body; the
Jews still regarded the body with reverence as the creation of
God, while the Christians succumbed to the Hellenistic idea
that the body was the prison of the soul, the possession and
province of Satan.

There was also less *individualism* in the Jewish concept of the
Messiah than in the later Christian concept.[5] The Messiah was
not a Saviour who came to rescue individuals from sin but a
representative of the Jewish people who came to provide the
culmination of the Jewish role in history. He represented the
fruition of the Jewish idea of their own mission. While the
Christian concept centres round the *person* of the Messiah/
Christ who descends from an extra-historical dimension to save
the believer, the Jewish Messiah represents an *era* rather than a
person; he is the figurehead of a stage of human development.
There is hardly any reference in the Prophetic writings of the
Old Testament to the Messiah as a person. There is no splendid
shining figure judging mankind, coming very near to eclipsing
God Himself by his glory. Instead, the vision is one of a world
at peace when people will have a "new heart" and "the earth will
be full of the knowledge of the Lord as the waters cover the
sea."[6]

Just as it would be wrong to read into the Messianic
expectations current in Jesus's time the more "spiritual" connotations of a later period, so it would be wrong and superficial

to regard the Messianic hope as merely political and nationalistic. If the longing for the Messiah had been no more than a desire for political independence it would not have had the power to inspire such extraordinary resistance. In other countries patriotism had produced great heroism against Rome but nothing so prolonged and determined as the Jewish efforts which by their obstinacy and courage aroused the wonder, fear and hatred of Roman historians. The Messianic ideal arose from the whole "weltanschauung" of the Jewish people which was unique in the ancient world. The Messianic ideal arose out of *monotheism*.

Monotheism unified human history into a single process tending towards one final aim, the fulfilling of the purposes of God in creating the world. The idea of a Messianic age providing the dénouement of the cosmic drama is inherent in monotheism. Polytheism, on the other hand, provided no such cosmic drama. Each nation had its own gods and there was no overriding purpose for mankind. History, in polytheistic cultures, was regarded as cyclic. Nations like individuals had their life-cycles of youth, maturity and decline. Even the gods had these life-cycles; and above both gods and men was an inexorable, indifferent Fate. Only the Jews claimed to be in contact with this supreme immortal Fate, claiming also that it was not indifferent to mankind but a loving Father who moulded the process of history. This concept of progress in history towards a final Utopia has been the inspiration of the progressive and utopian tradition in Western culture—so much so that it is difficult nowadays to visualize the *uniqueness* of this idea in the ancient world.

As well as being a source of unquenchable optimism, Monotheism was unable to acknowledge defeat. Polytheistic nations could admit that their gods had proved weaker than those of Rome; or could succumb to Roman syncretism by which the undefeated gods were *identified* with the gods of Rome, (e.g. Jupiter/Zeus/Ammon). The Jewish God, the creator of Heaven and Earth, could not submit to such annexation. Some Roman emperors, to show their religious toleration, built "pantheons" (i.e. temples of all the gods). One emperor, as a generous gesture to the Jews, included in his pantheon an effigy of Abraham! (This Roman religious "tolerance" was really a sort of collector's passion; and the Jewish God, the God of all the Universe, would not be collected in this way.) When the Jews were in fact defeated it meant not that God had been defeated but that God's people had failed in their mission and must re-dedicate themselves by repentance. This is the meaning of the campaigns of repentence (e.g. by John the Baptist) which often preceded or accompanied a Messianic movement.

Monotheism also carried a revolutionary social message. Since all mankind were created by the One God all mankind were brothers. Monotheism began as the religion of a band of runaway slaves; and it expressed their determination not to submit to any oppressive individual or class again. Polytheism lent itself to aristocracy; for kings and ruling classes could claim to be descended from gods, or, in some cases, even to *be* gods. Monotheism outlawed the cult of the god-king. As the Jewish Scriptures show, it kept a watchful, critical eye on all rulers. It stressed the concern of the One God for each individual, without intermediary gods, demigods or semidivine priests; and one of its chief preoccupations was social justice. This aspect of Judaism too was a powerful factor in the struggle against the Roman Empire.

Monotheism, it can be said, was the deepest source of the Jewish Resistance.

8

Realism and Mysticism

We have seen that Messianism, rooted in the monotheistic vision of history, was the mainspring of the Jewish spirit of resistance. Even the Sadducees, the only religious group to collaborate with the Romans, subscribed to these views. But they relegated the triumph of monotheism over paganism to the distant future, and in their comfortable aristocratic position they did not have the sense of despair and urgency of their less well-off brethren.

It would be wrong to suggest that religion was the *only* motive force in the Jewish resistance—that the Jews were blinded by their religious dreams in which they played the chief role in history to the plain facts of Roman power and the likelihood of failure of any rebellion. Even the Zealots, the most adventurous of the organised parties, were not such deluded fanatics as they are sometimes made to appear. There were practical considerations which made success against Rome a rational possibility. Common-sense and the assessment of practical possibilities did play some part in the plans of the resistance leaders.

We must remember that at this time the Romans were relative newcomers on the scene. We tend to think of the

Romans in the light of 400 years of subsequent history; but at
this time it was by no means certain that the Romans were
destined for a long-lived hegemony. Only a few years earlier
the Roman Empire had split into two halves grappling at each
other's throats in the war between Antony and Octavian. Such
internecine strife between rival Roman power blocs was always
a possibility; and the Jews remembered that it was precisely this
kind of instability in the Greek Empire, after the death of
Alexander the Great, that had enabled the Maccabean revolt to
succeed. The Romans did not appear any more formidable to
the Jews than the Greeks had been; indeed it was from the
Greeks that the Romans had learnt their methods of warfare.
With their long perspective of history the Jews were able to
compare the Romans with many previous conquerors who had
had their day and disappeared from view.

The vulnerability of Rome had been shown in the heavy
defeats she had suffered at the hands of the Parthians (53 B.C.)
and the Germans (9 A.D.). Both these defeats, incidentally, had
given a particular boost to Jewish morale because of the Roman
generals involved. In the case of the Parthian debacle the
Roman general so ignominiously defeated was Crassus, who
had robbed the Jewish Temple of its treasures. In the German
defeat, one of the greatest disasters in Roman history, the
Roman general was none other than Varus who, when Prefect
of Syria, had crucified 2000 Jewish rebels (6 A.D.). The Jews
must have thought that the hand of God had struck.

Eighteen years before his defeat by the Parthians, the
money-hungry Crassus had commanded the Roman army
which finally put down the slave-revolt of Spartacus in Italy
itself. In 73 B.C., just when Rome had emerged as the greatest
power in Europe, she suddenly found her power set at nought
by a band of escaped slaves in her own territory. The slaves
were of different origins: Thracians, Gauls, Germans, even
Italians, the human loot of Roman conquests. Their leaders,
including Spartacus himself, were gladiators, men who had
been set to kill each other for public entertainment. Spartacus,
an excellent general, defeated three Roman armies sent against

him and roamed unchecked through Italy for two years. He wished to lead the slaves out of Italy to found a new state of their own but his plan was rejected and the slaves, degenerating into mere looters, were eventually defeated.

This was an episode that struck at the root of all civilisation as it was understood in the ancient world. It aroused an unparalleled horror among the Romans. Spartacus's name became a bogy used long afterwards by Roman nurses to frighten naughty children. When the revolt was defeated the Romans set up a line of crucified slaves along the whole of the Appian Way, a line of 6000 crosses. It was a scene which was often to be repeated in Palestine. But the years in which the army of Spartacus triumphed gave hope to all those who groaned under the Roman yoke.

There is no record of Jewish opinion of the Spartacus revolt but it must have reminded them of their own origins as a band of slaves rebelling against the power of Egypt. After all, what Spartacus had wished to do Moses had done; the Jewish state was a successful Spartacist revolt. The episode also showed Rome to be vulnerable, and must have been in the minds of the Zealots whose social aims were no less revolutionary than those of Spartacus.

The Parthians who defeated Crassus and poured molten gold into his dead mouth (in scorn of his avariciousness) represented another hope of escape for the Jews. The Parthians were a mixed Scythian (Mongolian)–Persian people who had formed an empire in the East under Mithridates I (about 150 B.C.) by defeating the Greeks. Their religion was Zoroastrianism which they practised in a casual, unenthusiastic way (unlike the fanatical, intolerant Sassanian Persians of later times). Their empire was loose and disorganised and for this reason (rather than from positive friendliness) they allowed the large Jewish community of Babylonia which stemmed from the days of the Babylonian exile considerable freedom and self-rule. The Babylonian Jews were rich. They were also very loyal to Judaism and to the homeland, Palestine, to which they sent generous offerings every year under strong armed guard

for the maintenance of the Temple. Moreover, the kingdom of
Adiabene which was independent but within the Parthian orbit
became converted to Judaism in about 30 A.D. Queen Helen of
Adiabene visited Jerusalem to scenes of great enthusiasm in 43
A.D. This too made the Palestine Jews look towards the
Parthian sphere of influence for help in their distress. Groaning
under exorbitant Roman taxation and the crass oppression of
such governors as Pilate, they must have envied their brethren
under Parthian rule.

These, then, were the kind of practical reasons that reinforced religious considerations in the Jewish resistance against
Rome. This kind of calculation, however, was open to other
subject peoples as well as to the Jews. But, as we have seen,
their religions did not provide the same motivation, partly
because polytheism could not give the same sense of historical
mission as monotheism and partly because Judaism had a
revolutionary content. There was, however, another very
important reason in the religious field for their relative quies-
cence. This was the phenomenal growth of *other worldly* religion
in the Hellenistic world. This feature is so important for the
study of the background of the events described in the Gospels
and is such an important influence on the tone of the Gospels
themselves that it deserves some special consideration.

From very early times "mystery-cults" had been a feature of
Greek religious life. In the Eleusinian and Orphic "mysteries" a
secret ritual took place in which initiates went through
purification ceremonies which put them into a special relation
with the divine. However, these "mysteries" were not in the
mainstream of the religious life of the community. They were
essentially a private, individual matter. For the majority of
people religion was a matter of public worship of the Olympian
gods, and this worship was firmly centred in the life of the
everyday world over which these gods presided. Greek religion
in its greatest days, in Athens, was humanistic in tone, and the
art and ceremonies of this religion breathe an unexampled love
of the beauty of this world and of the human body. But after the
degeneration and fall of Athens, after the life of the Greek

city-states had been swallowed up in huge militaristic king-
doms following the death of Alexander, a great change of
emphasis took place. The mystery-cults began to assume a
much more important role and their character began to change.
They took on a more passionate tone, and they began a fevered
missionary activity. Their role became that of a *consolation* for
the miseries of life and a promise of a better life in another
world. They began to promise their initiates immortality, not
in the sense that their bodies would live for ever but in the sense
that their souls would be freed from the bodily clay and ascend
to the world of the Spirit.

As the civilization of Greece took over other cultures, its own
mystery-cults began to imbibe and become infected by the
mystery-cults of other nations. The Hellenistic world was a
melting-pot of religions, and in the political disillusion of the
time it was the world-weary, consolatory, ecstatic elements
that came to the fore. From Egypt came the cult of Isis and
Osiris, from Asia Minor the cult of Attis and the Great Mother,
from Persia the cult of Mithras. These cults had a long history
behind them and were derived ultimately from pre-historic
vegetation-religions designed to promote the fertility of the
earth. In their original form they were cults of human sacrifice
in which a chosen victim was killed in order to replenish the
vigour of nature. The victim came back to life as a god and was
worshipped. In their later Hellenistic manifestations, however,
these religions were no longer human-sacrificial. They had
become spiritualized and allegorized, and were no longer
associated with fertility but with the renewal and salvation of
the individual soul. They were still concerned with the death
and resurrection of a god, and the object of the mysteries was to
enable the initiate to take part in this death and resurrection and
so attain immortality and god-like status himself. In some of
these rites the initiate literally bathed in the blood of an animal
which was sacrificed to represent the slain god. In others, the
sacrifice was replaced by a solemn ritual in which the initiate ate
the body and drank the blood of the sacrificed god and so
attained identity with him. The time of the enactment of the

death and rebirth of the Phrygian god Attis, one of the most popular of these deities, corresponded to Easter-time; and the period between the death and rebirth of the god was frequently three days, (this being probably a remnant of moon-worship, since this is the time between the death of the old moon and the birth of the new).[1]

In addition to the mystery-cults, and partly derived from them, was the movement known as Gnosticism which derived elements from Stoic philosophy and from Babylonian astrology. It used to be thought that the Gnostic sects, of which there were many, were all heresies derived from Christianity, but it seems probable that Gnostic sects existed before Christianity began, and it may be closer to the facts to explain Christianity in terms of Gnosticism than the reverse. In Gnosticism there was a Saviour (in Greek, "Soter") who was one of a Trinity of divine beings. This Saviour was also called the "Son of God." In order to save mankind from its sufferings in this world of Darkness, under the tyranny of the Seven Planets, the Saviour voluntarily undertook a journey from his place in the world of Light. He redeemed mankind by his suffering and then ascended to Heaven to sit by the side of his Father in glory. An interesting and significant fact is that the Gnostic writings, even before the birth of Christianity, were bitterly anti-Jewish. They were composed in centres like Antioch and Alexandria where Greek-Jewish cultural rivalry was strong. The Gnostics included the Jewish God, Jehovah, in their speculations, but as a kind of Devil, the Creator (Demiurge) of this evil fallen world from which the Saviour comes to release us. The Jews themselves, however, were not wholly immune to the attraction of Gnosticism, and some of it got into their mystical tradition cultivated unofficially and in small circles later called the Kabbalah. On the whole, however, the Jews resisted Gnosticism because it was an expression of a dualistic view of life, a hatred of the world and of the body, a dichotomy between the body and the soul, which was alien to Judaism. A cardinal doctrine of Gnosticism was "the body is a tomb," (in Greek this is a pun: "soma sema"). An important characteristic of Gnosticism was its loathing of the sexual side of human nature. Gnostic sects were usually rigidly ascetic, forbidding sexual intercourse even for the sake of procreation; but sometimes (a tendency in all extreme ascetic groups) they would go the opposite extreme and indulge in wild sexual orgies in an attempt to rid sex of all contaminating guilt.[2]

All the religions and sects described above share the same characteristics: a movement away from life towards a dream-world, a movement away from concerted action in politics towards a concentration on the individual soul. One may regard these movements as showing an increased "spirituality," a distaste for materialism and a concern for the development of a divine potential in human nature. On the other hand, one must recognise behind these movements a sense of despair. Their object is Salvation, being rescued from the human condition which is regarded as irremediably fallen and degraded. Gilbert Murray justly called the whole spiritual movement of the Hellenistic world "a failure of nerve," and he refers to it as "the Great Failure."[3] The failure is to be seen not only in religion but also in the field of philosophy, that great humanistic enterprise which Greece gave to the world in her days of confidence and élan. The philosophies of the Hellenistic world were Stoicism and Epicureanism, both of them noble philosophies which inspired many great men and even at times moved individuals to noble action. But both were ultimately sad and resigned, seeing wisdom in damping down one's emotions and enthusiasms; and seeing no real hope in politics or in the mass co-operation of human beings. Where Plato and Aristotle had made the City the centre of their thoughts, regarding the philosopher as a citizen and constitution-maker, the Stoics and Epicureans saw the philosopher as an alienated individual making the best of a bad world.

This despair arose, no doubt, from a desperate political situation. More and more people, as the military despotisms developed, saw their right of self-determination taken away from them and found themselves in a complex world so dominated by irresistible power that external action seemed pointless. They turned in upon themselves. The Hellenistic world did not suffer from the decay of religion, as is often said. There had never been so much religion. It is not the case at all that Christianity came to a world starving for spiritual doctrines about salvation, the soul and the promise of Heaven. It was only the most successful of the salvation-religions. Christianity was not fighting against the stream, but was very much borne along by it. The religion that did stand out against the tendencies of the time was Judaism.

Two nations remained relatively impervious to the flood of mystical, consolatory religion: the Romans and the Jews. Despite Roman brutality to the Jews, despite the wars in which the Jews flung themselves against their masters, there was something in common between them. They both lived firmly in this world. It is a curious fact that the Romans were never really anti-Semites like the Greeks. They vilified the Jews often enough for their rebelliousness, but they never did the true anti-Semitic thing which is to cast the Jews for a cosmic role as the earthly representatives of the Evil Principle. After the two Jewish-Roman wars, from about 200 A.D., the Romans treated the Jews with respect right up to the time the Roman Empire became converted to Christianity, when the long nightmare for the Jews began.

The Jews were not entirely impervious to the religion of despair. Their apocalyptic literature, such as the Book of Enoch written shortly before the time of Jesus, shows a dualistic, hysterical tone which is foreign to the spirit of the Old Testament. Even this, however, is very different from the Gnostic or mystery-cult writings. The apocalyptic writings have lost all sense of political reality and look forward to vast supernatural happenings which will lead to the redemption of Israel, but the upshot of these happenings is a Kingdom of God *on earth* not in Heaven. Even the Essenes, who retired to a monastic life and opted out of practical politics, had a vision (as the Dead Sea scrolls show) of a final real-life battle which would result in the defeat of the Romans and the establishment of a Kingdom of peace and prosperity on earth. They had not retired into a fantasy-world, populated by imaginary beings, where the Romans no longer existed, and where earthly matters were of no real significance. Even so, the apocalyptic writings were on the lunatic fringe of Jewish life. They were never accepted into the canon by the Pharisees as holy writings; and it was only their importance to the Christian Church that preserved them. The Book of Enoch, for example, which is quoted in the New Testament,[4] was preserved by Christians. The whole Enochian angelology was regarded by the Rabbis as bordering on the idolatrous, and Enoch himself is never mentioned in the Talmud except in one rather deflating passage.[5]

The Jews were never induced by despair to succumb to the religious standpoint which regarded human life as evil. They did have a doctrine of immortality, but it took the form of a Resurrection of the Body not of an escape of the soul from the prison of the body to live in another world. Believing that the human body was created by God, not by an evil Demiourgos, the Jews could not detach themselves from earthly life. This is the fundamental thought of Judaism and accounts for its continual concern to develop a law to cope with the difficulties of ordinary human existence. This too is the basic reason why the Jews could not give up their communal ideal and accept enslavement. The Kingdom of God on earth was the vision which launched them against the Romans.

9

What Really Happened

It is time to consider, in the light of conditions in Palestine, the true facts that underlie the Gospel account of the life of Jesus. If we stand back from the Gospel narrative and concentrate on the bare bones of the story, we see the four following stages in Jesus's life:

1. Jesus began his public career by proclaiming the coming of "the kingdom of God."

2. Later, he claimed the title "Messiah" and was saluted as such by his followers.

3. He entered Jerusalem to the acclamation of the people and took violent action in "the Cleansing of the Temple."

4. He was arrested, became a prisoner of Pilate the Roman Governor, and was crucified by Roman soldiers.

From previous chapters we can understand what it meant in first-century Palestine to proclaim the "kingdom of God" and to assume the title of "Messiah." These were not (as they later became in the Gentile-Christian Church) purely "spiritual" expressions. They were political slogans which put those who used them in danger of their lives from the Roman and pro-Roman authorities, just as the use of expressions such as "the dictatorship of the proletariat" would attract police atten-

tion in Tsarist Russia. They were expressions of revolutionary
content. Time and again, as we see from the pages of Josephus,
these watchwords were raised in the troubled period with which
we are concerned; and those who used these phrases became the
targets of the Roman occupying forces and the native quislings
and in many cases died by crucifixion. If we fix our attention on
the *facts* of Jesus's life and death (as opposed to the interpretations of the facts added by the Gospels) we shall see that Jesus
was a Jewish Resistance leader of a type not unique in this
period.

The Gospels tell us that when Jesus used expressions such as
"kingdom of God" and "Messiah" he meant something quite
different from the meaning attached to them by all the other
Jews of his time. This is inherently unlikely. If he meant
something entirely different why did he use these expressions
at all? Why say "dictatorship of the proletariat" when what you
really mean is "God bless the Tsar"? If Jesus wanted to say that
his kingdom was not of this world, that he had no political aims
and that he had nothing to say against the Roman occupation of
the Holy Land, why would he use expressions which were
understood by the entire body of his compatriots to be political
and revolutionary in meaning?

The Gospels have undergone a process of distortion by
which the political dimension has been removed. This is not
only a matter of depoliticizing key phrases such as "kingdom of
God," "Messiah," "gospel," "salvation," and "son of David";
the actual political atmosphere of Jesus's time has been altered
out of recognition. Instead of a situation of seething political
discontent, we have the picture of a settled Roman province.
Jesus lived at a time when hardly a day passed without some
incident of oppression or revolt; when the presence of Roman
soldiers in the Holy Land was a constant provocation to the
inhabitants. Jesus himself lived in Galilee, a centre of revolutionary activity. Yet the picture we are given in the Gospels is of
a land in which the Roman presence is so unobtrusive as to be
nearly invisible. If a Roman does briefly appear, it is to act as a
benevolent restraining influence or as an example of Gentile

superiority. The contrast between this bland portrayal and the raw political reality should be the starting-point of any interpretation of the Gospels; yet the vast majority of New Testament commentaries do not even mention it. One may search through libraries of books about the Gospels without ever encountering the obvious and vital question, "Why does Jesus never criticise the Romans?"

The Gospels were written about 40–80 years after the death of Jesus, at a time when conditions were very different from those prevailing during Jesus's lifetime. Moreover, they were written outside Palestine, in a non-Jewish language, Greek, and by writers with a Hellenistic, not a Jewish, outlook. These writers were in fact pro-Roman and anti-Jewish.* It is not surprising, therefore, that in their hands the life-story of Jesus suffered considerable distortion. Fortunately the Gospels are not all of a piece; they contain certain elements or strata which survive from earlier and more authentic accounts of Jesus's life. It is possible to recognize these earlier elements because they ring true to the conditions which actually existed in Jesus's lifetime; they make sense in the context of early first-century Palestine while the later elements do not. In coming chapters these tell-tale survivals in the narrative (often preserved by only one or two of the four Gospel-writers) will be pointed out.

Even without such helpful indications, however, it is possible to recover the main outlines of the real story by looking at key concepts such as "Messiah." What did Jesus mean when he claimed to be the "Messiah"? What did Peter mean, in the first place, when he hailed Jesus with the words "Thou art the Christ"? (This was the incident known as the "Salutation," a turning-point in Jesus's career.) As a Jew with a background of Pharisaism and Zealotism (as his sobriquet "Barjonah" shows) Peter certainly did not regard "Messiah" as the name of a divine being. He had no idea of the later connotations that this title would acquire in Gentile hands; he had no conception of

*See Chapter 8.

"Christ" as the mystic *surname* of a divinity on the Hellenistic
Gnostic model, who descended from the World of Light in
order to act as a divine sacrifice in the World of Darkness.* And
the notion that the man Jesus standing before him was God
would have seemed to him bizarre and insane. He revered Jesus
as his teacher and Prophet and he now acknowledged him as his
King. But the picture evoked for him by the word "Christ" or
"Messiah" was that of someone like King Solomon, or King
Hezekiah, both of whom were "Christs." What he had in mind
was Jesus, or rather King Jesus, reigning in Jerusalem on the
throne of Solomon, bringing peace and prosperity to his people
and acting as a "light to the Gentiles." The notion of "Christ"
carried for him no associations of either sacrifice or divinity.

Now if Peter's notion of Messiahship was modelled on
someone like King Solomon, then his action in saluting Jesus as
the Christ was a revolutionary, rebellious deed. He was
challenging the power of Rome and declaring the Roman
Occupation to be at an end. In the Gospels as we have them,
this fact is thoroughly obscured. The concept of "Christ" has
completely changed and carries no revolutionary significance; it
is no longer a political, but a heavenly, title and conveys no
more threat to the Romans than if Jesus had been hailed as the
Archangel Gabriel. The Gentile-Christians for whom the
Gospels were written were in a situation which was very
different from that of Peter or Jesus himself. They were not
Jews, and were not living in a country occupied by a hostile
power. They were anxious not to give the impression of being
subversives or rebels; but they had a problem on their hands,
for their object of worship was a Jew who had been crucified for
the offence of rebellion against Rome.* It was therefore
important for the Christians to argue that Jesus, despite all
appearances to the contrary (the most damning being the
crucifixion itself), was a non-political figure. The depoliticiza-
tion of the term "Messiah" was an important element in this

*See Chapter 16(i).

strategy; with the result that a Hebrew word with a definite historical meaning acquired a non-Jewish meaning that Jesus himself would have found unrecognizable.

Jesus and his followers were Jews to whom the whole idea of a man-god was alien and repugnant, a direct contravention of the first and most important of the Ten Commandments. To the Jews, the title "Messiah" or "Christ" was a human not a divine title. When Jesus claimed the title "Messiah" he was not claiming to be God. This statement alone, if we follow through its implications, is a clue to what really happened.

According to the Gospels, the chief thing that brought Jesus to his death was his blasphemy in claiming to be the Messiah or Christ. Yet this claim would not have been regarded as in any way blasphemous by the Jews of the time, whatever their party. This title, in Jewish eyes, belonged to royalty, not divinity. Even the title "Son of God" was to Jews (but not to Gnostics) a human title applied at various times in the Hebrew Scriptures to kings such as King David, to ordinary Jews, and to non-Jews (by virtue of the common Fatherhood of God). The title "Son of Man" also was not a divine title. In certain esoteric writings it was the name of an angel (never of God); but the expression was far better known as a mode of address to a prophet (see Ezekiel, passim), and the expression was also in common use to mean simply "human being." There could be no grounds for a charge of blasphemy in Jesus's use of this designation.*

In addition to the offense of blasphemy, Jesus is represented in the Gospels as having offended against the Jewish religion in other ways, thus incurring the enmity of the Pharisees. The stories of Jesus's clashes with the Pharisees, however, do not stand up to examination. Many concern his alleged offence of healing on the Sabbath, but Pharisaic law did not forbid such cures. The Pharisees were very different from the reactionary hypocrites portrayed in the Gospels. The "new truths" enun-

*See Chapter 7.

ciated by Jesus were in fact ideas which had been previously formulated by Hillel and other Pharisee thinkers, and which were accepted in the Pharisee movement. Moreover, the arguments which Jesus is represented as using *against* the Pharisees are Pharisee arguments. Jesus's style of preaching also is typically Pharisee. He was himself a Pharisee, and the portrayal of him as an anti-Pharisee is part of the attempt to show him as a rebel against the Jewish religion rather than a rebel against Rome.*

There is no need to doubt that Jesus often spoke to the people on purely religious and moral topics, like any other Pharisee teacher, but if he had confined himself to these topics he would never have ended his life on a Roman cross. The emphasis in the Gospels is on Jesus's preaching, teaching and healing activities, to the exclusion of any awareness on his part of the overwhelming political reality of Roman occupation. The picture we have is that of a preacher and healer who suddenly, without previous preparation or indication, performed a political act by entering Jerusalem in his Triumphal Entry and who then immediately lapsed back into preaching and waited passively to be arrested and executed. This is a false picture, for Jesus's public speaking had a strong political aspect from the beginning. As a preacher of the "kingdom of God" he was announcing the end of Roman rule; his preaching must have contained denunciations of the Roman rape of the Holy Land, fiery prophecies of the imminent defeat and ejection of the Romans, and appeals to the revolutionary fervour, religious love of liberty and patriotism of his listeners. All this is omitted from the Gospels, and the "kingdom of God" has been emasculated of its political content and turned into a remote other-worldly place of individual salvation.

If Jesus had confined his activities to preaching and healing he would never have aroused the hostility of such political figures as Herod Antipas and Caiaphas. The Herodians and the

*See Chapter 5, and Appendices 4, 5 and 7.

Sadducees (of whom these two men were the leaders) were the Jewish quislings. They were watchdogs for the Roman occupying powers, and were profoundly indifferent to purely doctrinal matters. These, not the Pharisees, were the enemies of Jesus among the Jews. A crucially important passage in the Gospels is the following (Lk. xiii. 31):

> The same day there came certain of the Pharisees, saying unto him,
> Get thee out, and depart hence: for Herod will kill thee.

This passage has survived in only one of the four Gospels, and is one of those key passages which give us a glimpse into the true story lying behind the revisions of the Gospel-writers. It explodes the myth of the enmity between Jesus and the Pharisees, showing how the Pharisees saved Jesus's life.[1] It also proves that Jesus, like John the Baptist, was in danger of his life from the collaborators who cared nothing for religious matters but were much concerned about revolutionaries.

Also illuminating is the following passage (Lk. xxiii.2):

> We found this fellow perverting the nation, and forbidding to give tribute to Caesar, saying that he himself is Christ a King.

This is presented as a false accusation, invented by the Jews to discredit Jesus with Pilate. It is in fact a true description of Jesus's activities, given by the Jewish quislings to Pilate when they handed him over to the occupying power as a dangerous Resistance leader. The reference to the term "Christ" in its authentic political sense is unique in the Gospels, and makes nonsense of the contention elsewhere in the Gospels that a claim to Christhood could be made the basis of a religious charge of blasphemy rather than a political charge of subversion. If Caiaphas (who was appointed to his office by a Roman Procurator) had regarded Jesus's offence as purely religious he would have taken no action. If Jesus had put himself forward as God, he would have been regarded by Caiaphas as a harmless lunatic; and as for any alleged criticisms made by Jesus against the Pharisees, Caiaphas, as a Sadducee, would have regarded them with the greatest satisfaction. But to "pervert the nation" (i.e. stir them to rebellion against Rome), to forbid giving the tribute, to make the explosively political claim of being "Christ a King"—these are the very charges that would have made Caiaphas hand Jesus over to the Romans.*

But surely Jesus expressly refused to commit himself to an anti-Roman standpoint on the question of the tribute? No passage in the Gospels is better-known or more often quoted than Jesus's reply to the question, "Is it lawful to give tribute to Caesar or not?" Jesus's reply was "Render to Caesar the things that are Caesar's and to God the things that are God's" (Mk. xii. 17). This is the only passage in the Gospels in which Jesus is shown actually dealing directly with the fact of the Roman occupation. His answer appears to mean that the Romans were *entitled* to levy tribute from the Jews. If this was Jesus's meaning, he was endorsing the Roman invasion of Palestine and other countries, their subjugation, by force, of native liberty, their naked imperialism and wholesale plundering of weaker nations. The Romans had no more right to be in Judaea than the German Nazis had to be in occupied France, and in many respects the Nazi rule was the less cruel and greedy. Even the Sadducees and Herodians who collaborated with the Romans would not have adopted such a servile position. Like the Pétainists in France, they would have argued that collaboration was an evil and regrettable necessity. Jesus's actual words on the tribute may have been correctly reported in the Gospels, but if so they have been misinterpreted.† The accusation made against Jesus when he was handed over to Pilate, that he was "forbidding to give tribute to Caesar," was the literal truth, the necessary corollary of his preaching the "kingdom of God" and claiming the Messiahship.

---

*See Chapter 14.
†S.G.F. Brandon has argued that Jesus meant "Let Caesar go back to Rome where he belongs, and leave God's land to the people of God." In other words, he meant to forbid the giving of tribute not to allow it.

We see then that the whole trend and emphasis of the Gospel narratives are misleading. Jesus was not a harmless preacher who erupted into action only once in his life (the Triumphal Entry and the Cleansing of the Temple) and then relapsed into his previous passivity. He was not primarily a teacher of doctrines who incurred doctrinal and theological antagonism which brought about his tragedy. From the first, he was a man of action. From the moment that he began to preach the advent of "the kingdom of God" he was a marked man, and when he claimed the Messiahship he was in head-on collision with Rome. From the outset of his public career he was on the run from the pro-Roman Jewish authorities, i.e. the Herodians and the Sadducees, and from the Romans themselves; this is the reason for his poignant cry, "The foxes have holes, the birds of the air have nests; but the Son of man hath not where to lay his head."[2] Jesus's intervention on the political scene in his Triumphal Entry and his forcible reform of the Temple are not therefore inexplicable eruptions of violent action, but the culmination of his whole career. This was his bid for power; and when he failed, it was not because of the opposition of religious leaders but because the forces of Roman imperialism were too strong for him. Like many a Jewish patriot, both before and after him, he died on the Roman cross; and the people and their leaders the Pharisees mourned for him as a Jewish hero and martyr.

10

Jesus, Rabbi and Prophet

In the last chapter the view was put forward that Jesus was a rebel against Rome, not against Judaism; that his kingdom *was* of this world; that his aim was to be an earthly king on the throne of David and Solomon, not an angel sitting on a cloud. One of the implications we can now draw is that Jesus *did not go to his death voluntarily*. The whole idea of a god-man who sacrifices himself in order to atone for the sins of mankind is alien to the Jewish tradition. It is part of the sadomasochistic romanticism of the Hellenistic mystery-cults, with their irresistible appeal to those who found the burden of guilt unbearably heavy and who longed for it to be taken away from them by some charismatic divine figure. To the Jews, such a get-out from the moral burden held no attraction; moral responsibility was for them not a burden but a privilege.

When Jesus entered Jerusalem in his final bid for power he knew he was risking his life; but he did not *aim* at losing his life. He aimed at success, at defeating the Romans and establishing the kingdom of God on earth. He failed, and was crucified, just as 100 years later Rabbi Akiva failed and was torn to death by iron combs. Both Jesus and Akiva were Jewish heroes whose significance lies in their lives, not in their deaths. It was left to later death-worshipping mystagogues to exalt that instrument of torture, the Roman cross, into a religious symbol and to see more meaning in Jesus's death than in his life.

So much we can say with confidence. But can we venture further in exploring the details of Jesus's life? Can we know anything about his childhood, about the successive stages of his career, about his practical decisions and style of leadership, about the actions that led to his being a hunted fugitive, about the climactic incidents of his campaign of revolt? It might be thought that the Gospels are so distorted by an anti-Jewish bias that we must abandon the search for a reasonably detailed life of Jesus. Fortunately, however, we have four Gospels, not just one, and by comparing them and noting their inconsistencies many facts can be gleaned, especially when their order of composition is taken into account. Often a revealing and significant fact is retained in one of the Gospels though it has been censored in the other three. If such an incident *contradicts* the prevailing pro-Roman tenor of the narratives one can assume it is authentic, since such an incident would not have been added at a late stage in the development of the Gospels and must be a survival from the earliest versions.

The most important result of New Testament scholarship is that the earliest Gospel is that of Mark; this fact alone is useful in recovering the real facts of Jesus's life. Often we can discover the truth by taking into account the "spiritualization" of the narrative and translating it back into the more earthy terms appropriate to the background and period. Peter's "Salutation," for example, can be seen as the proclamation of Jesus as King of the Jews, heir of David and Solomon, rather than as a sacrificial god.

All that we know about Jesus's childhood is that he was born and brought up in Galilee, and trained as a carpenter. Two of the Gospel writers, Matthew and Luke, represent him as having been born in Bethlehem, claiming that his parents had to go there from Galilee for the purpose of a census. However, the only census in Jesus's lifetime took place in Judaea when Jesus was ten years old, and it did not affect the inhabitants of

Galilee; nor were people required to register at any place other than their usual residence.[1] The whole story was invented to strengthen Jesus's claim to be the Messiah, who, according to the prophecy of Micah, would be born in Bethlehem like his ancestor David.

We can dismiss as legend the story of Herod's Massacre of the Innocents (derived from the Biblical story of Moses), the story of the journey of the Magi (derived from an extra-Biblical legend about Moses), the story of the Virgin Birth, or miraculous impregnation of Mary by God the Father (part of the later deification of Jesus, and paralleled by countless mythological stories of the birth of heroes and demi-gods), and the story of Jesus's birth in a manger or cave (as in some apocryphal Gospels), and being greeted by shepherds (taken from the legend of the birth of Mithras). None of these stories is to be found in the earliest Gospel, Mark. They are trappings to the developing dogma of Jesus's divine origin, and are all designed to assimilate Jesus to previous heroes of legend and myth. There is no historical value whatever in these stories.

Jesus was not known to be descended from King David. Very few people among the Jews at this time could trace back their ancestry so far. The genealogies inserted in two of the Gospels showing that Jesus through his father, Joseph, was descended from David are later fabrications invented to support the claim that Jesus was the Messiah. Not only do these genealogies contradict each other, they totally contradict the story of the Immaculate Conception and the Virgin Birth.

What about Jesus's education? There can be no doubt that he was educated as a Pharisee; for this was the only kind of education available to the poor, and Jesus's style of teaching and preaching is stamped with Pharisaic characteristics (e.g. his use of parables, and his use of actual Pharisaic maxims). The contention of John (the latest Gospel writer) that Jesus was an uneducated man was probably invented to enhance the miracle of his alleged theological victories over learned Pharisee opponents, and to stress the primacy of faith over reason, an emphasis characteristic of ecstatic sects. Jesus's own sayings, his detailed knowledge of Scripture, and the fact that he was addressed as "Rabbi," all show him to have been highly educated. There was an enthusiastic brotherhood of Pharisee teachers centred in Galilee, so there would have been no difficulty for a bright youngster to receive a thorough grounding in Scriptural and traditional learning, together with calendrical astronomy and the other Pharisaic disciplines.

Jesus, then, became qualified and accepted as a Rabbi; but this does not mean that he ceased to be a carpenter. He probably continued in his craft until he undertook his mission as a Prophet. The Pharisees disapproved of religious professionalism, and the Rabbis would earn their living by ordinary trades and professions. Great leaders like Hillel and Shammai never accepted payment for their services as Rabbis.

Jesus was not only educated as a Pharisee; he remained a Pharisee all his life. Many readers may find this statement surprising in view of the alleged hatred of the Pharisees for Jesus, and Jesus's own denunciations of the Pharisees as hypocrites and oppressors. These passages in the Gospels are unhistorical, and arose out of the later history of the Christian Church, which *at the time when the Gospels were written* (40-80 years after Jesus's death) was in a state of enmity with the Pharisees. In fact, as we have seen, the Pharisees of Jesus's lifetime had no reason to hate him; and the Gospels themselves retain incidents which show the friendship that in reality existed between Jesus and the other Pharisees. The "anti-Pharisee" passages in the Gospels have been doctored in many ways. In several passages the word "Pharisees" has clearly been inserted where the original story had "Sadducees"; in these episodes (dealing, for example, with Sabbath-healing) Jesus is taking the typical Pharisaic line against a Sadducaic standpoint. In some episodes, the word "Pharisees" has not been substituted but *added*, with the absurd result that the Pharisees are several times bracketed together with the Herodians in plotting against Jesus! (This is like bracketing Gaullists and Pétainists together as companions-at-arms in war-time France.) Jesus's alleged denunciations of the Pharisees are late insertions, and some of them (especially Matthew xxiii) are disgraceful examples of Hellenistic anti-Semitism. Jesus himself would have been saddened and horrified by the speeches put in his mouth, in which he is represented as saying that the Jews and the Pharisees are the archvillains of history.[2]

As a Rabbi, Jesus was a typical Pharisee teacher. Both in style and content, his religious teachings show an unmistakable affinity to Pharisaism, and especially to the teachings of the great apostle of Pharisaism, Hillel. (Jesus's Golden Rule for example, is almost identical with Hillel's).'* Like other Pharisees, Jesus laid stress on the mercy and love of God, on love towards enemies, and forgiveness towards the repentant.

There is no evidence in the Gospels that Jesus tried to found a new religion. He accepted the Hebrew Scripture as the word of God, and made no attempt, for example, to abolish the Jewish dietary laws or the laws of ritual impurity. Like other Pharisee rabbis, he had his individual views on some points: he had uncharacteristically severe views on divorce; he may have objected to the practice of hand-washing before meals; he is represented as over-fond of threatening hell-fire to sinners (the Sermon on the Mount is punctuated by such threats which may well be a later importation derived from Gnostic dualism).[3]

Certain sayings of Jesus have been preserved which show that he had no intention of subverting Judaism. Of the Scriptural Law, he had this to say:

> Whosoever therefore shall break one of these least commandments, and shall teach men so, he shall be called the least in the kingdom of heaven: but whosoever shall do and teach them, the same shall be called great in the kingdom of heaven (Mt. v. 19).

Of the Pharisaic additions and reforms he had this to say:

> The scribes and the Pharisees sit in Moses' seat. All therefore whatsoever they bid thee observe, that observe and do (Mt. xxiii. 2).

*See Appendix 4A.

These statements are entirely at variance with the later teaching of the Gentile-Christian Church, by which Jesus was held to have abrogated the bulk of the Law contained in the Hebrew Scriptures, and to have repudiated Pharisaism altogether. Yet even the Gospels, despite the re-working they have undergone, do not show Jesus as flouting or attacking a single Biblical law. He did not abrogate the Sabbath. He advocated leniency in its practice, (his maxim, "The Sabbath was made for man, not man for the Sabbath" was a well-known Pharisaic saying). He did not abrogate the dietary laws, which continued to be observed by his immediate disciples in the Jerusalem Church after his death. He did not abrogate the laws of ritual purity, (after curing a leper, he told him to "offer for thy cleansing those things which Moses commanded"—Mk. i. 44). The only "impurity" law he is said to have criticised is the non-Biblical custom of hand-washing mentioned above.

The authenticity of his reported criticism of the Pharisees for "making the word of God of none effect through your tradition" (Mk. vii. 13) is doubtful. This criticism is a typical *Sadducee* complaint, made on the grounds that the Pharisees had nullified, by their reforms, the ancient laws of the Hebrew Scripture ("the word of God"). This complaint, if genuine, would mean that Jesus disapproved of all the reforms by which the Pharisees had made Scriptural law less primitive and severe. It would mean that he advocated a return to the literal interpretation of the "eye for an eye" law, to the ordeal by "bitter water" for suspected wives, to the parading of the "proofs of virginity" for a bride, and other primitive Biblical institutions abolished by the Pharisees through their "traditions." It is clear, however, from Jesus's other sayings that, far from disapproving of these Pharisee "additions," he advocated them strongly, (though the editors of the Gospels hide the fact that Jesus was advocating Pharisee reforms, and suggest that they were original moral doctrines of Jesus himself).

We have seen in Chapter 7 that Pharisaism was a movement of the poor and oppressed, as opposed to the Sadducees, the party of the rich. Such sayings as, "It is easier for a camel to go through the eye of a needle than for a rich man to enter into the kingdom of God," are characteristics of the Pharisees, and especially of their extreme wing, the Zealots, whose aims were communistic. The opening of the Sermon on the Mount, "Blessed are the poor in spirit: for theirs is the kingdom of heaven," breathes Pharisaism, as well as echoing many passages in the Hebrew Scriptures. A knowledge of the historical Pharisee party, as opposed to the malicious caricature of it found in the Gospels, leads inescapably to the conclusion that Jesus was a member of this party.* Some of the bitter arguments between Jesus and the "Pharisees" reported in the Gospels were probably amicable discussions in the original version. By comparing Mark's version of Jesus's conversation with the "scribe" (Mk.xii) with the later versions of the same incident (Mt.xxii and Lk.x), one can see the actual process of editing taking place within the Gospels themselves.

As a Rabbi, Jesus would have concentrated on teaching, but when he became a Prophet his life would have taken on a much more political, activist aspect. In the Gospels as we have them, however, Jesus's *teachings* become the central preoccupation of his life. This emphasis is achieved by exaggerating their originality so that he could appear as an epoch-making pioneer who was bound to arouse the antagonism of the Jewish leaders of his day. All this was part of the campaign to disguise the real reason for Jesus's death, namely his opposition to Rome.

In this connection, one particular aspect of Jesus's teaching requires comment: his alleged pacifism. If Jesus really was a pacifist, of course, he was no threat to the Romans. However, if he was a pacifist, certain episodes recorded in the Gospels are very hard to understand. Why did he drive the money-changers out of the Temple with a whip? Any money-changer on whose shoulders Jesus's whip descended would be justified in regarding Jesus as an odd kind of pacifist. Are we to understand that

*For more detailed comment on Jesus's Pharisaism, see Appendix 4 "Jesus as Pharisee."

Jesus was a pacifist only towards Romans, and not towards Jews? If he objected so strongly to profanation of God's Temple by Jewish money-changers, why did he not object equally strongly to the profanation of God's Holy Land by Roman idolaters?

If Jesus was a pacifist, why did he say "I came not to send peace but a sword" (Mt.x.34)? And why, on the crucial night of his career, after the Last Supper, did he distribute swords to his disciples? (This incident slipped through the net of censorship in only one Gospel, that of Luke.)

Clearly Jesus was not a pacifist at all. His "pacifism" is part of the story of his harmlessness and lack of antagonism towards the Roman Empire; the story by which the Christian Church hoped to lull the suspicion of the Romans that the Christians were a subversive group.

Matthew represents Jesus as saying:

> But I say unto you, that ye resist not evil: but whosoever shall smite thee on thy right cheek, turn to him the other also. And if any man will sue thee at law, and take away thy coat, let him have thy cloak also.

These sentiments are a perfect recipe for the proliferation of evil. "Resist not evil" is formula of appeasement. What Jesus may have said was "Recompense not evil" (derived from Proverbs xx.22), meaning "Do not seek a tit-for-tat revenge. Two wrongs do not make a right." The saying "Resist not evil" is a negation of everything the Jews stood for. Hebrew Scripture is full of examples of people who resisted evil—the "saviours" who fought against the oppression of Philistines, Assyrians, Greeks, and evil Jewish rulers. To Hellenistic mystics, driven inwards by political despair and a sense of powerlessness, the saying might give comfort, but to the Jews, with their unquenchable hope of the kingdom of God on earth, it was meaningless. Only the forlorn circumstances of the post-70 A.D. Christian Church could have led to the ascription of this saying to Jesus.

Brought up in Galilee, at the centre of the idealistic Resistance to Rome, the birthplace of the Zealot movement and of its leader, Judas the Galilean, Jesus would have been aware of the tragedy of the loss of Jewish independence, and of the presence of ruthless idolaters in the holy places of the people of God. He would have looked forward with eagerness to any signs of approaching redemption, of a saviour sent by God to rescue the Jews from foreign occupation. He would have felt the nation-wide shock at Pilate's attempt to desecrate the Holy City. This was in 26 A.D. when Jesus was 30 years old, and had already qualified as a Rabbi. He would have been excited by the advent of John the Baptist, with his prophetic message of the coming of the kingdom of God. And shortly afterwards he felt the call to a similar prophetic mission himself.

It is quite clear from the Gospels that Jesus's first appearance as a public figure was as a *prophet*, not as a Messiah or Christ. Like John the Baptist, he proclaimed the coming of the kingdom of God and called on the people to believe the "good news" and to repent. During this period he always describes himself as a "prophet"* (except in the Gospel of John, which differs from the earlier Gospels in its presentation of Jesus's personality and life-story and which, as we shall see, was very much a product of Church mythologising and Christology).

It is also clear that John the Baptist never subordinated himself to Jesus. On the contrary, John's movement and Jesus's movement were similar in their aims and even displayed a certain rivalry. Scenes describing John acknowledging Jesus's superiority ("the latchet of whose shoes I am not worthy to stoop down and unloose") are contradicted by other incidents preserved in the Gospels showing John adopting an attitude of equality. We know that John the Baptist's movement continued after his death, and that it was only gradually that his followers became absorbed into the Christian Church. The scenes in which John is shown subordinating himself to Jesus are intended to promote and hasten this absorption, and have no

*e.g. Mt. xiii. 57.

historical value. Luke's Introduction to his Gospel, written in a careful imitation or pastiche of Old Testament style contains an incident in which the unborn baby John leaps in his mother's womb in acknowledgement of the superiority of the unborn baby Jesus![4]

The "kingdom of God" heralded by both John the Baptist and Jesus was not a "spiritual" kingdom situated in the remote heavens or at some remote point in time; it was an earthly kingdom situated in Palestine in the immediate future. The phrase "the kingdom of God" was the watchword of the Zealots and other anti-Roman groups; it meant the *reign* of God (not His heavenly territory) and referred to a projected return to the Jewish system of theocracy—a return which could come about only by one means, the ejection of the Roman occupying forces.

By omitting everything of political significance from their accounts, the Gospels give a misleading impression of the popular movements of John and Jesus. The fact that Judaea was in a state of political ferment, and that a seething discontent with Roman rule constantly erupted into revolutionary apocalyptic movements, is scarcely hinted at. On the contrary, the Gospels give the impression of a settled province of the Roman Empire, long reconciled to Roman rule.

John the Baptist himself was a figure of strong political significance. He called for "repentance," which, combined as it was with the "good news" of the coming of the kingdom of God, was a call for preparedness for the overthrow of the Romans. It meant that the great days forecast by the Prophets were at hand; the days when foreign invaders would be defeated and the Jews would be a sovereign people to whom all nations would defer. It was vital to "repent" because the coming of the great day would be hastened by such turning-back to God; and also because the coming of the kingdom of God would be accompanied by great wars and upheavals in which many Jews would die and only those who had been thoroughly purified by repentance would survive. It was to symbolize this eligibility for survival that John used in his campaign the ancient Jewish ritual of baptism.

Jesus, at first, was almost exactly the same kind of figure as

John, i.e. a prophetic precursor-figure, preparing people for the coming of great events but not seeking to bring them about directly himself. There was a great change in Jesus's life when he took up the career of a Prophet. Instead of being a sedentary Rabbi, centred in one spot and ministering to a local community, he became a national figure, with a mission to the Jewish nation as a whole. This entailed a life of travel; he moved from town to town and from province to province, gathering a crowd in each place and exhorting the people, saying "The time is fulfilled, and the kingdom of God is at hand: repent ye, and believe in the gospel." He built up a small band of special disciples with whom he formed a travelling commune; this was the age-old pattern of Jewish prophetic organisation, as we see from such prophets as Elijah and Elisha in the Old Testament. He was not at this time a military leader; his mission was to act as a herald and a "preparer of the way." Nonetheless, he was unmistakably a *political* leader. The purpose of his mission was to prevent the people from sinking into submission to Rome and to raise their hope of deliverance in the near future. His activities, therefore, were carried out at the risk of his life; such prophet-figures aroused the immediate hostility of the Roman and pro-Roman authorities and nearly all came to a violent end. Josephus makes it clear that John the Baptist, for example, was executed for political reasons.[5]

In the records of Jesus's preaching preserved in the Gospels, we can see that the predominant note was "apocalyptic," i.e. an impassioned prophecy of the imminent arrival of the "kingdom of God." Parable after parable drives home the same points— that the advent of the kingdom of God will be sudden, and that those who have prepared for it will be saved and the unprepared will perish. This is the preaching of a man whose message is urgent and practical. It is not the preaching of a man whose message is primarily doctrinal, who is trying to found a new religion, or who is advocating new moral attitudes or spiritual insights.

It must be said that Jesus's mission as a prophet was exclusively directed towards the Jews, not towards the Gentiles. The idea that Jesus rejected the Jews and transferred the Old Testament "promises" to the Gentiles was a later invention of the Gentile-Christian Church.* Jesus stressed repeatedly that his mission was to "the lost sheep of the house of Israel," i.e. to the sinners among the Jews who stood in danger of annihilation in the troubles which would accompany the arrival of the kingdom of God ("the birth-pangs of the Messiah"). Jesus, in a passage which must be authentic because it contradicts so strongly the later trend of Christian thought, repudiated the Gentiles as "dogs" to whom it would not be meet to cast "the children's bread," (Mt. xvi. 26; Mk. vii. 27).

As a popular leader, then, Jesus was a prophet and a "preparer of the way." But soon a new and even more dangerous phase in his career opened out. He became convinced that the Messiah and deliverer whose advent he had been prophesying was none other than himself.

---

*For explanation of the term "Gentile-Christian Church," see Chapter 16, ii, and Appendix 8.

11

The Kingdom of God

The apocalyptic movement of which Jesus was the leader achieved great popular support, partly as a result of his success as a miracle healer (see Appendix 6). The death of John the Baptist meant that Jesus was the only remaining prophet-figure, although John's movement continued to have an independent existence. For a short period in Jewish history Jesus became the sole hope of a great number, perhaps even the majority, of the Jewish people. Jesus must have pondered deeply on the meaning of John's disappearance and on the relationship between John's movement and his own. These questions puzzled his disciples too, and they pressed him for an explanation.[1] The situation could not remain static. So far Jesus had played the role of a precursor or herald, pointing to events about to occur in the near future. Now the death of John and the explosive growth of his own movement made this waiting role impossible. His followers, convinced of his greatness, expected some bold developments from him. They pressed him to reveal himself and to take the national stage openly in Jerusalem.[2] Jesus himself must have been convinced by the success of his movement that a greater role awaited him than he had hitherto supposed.

It is worthwhile to pause here to consider the nature of Jesus's prophecies, made during the earlier part of his career, about the coming "kingdom of God." What kind of events did Jesus expect to take place when this great event actually began to occur?

The chief aspect stressed by Jesus in his prophecies, parables and other apocalyptic sayings is the *suddenness* with which the kingdom of God would arrive. He expected salvation to take place by miraculous means and with breathtaking swiftness.

> Then shall two be in the field; the one shall be taken, and the other left. Two women shall be grinding at the mill; the one shall be taken and the other left. Watch therefore: for ye know now what hour your Lord doth come (Mt. xxiv).

What kind of event would take place with such suddenness? Jesus himself was concerned with the concept of the "day of the Lord" which he derived from the Hebrew prophets. These obscure and lofty prophecies spoke of a "great and terrible day" when God would overthrow the foreign enemies of his people. They spoke of a great final battle in "the valley of decision."

> Let the heathen be wakened, and come up to the valley of Jehoshaphat: for there will I sit to judge all the heathen round about. . . . Multitudes, multitudes, in the valley of decision: for the day of the Lord is near in the valley of decision. The sun and the moon shall be darkened, and the stars shall withdraw their shining. The Lord also shall roar out of Zion, and utter his voice from Jerusalem; and the heavens and the earth shall shake: but the Lord will be the hope of his people, and the strength of the children of Israel (Joel, iii).

Jesus spoke frequently of "that day," saying for example, "But of that day and hour knoweth no man, no, not the angels of heaven, but my Father only."

The prophets spoke of the terrible enemy who would oppress the Jews:

A fire devoureth before them; and behind them a flame burneth: the land is as the garden of Eden before them, and behind them a desolate wilderness; yea, and nothing shall escape them. . . . They shall run like mighty men; they shall climb the wall like men of war; and they shall not break their ranks.

This must have seemed an excellent description of the Romans. But the answer, says the prophet, is repentance:

. . . turn ye even to me with all your heart, and with fasting and with weeping and with mourning: and rend your heart, and not your garments, and turn unto the Lord your God: for he is gracious and merciful . . . Then will the Lord be jealous for his land, and pity his people . . . I will remove far off from you the northern army, and will drive him into a land barren and desolate. . . . The sun shall be turned into darkness and the moon into blood, before the great and terrible day of the Lord come. And it shall come to pass, that whosoever shall call on the name of the Lord shall be delivered: for in mount Zion and in Jerusalem shall be deliverance, as the Lord hath said, and in the remnant whom the Lord shall call (Joel, ii).

Only a "remnant" would be saved, those who repented in time. The other Jews would perish in "the great and terrible day of the Lord." As Jesus said, "One shall be taken and the other left." That was why it was so urgent for Jesus to bring his message of repentance to the "lost sheep of the house of Israel."

It is in his preaching on repentance that the characteristic voice of Jesus can be heard. It is this that raises him from the status of a blood-and-thunder "end-of-the-world" revivalist. In a wonderful series of parables Jesus expressed Pharisaic themes of God's mercy and the efficacy of repentance in a manner hardly rivalled in the Pharisaic literature. These parables are so redolent of the spiritual atmosphere of Pharisaism that they are the strongest proof that Jesus really existed, and was a Pharisee teacher of original power.

The Pharisees were the creators of the parable as an art-form. Its homely vividness, drawing on familiar scenes such as sowing and harvesting, expresses their concrete, direct approach to life. (It is noteworthy that John's Gospel, the most Hellenistic of the Gospels, contains no parables in the true sense of the term.) The Pharisees used parables in order to make their discourses more attractive and easier to understand; this was part of their effort to reach the ordinary people.* Unfortunately, the Gospel-writers represent Jesus's parables as *riddles*, composed by Jesus in order to *prevent* the majority of his hearers from understanding his message (see Mk. iv. 11). This is part of the later Gentile-Christian portrayal of Jesus as alienated from his own people and having no serious intention of winning them over.

Perhaps the finest example of Jesus's repentance-preaching is the parable of the Prodigal Son (Lk. xv). The moral of this parable introduces it: "I say unto you, that likewise joy shall be in heaven over one sinner that repenteth, more than over ninety and nine just persons, which need no repentance." This is similar to the Talmudic saying: "Where the repentant sinners stand in the World to Come the perfectly righteous are not permitted to stand."[3] For the Prodigal Son who returned to his father in repentance the fatted calf was killed; and when the faithful elder son protested, his father replied, "Son, thou art ever with me, and all that I have is thine. It is meet that we should make merry, and be glad: for this thy brother was dead, and is alive again; and was lost, and is found." With this kind of parable, Jesus assured the sinful and despairing that it was not too late for them to turn back to God; that even though the "day of the Lord" was close at hand it was possible for them to enter the kingdom of God at the last minute if they truly repented; more, that their place in the kingdom would be higher than those who had never sinned, for "the last shall be first," and the last-hired labourers would receive their penny before those

*See Appendix 7.

"which have borne the burden and heat of the day" (Mt. xx). Similarly, in the Talmud it is said, "There are those who gain a place in the World to Come after many years, and there are those who gain it in a moment."[4] Sincere repentance can wipe out a whole lifetime of wrong-doing even for reprobates and gangsters like the "publicans."[5]

Though Jesus believed that his prophetic mission was to the Jews alone and especially to the sinful among them, this does not mean his attitude was parochial. He regarded the Jews as the key factor in world history; for the Hebrew prophets had taught that the "day of the Lord" would inaugurate an era of universal peace when the swords would be beaten into ploughshares and the wolf would lie down with the lamb. His call for repentance was a demand for a special spiritual effort by a dedicated nation whose role it was to achieve a breakthrough to a new world-era. Jesus aimed at the re-dedication of the whole Jewish people, basing his effort on the dedicated nucleus of Pharisees that already existed, and having in mind the salvation of the entire world from the rule of the sword.

We may sum up Jesus's beliefs and aims as follows. He believed that the time for the fulfilment of the prophecies of Zechariah, Joel and Isaiah had come, the foreign enemies spoken of in those prophecies being the Romans; that a great battle would take place against the Romans, in which the Jews would be led by a descendant of King David, a Messiah or Christ, who would be the lawful king of the Jews; that the battle would be accompanied by miracles (including an earthquake and plagues) in which the Romans and the unworthy among the Jews would perish; that the battle would be a victory for the Messiah and the Jews, who would then embark on an era of independence; and that this would also be an era of peace and spiritual advance for the whole world, when the God-given mission of the Jews as the people of God would be acknowledged by all nations, and the Temple in Jerusalem would be regarded as the spiritual centre of the world. The principles of social justice and freedom as expounded in the Hebrew Scriptures and in the Jewish tradition would be accepted by the

peoples of the world, and the era of robber military empires
would be at an end.

If this was Jesus's vision (as seems very probable from his
special dependence on the prophecies of Zechariah and Joel), it
was a noble one. It was also a revolutionary vision, involving
the overthrow of Roman power.

At the same time, it must be realized that Jesus was not a
Zealot. As we have seen, the Zealots, despite their religious
fervour, were committed to a realistic programme of long-term
guerrilla fighting, and apocalyptic visions played little part in
their thinking. They claimed no prophetic powers, and many
of them were too republican in sentiment to believe in the
advent of the Messiah. Jesus was first and foremost an
apocalyptist: he believed in the miraculous character of the
coming salvation, as described in the writings of the Scriptural
prophets. Again and again he described its sudden, miraculous
appearance; it would come "like a thief in the night," "as the
lightning cometh out of the east," "in such an hour as ye think
not." The important thing was spiritual preparedness, not
military preparedness, though when the hour finally came
fighting would be required, for the prophets had said that there
would be a battle. Jesus probably had in mind the example of
Gideon, to whom God said, "The people that are with thee are
too many for me to give the Midianites into their hands, lest
Israel vaunt themselves against me, saying, Mine own hand
hath saved me." Gideon's army was accordingly reduced
from 22,000 to 300. Yet those 300 still had to fight and it was
those who were "fearful and afraid" who were sent away.
Salvation would have a military aspect and the faithful would
not be mere onlookers at God's miracles; but the glory of the
victory would be primarily God's.

Jesus then was not a guerrilla leader. He did not train his
followers in military exercises or engage in skirmishes with
Roman troops. From the point of view of twentieth-century
scientific scepticism he may seem a self-deluded dreamer, yet
he was following a pattern common enough in Jewish history
and would not have been regarded as insane by current

standards of Jewish belief. (On the other hand if he had declared himself to be God and announced an intention of voluntarily undergoing crucifixion he would certainly have been thought to be mad.) Other anti-Roman groups would not have regarded his activities as in any way opposed to their own. Even those who did not join his movement would have followed his career with admiration and hope. And there would have been a constant flow of new adherents—men attracted by the daring of Jesus's claims, by the charisma of his personality, by the fame of his miracles, and by the prospect of a swift victory over the Romans instead of a long-drawn campaign. This explains why five of Jesus's closest disciples, the Twelve, came from the ranks of the Zealots (Simon the Zealot, Judas Iscariot, Simon Peter, known as Barjonah, and James and John, the sons of Zebedee, known as Boanerges, or "sons of thunder"). These disciples retained their Zealot nicknames even after joining Jesus, which suggests there was no fundamental disparity between Jesus's aims and those of the militant Zealots.[6]

The impression given by the Gospels is that Jesus was isolated from the mass of the Jewish people and from the religious and political currents of his time, from the Pharisees, (the "scribes," the "lawyers") as well as the Sadducees and the Herodians. As for the Zealots, they are not even mentioned. The sense of isolation is strongest in the Gospel according to John, in which Jesus's enemies are characterized simply as "the Jews," Jesus himself having become so other-worldly that he is not thought of as being a Jew at all. By the time the Gospels reached their final form the Jews were so hated by the members of the Gentile-Christian Church, with their background of Hellenistic anti-Semitism, that they could not believe that Jesus had ever seriously intended to win over the Jews. On the contrary, it was now believed that the Jews, as an accursed nation, were destined to bring about Jesus's death, and unwittingly to bring about the salvation of all mankind except themselves.

The impression of Jesus's isolation is reinforced in the portrayal of Jesus as being at odds with his own family. Jesus's "brethren" and "kinsmen" are shown as regarding him as a madman and as not believing in him. Yet this cannot be so, for Jesus's brother James became the leader of the movement (the Nazarenes, or Jewish-Christians) immediately after Jesus's death, and another brother, Judas, was also prominent in the Jewish-Christian Church and is credited with an Epistle in the canon of the New Testament. These two brothers were probably members of the Twelve during Jesus's lifetime, and are to be identified with James the Less and Judas Thaddaeus.* This has been suppressed in the Gospels in order to emphasise Jesus's isolation.

We have now come to a crucial point in Jesus's career. His movement has achieved a startling success—so great as to pose difficult problems for him. He is acclaimed by huge crowds who look to him for some important move. Herod Antipas, the pro-Roman ruler of Galilee, has become aware of the danger of Jesus's movement and is seeking to arrest him. Yet the Messiah prophesied by Jesus has failed to arrive, and John the Baptist, his fellow-prophet, has been arrested and killed. Jesus consults with his closest disciples, the Twelve, and the solution is found. Here is the account of this important consultation in the Gospel according to Mark:

> And Jesus went out, and his disciples, into the towns of Caesarea Philippi: and by the way he asked his disciples, saying unto them, Whom do men say that I am? And they answered, John the Baptist: but some say, Elias [i.e. Elijah]; and others, One of the prophets. And he saith unto them, But whom say ye that I am? And Peter answereth and saith unto him, Thou art the Christ.

Here the true meaning of "Christ" ("Messiah"), i.e. "anointed one" or "king" must be kept in mind. Peter hailed Jesus, for the first time, as King of Israel. Note how clear it is from this passage that the idea of Jesus as a Christ or Messiah

*See Appendix 3.

was at this time entirely new. The switch in role from Prophet to King was a dramatic one, unprecedented in Jewish history. Here, if anywhere, the uniqueness of Jesus is to be found. There had been Prophet-Rulers before (e.g. Moses, Samuel), and there had even been Kings who had prophetic, or near-prophetic, status (e.g. David and Solomon, both authors of canonical works), but there had never before been a Prophet who, in mid-career, had announced himself to be King. Yet there was nothing in this that ran counter to Jewish ideas. The King whom Jesus now announced himself to be was no ordinary king, but the final King-Messiah whose advent was the culmination of human history, the holy King to whom the world would turn as its spiritual head. It would have seemed very fitting that this King should have proved himself to have prophetic gifts. By becoming King, he did not cease to be a Prophet. He would in fact become the first King who was also a major Prophet; in him, the Monarchy and the Prophetship, so often at loggerheads, would be united and reconciled, and the days of the Prophet-Judges (such as Deborah and Samuel) would return, enhanced by the charisma of the Davidic throne. The rift between the spiritual and the secular powers, of which the prophet Samuel had so powerfully warned, would at last be healed.

The Hasmonean kings had attempted to heal the rift by combining the Monarchy and the *Priesthood*. The Pharisees strongly opposed the Hasmonean innovation, because it corrupted the Priesthood and confused two institutions which they thought it better to keep separate. The Prophetship, however, was not an institution in the same sense as the Priesthood. A man became a Prophet by the election of God, not by human procedures, and if God chose to give his Holy Spirit to his anointed Messiah, this could only be regarded as a sign of the greatest Divine grace. Jesus, by combining the Prophetship with the Messiahship, was not setting up a new institution, but bringing together two functions that might never be brought together again.

The Pharisees believed that there had been no true Prophet

in Israel since the death of Malachi, nearly 400 years before.
However, they did not think that prophecy was gone for ever,
and were always ready for a new prophet,[7] especially as they
believed that the renewal of prophecy would be the sign of the
arrival of the Messianic age. Jesus's claim to be a prophet was no
everyday thing, for very few such claims were made; but his
conception of being a Prophet-King was awesome and inspiring. It must have aroused tremendous enthusiasm in his
followers, and great hopes in the country generally. This lofty
new conception, combined with Jesus's own charismatic personality and gift of healing, accounts for the fact that Jesus,
unlike other Messianic claimants, was not forgotten after the
failure of his bid for the throne. His followers could not believe
that his crucifixion was the end. They believed that, like Elijah,
he was still alive and would soon return to lead them to victory.
This belief degenerated in the Gentile-Christian Church,
under the influence of Paul, into an idolatrous belief in Jesus's
divinity. In the Jewish mind, the idea of resurrection was not
associated with divinity. We see in the passage quoted above,
how natural it was for the Jews to suppose that Jesus himself
was the resurrected John the Baptist—even though the lives of
these two men overlapped. The Pharisees believed that all the
heroes of Jewish history would eventually be resurrected,
together with the righteous of every generation, including
righteous non-Jews. So the association between resurrection
and divinity which seemed so inevitable to Gentile-Christians
was quite foreign to the Jews.

Jesus, then, with his unique claim to be a Prophet-King, had
embarked upon a new and fateful phase of his career. Even as a
Prophet, his life was constantly in danger, for the aim and effect
of his preaching was to rouse the people from acquiescence in
Roman rule, and to keep alive their hopes of deliverance. But
now he was announcing the deliverance itself, and laying claim
to the title of Deliverer. By accepting Peter's salutation as
Christ or Messiah, Jesus raised the banner of revolt against
Rome. We now have to ask the question (necessary because of
the Gospels' attempt to disguise the whole matter), "What steps
did Jesus take to press his claim to be the King of the Jews?"

12

King of the Jews

The Gospels say as little as possible about Jesus's claim to be the King of the Jews. This expression appears with great abruptness when Pilate asks Jesus, "Art thou the King of the Jews?" Nowhere in the Gospels do we find the events or activities which such a question would lead us to expect: the proclamation of Jesus's accession to the throne, the anointing of Jesus as King, the appointment of officials of his court, the planning by Jesus of his royal regime. When Jesus appears before the Jewish Court, not a word is said about his claim to the throne; instead he is charged with blasphemy. Yet when he enters Jerusalem in his Triumphal Entry the people evidently know of his claim, for they greet him by the royal title "Son of David" and (according to Luke) "King." Jesus himself eventually disclaims any intention of being an earthly king by telling Pilate "My kingdom is not of this world" (according to John only); which makes his Triumphal Entry seem a pointless deception of the people. Though the Jewish Court says nothing during his trial about his claim to the throne, they make this claim the basis of their denunciation of him to Pilate, and the charge actually inscribed on his cross is "King of the Jews." The Gospels are extremely confused on this matter, and the usual interpretation (that Jesus claimed this political title without having any political intentions) only adds confusion.

These difficulties arise because the Gospel-writers, while they could not deny Jesus's royal claim, found it extremely embarrassing since they knew it constituted rebellion against Rome. They therefore disguised it in every way they could: by pretending that it was metaphorical only, by suppressing details connected with it, and by representing it as an invention of his enemies designed to get him into trouble with the Romans. While Jesus's claim to be the "Messiah" or "Christ" is pressed strongly in the Gospels, the title is divested of its political content, and the Jews are shown as not understanding the meaning of this concept, which arose from their own literature and history.

However, when we take a closer look at the Gospel accounts (especially those of the three "Synoptic" Gospels, Mark, Matthew and Luke), we find that the facts are not so much suppressed as disguised. If we adopt the method of "de-spiritualization" (i.e. translating terms like "Christ" back into their original political context and meaning), we can recover a great deal of the history of Jesus's short reign as King of the Jews. The Synoptic Gospels (unlike that of John) are, in the main, following the outline of an earlier gospel, or group of gospels, in which a Jewish-Christian* account of Jesus's career was given; an account in which Jesus was portrayed as a human Prophet and King, not as a divine sacrifice. This original account can be discerned beneath the "spiritualizing" devices employed by the Synoptists.

The first important event we can recover in this way is nothing less than Jesus's Coronation as King of the Jews. Following Peter's Salutation of Jesus as "Christ" (i.e. "King"), comes the mysterious incident known as the "Transfiguration." This incident, on examination, turns out to be a disguised, "spiritualized" account of Jesus's coronation.

*See Appendix 8.

Let us look at the account of the Transfiguration given by Mark:

> And after six days Jesus taketh with him Peter, and James and John, and leadeth them up into an high mountain apart by themselves: and he was transfigured before them. And his raiment became shining, exceeding white as snow; so as no fuller on earth can white them. And there appeared unto them Elias with Moses: and they were talking with Jesus. And Peter answered and said to Jesus, Master, it is good for us to be here: and let us make three tabernacles; one for thee, and one for Moses, and one for Elias. For he wist not what to say; for they were sore afraid. And there was a cloud that overshadowed them: and a voice came out the cloud, saying, This is my beloved Son: hear him.

Despite the miraculous trappings with which the incident is here invested, the underlying Coronation-account can be discerned. The announcement "This is my beloved Son" is taken from the Coronation Psalm (Ps. ii), which was recited at the coronation of every Jewish king. (It should be remembered that "Son of God" was a royal title, and carried no connotations of divinity.) It was a regular feature of a Jewish coronation that the king was crowned (or rather anointed) by a prophet, who addressed the king and was answered by him. In the absence of an actual prophet, someone would represent the prophet. In Jesus's coronation, two people evidently performed this function, representing Moses and Elijah. The presence of Elijah is natural, since the Messiah's advent was to be preceded, in Jewish belief, by the coming of Elijah, who would perform the function of prophet at the Messiah's coronation. The presence of Moses in addition can perhaps be explained by the fact that Jesus was the culminating Messiah, and was himself a prophet, so Moses himself, the greatest of all the prophets, was required to assist at his coronation.[1]

The making of the "tabernacles" by Peter can be explained by the fact that it was a feature of Near Eastern coronation rites, including the Jewish ones, to enthrone the king in a "taberna-

cle" or booth (Hebrew, "succah"). This feature of the "Transfiguration" had become so unintelligible to the Gospel-writers
that they represent Peter as not knowing what he was saying
when he offered to make the tabernacles. Peter probably made
only *one* tabernacle, for Jesus himself. The other two may have
been added by the Gospel-writers out of respect for Moses and
Elijah, and in ignorance of the true significance of the tabterna-
cle.

An interesting point is that the "Transfiguration" took place
at a specified interval of "six days" after the Salutation. One of
the features of Near Eastern coronation rites was that there was
a Proclamation, followed a week later by the full coronation
ceremonial. This is one of the few instances in the Gospels of a
specific interval being recorded between two events. Evidently
the Gospel-writers knew dimly that there was some
significance in the interval. We see now that the Salutation of
Peter, when he hailed Jesus as the "Christ," was not just a
chance event but a formal part of the coronation ritual, i.e. the
initial stage, or Proclamation.

An important feature of Near Eastern coronation rites was
that they took place on a mountain. The site of Jesus's
coronation was in fact Mount Hermon, which was close to
Caesarea Philippi where Peter gave his Salutation. Mount
Hermon is the highest mountain in Palestine, an awe-inspiring
spot which must have seemed to Jesus the ideal Coronation-
place. We see again that Jesus's journey to Caesarea Philippi
(outside the territory of Galilee) was not just a fortuitous
expedition, as it appears in the Gospels, but was made for the
express purpose of his Coronation.

Another feature of a Jewish Coronation was the presence of
representatives of the Twelve Tribes of Israel. This would
explain the presence of Peter, John and James, leaders of the
Twelve apostles, who themselves represented the Twelve
Tribes. Peter's rather strange remark, "Master, it is good for us
to be here," may represent some formula by which the leaders
of the Tribes acknowledged the sovereignty of the new King.

Finally, the term "transfiguration" itself signifies a regular
feature of the coronation ritual. The new king was regarded as

being re-born, and went through a certain ritual to show that he was "turned into another man" (I. Samuel. x. 6). This does not mean he was deified; but it lends itself to imaginative exploitation by the Gospel-writers in the direction of deification. Jesus was in fact no more deified or "transfigured" by this aspect of his coronation than Saul, David, Solomon, and all the other Jewish kings who underwent the same ceremony. However, the Gospel-writers used this feature of the Jewish coronation ceremony as the basis for their concept of the "Transfiguration" as an epiphany or assumption of deity by Jesus, and they combined it with other features taken from the experience of Moses on Mount Sinai (the divine cloud and the shining of Jesus's clothes and face) thus suggesting that this event constituted a new Revelation and the foundation of a new religion.

We see then that Jesus's Transfiguration was neither more nor less than his Coronation, carried out in magnificent traditional style on a carefully-selected spot, the lofty mountain-top of Mount Hermon, associated with anointing-ceremonies in the Psalms (Ps. cxxxiii. 3). From now on he was in truth King Jesus; and his actions, properly understood, show him to be conscious of his royal status, and determined to fulfil his duty to free his subjects from the cruel, greedy invaders who had deprived them of independence and liberty.[2]

Following his Coronation, Jesus began a royal progress towards his capital, Jerusalem. One of the regular rites or customs for a new king was to make an inaugural tour of his kingdom. Jesus could not do this immediately, because his first task was to make his appearance in Jerusalem and to take action against the Romans. But he planned to make his inaugural tour of the whole of his realm as soon as he was free to do so. This is shown by the verse in Luke, shortly after the account of the Transfiguration (Lk. x. 1): "After these things the Lord appointed other seventy also, and sent them two and two before his face into every city and place, *whither he himself would come.*" This is another instance of Luke carelessly leaving in a passage which the other Gospel-writers censored. It is clear from the subsequent instructions to the Seventy that they were being sent not to the few cities which lay in the path of Jesus's progress to Jerusalem, but to the majority of the inhabited places of Palestine. This body of Seventy is not even mentioned by any of the other Gospel-writers. The number seventy is significant, because this was the number of a Sanhedrin. Jesus, as Prophet-King, appointed his Sanhedrin and sent them to prepare the towns and cities of his realm for his inaugural tour. Clearly, Jesus had no intention or expectation of dying on the cross in Jerusalem; he was planning a tour of his kingdom to take place *after* his appearance in Jerusalem.

The Gospels, however, show Jesus, at this stage in his career, repeatedly prophesying his own death in Jerusalem and subsequent resurrection. The disciples are shown as failing to understand these prophecies, and at one point there is even a serious quarrel between Jesus and Peter on this very issue. While we may reject the idea that Jesus expected his own death in Jerusalem, it is quite possible that there was at this time some dissension between Jesus and his chief followers, the Twelve. The subject of dissension, most probably, was the plan of resistance to be followed against the Romans. Jesus's disciples, with their Zealot background, may have wished to organize full-scale military resistance. The country-wide enthusiasm for the advent of Jesus as Prophet-King must have seemed an ideal opportunity for mobilising a large army to engage the Romans in battle. Jesus, on the other hand, was a convinced apocalyptist, who considered that the fight against Rome would be won largely by miraculous means, and therefore made no serious military preparations. Peter, with his experience of Zealot fighting by which he had acquired the nickname of "Barjonah" ("Outlaw"), was especially persistent, but was brought to heel by a strong rebuke from Jesus. Judas Iscariot, another ex-Zealot ("Iscariot" is derived from "sicarius," or "dagger-man," another name for "Zealot"), was probably also prominent in these discussions, and this may account for the fact that in a later legend he was cast for the role of Jesus's betrayer. Jesus's personal charisma was so great that he was able to overcome his followers' doubts, and convince them that the miraculous intervention of God, as prophesied in the

Hebrew Scripture, would come, and that only a token military preparation was necessary. Jesus was no political or military opportunist. He was prepared to stake his life on his belief that his mission was of cosmic proportions. To drive out the Romans by force of arms, as Judas Maccabaeus had driven out the Greeks, was not his purpose; such success would only lead to the founding of one more dynasty like the Hasmoneans. Jesus would inaugurate the kingdom of God, a new era in world history, or nothing. It was this scorn of ordinary militarism that was perverted by the Gentile-Christian Church into a doctrine of pacifism. Jesus wanted victory, not his own personal victory, but the victory of God; in other words, the ideological world-victory of Judaism.

From Mount Hermon, Jesus, in his progress to Jerusalem, passed through Galilee, then through Peraea, on the east bank of the Jordan, until he reached Jericho. Here he was joined by a vast crowd in procession. Just outside Jericho, he passed the blind beggar, Bartimaeus, who greeted him as "Son of David." This is the first mention of this title in Mark's Gospel, and shows that Jesus's procession into Jerusalem was associated so strongly with his claim to the Jewish throne that even Mark cannot represent it as anything other than a Royal procession. *All* the Gospels record that Jesus, as he entered Jerusalem, was greeted by the crowd by unmistakeably Royal titles, such as "Son of David" and "King of Israel."

Acclaimed as the rightful King of the Jews, Jesus entered Jerusalem, riding an ass's foal in deliberate fulfilment of the prophecy of Zechariah (Zech. ix. 9):

> Rejoice greatly, O daughter of Zion;
> Shout, O daughter of Jerusalem;
> Behold, thy King cometh unto thee;
> He is just and having salvation;
> Lowly, and riding upon an ass;
> And upon a colt, the foal of an ass.

When the people greeted him as King, raised the ancient cry of independence, "Hosanna!" and strewed palms before him,

they were well aware that they were engaged in an act of
rebellion against Rome. Yet, according to the Gospels, Jesus
did not claim an earthly kingdom; his disciples misunderstood
him when they thought he was to achieve a triumph in
Jerusalem; the Jews as a whole were wrong in expecting him to
be the kind of Messiah described in their own tradition. He was
raising political hopes which he had no intention of satisfying,
and inducing the people of Jerusalem to engage in political acts
for which they would have to pay severe penalties. The Gospel
portrayal is hopelessly riddled with contradictions. The simple
solution is the obvious one: that Jesus was making a bid for
power as a literal, not metaphorical or "spiritual," King of the
Jews.

The Triumphal Entry was the high point of Jesus's political
career. The apocalyptic hopes which had centred round him,
first as a Prophet and then as a Prophet-King, burst into an
ecstatic welcome as the teeming crowds of Jerusalem, many of
them festival-pilgrims from the lands of the Dispersion, hailed
him with the cry, "Hosanna! Save us!"

What was the date of Jesus's Triumphal Entry? According to
the Gospels, it was at the time of the Feast of Passover, i.e. in
the spring. However, there are many indications that this was
not so, and that the Triumphal Entry in fact occurred in the
autumn, the time of the Jewish festival known as the Feast of
Tabernacles.[3]

The whole series of events from the Triumphal Entry to
Jesus's crucifixion (including an enquiry by the High Priest, a
trial before the Sanhedrin, a trial before Herod Antipas, and a
trial before Pilate, not to mention various previous activities,
such as the Cleansing of the Temple, the preaching in the
Temple and the Last Supper) is supposed to have taken only six
days (from Palm Sunday to Good Friday). This is an impossible
speeding-up of human political and judicial proceedings, even
if one does not allow for a full-scale insurrection. The theory to
be argued here is that Jesus's Triumphal Entry took place just
before the Feast of Tabernacles, and his execution took place on
the Feast of Passover, about six months later.

The most obvious feature that points to the autumn as the

date of the Triumphal Entry is the palms which were in evidence on Palm Sunday. At Passover time there are no palm branches in the region, and it is unlikely that Jesus's admirers would have greeted him with withered palm branches left over from the previous autumn. Furthermore, palm branches played (and still play today) an essential part in the rites of the Festival of Tabernacles. The "branches of trees" mentioned in the Triumphal Entry accounts are also important in these rites, being used in profusion to roof over the "tabernacles" or booths which give the festival its name, and to accompany the use of the palms (see Leviticus xxii. 40).

A curious confirmation of the autumn being the time of the Triumphal Entry can be found in the story of Jesus's cursing of the fig-tree, which happened immediately after his Entry. Jesus, apparently, came across a fig-tree without fruit, and said, "Let no fruit grow on thee henceforward for ever," whereupon the fig-tree withered away. Now this must have occurred in the autumn, as no one would expect to find a fig-tree bearing fruit in the spring. The reason for Jesus's angry reaction is probably this: the Hebrew Prophets had foretold that the time of the Messiah would be one of unprecedented fertility of plants and animals (e.g. Joel ii. 22: ". . . the fig-tree and the vine do yield their strength"). Jesus, with his Galilean belief in evil spirits, may have thought that the fig-tree contained an evil spirit that was fighting against the kingdom of God.

Use of the cry "Hosanna" by the crowd (Hebrew, "hosha-na," meaning "save, please") also confirms an autumn date for Jesus's entry. This cry has a special liturgical use in the rites of Tabernacles, and in no other festival.[4] The cry was addressed to God, not to Jesus, and meant something like, "Save us, God, through your Messiah." The word "save" is especially associated, throughout the Hebrew Scriptures, with God's mercies through rulers and fighters who protected Israel against their enemies. A prayer for such salvation was offered up in the Feast of Tabernacles and would have been especially fitting as an accompaniment to Jesus's Entry on a mission of salvation.

This leads us to an even more important point: that the Feast

of Tabernacles was in a special sense a Royal festival. In
general, the Jewish royal family had little part to play in the
ceremonials of the Jewish religion; but the exception was the
Feast of Tabernacles. In this festival, the King actually entered
the Temple Court and read aloud "the paragraph of the king,"
i.e. the portion of the Mosaic Law relating to his duties (Deut.
xvii. 14-20). The Mishnah describes this rite as follows:

> After what manner was the paragraph of the king? After
> the close of the first Festival day of the Feast of Tabernac-
> les, in the eighth year, after the going forth of the Seventh
> Year, they used to prepare for him in the Temple Court a
> wooden platform on which he sat. . . . The minister of the
> synagogue used to take a scroll of the Law and give it to the
> Prefect, and the Prefect gave it to the High Priest, and the
> High Priest gave it to the king, and the king received it
> standing and read it sitting. King Agrippa received it
> standing and read it standing, and for this the Sages
> praised him. And when he reached, "Thou mayest not put
> a foreigner over thee which is not thy brother," his eyes
> flowed with tears; but they called out to him, "Thou art
> our brother! Thou art our brother!" (Mishnah Sotah 7:8)

This passage shows that the Reading of the Law by the King
was performed every seven years. No doubt Jesus timed his
Entry to coincide with the end of the Year of Release, on the
expiry of which the King's Reading of the Law took place. He
would have carefully planned the timing of his Coronation and
his Royal Progress so that he arrived in Jerusalem just in time
for the Festival. He would then enter the Temple Court as King
and renew the rite performed by his great predecessors on the
Jewish throne. This act more than any other would signalize his
accession to the throne and his intention to carry out the duties
of a king and saviour.[5]

One particular figure must have been in Jesus's mind, namely
his great ancestor, King Solomon. Solomon was a king of
near-prophetic status, credited with the authorship of three
canonical works (Song of Songs, Proverbs and Ecclesiastes). It

was on the Feast of Tabernacles that Solomon performed the
Dedication of the First Temple, offering a long, moving prayer
to God, standing on a platform specially built in the Temple
Court.[6]

We can see now why Jesus's first action on entering
Jerusalem was the Cleansing of the Temple. This action has
been much trivialized by the Gospel-writers, who have represented it as an individual demonstration in which Jesus chased
out the money-changers with a whip. The action was far more
important than this: Jesus, as the rightful King, carried out a
thorough-going reform of the Temple, cleansing it from the
corruptions of its venal Sadducean High-Priesthood. Jesus now
was at the height of his power. Though he had no organised
army, the Jewish masses applauded his every move. The
Temple police, who would have acted sharply against mere
individual violence, were powerless to hinder Jesus's reforms.
He may even have appointed a new High Priest, which as King
he was entitled to do, (this is the first thing that the insurgents
did in the Jewish War of 66 A.D.).

Having cleansed the Temple administration, Jesus must
have carried through his plan of re-dedicating the Temple for
the Messianic age by appearing in the Temple Court, like
Solomon at the Dedication of the First Temple, to read "the
paragraph of the King." No doubt, like Solomon too, he took
the occasion to address a prayer to God for his new regime, and
perhaps to give a prophetic message to the people. So much we
can gather from a confused and garbled account, found only in
the Gospel according to John, of a visit by Jesus to the Temple
on the Feast of Tabernacles—though John represents this visit
as being a distinct occasion from the Triumphal Entry.[7]

The parallel between Jesus and Solomon throws light on a
charge that was later made against Jesus: that he threatened to
destroy the Temple, and rebuild it in three days. It is quite
possible that Jesus did declare an intention to destroy and
rebuild the Temple, once his Kingdom was fully established.
The Temple which Jesus now ruled had been built by Herod
the Great, known to the Pharisees as Herod the Wicked. The

Pharisees had given their reluctant consent to Herod's rebuild-
ing of the Temple, but despite its superb beauty, they never
expected his Temple to last into the reign of the Messiah. If
Jesus had indeed proved himself to be the King-Messiah by
expelling the Romans, the Pharisees would not have objected to
his destroying Herod's Temple and building another; they
would have expected him to do so. Why should not the
Messiah-King of the Last Days, a greater King even than
Solomon, build and dedicate the final Temple? Why should the
purified and re-dedicated Jewish people, restored to freedom,
worship God in a temple built by the corrupt Herod? There is
nothing here that the Pharisees would have regarded as blasphemous, or that would have frightened anyone except the
High Priest, Caiaphas, and his clique. The idea that the
Pharisees regarded the Temple as a sort of god, which it would
be blasphemous to alter, is entirely wrong. The charge of
planning to destroy and rebuild the Temple was part of the
indictment made against Jesus, not as a blasphemer or rebel
against Judaism, but as a rebel against the quisling regime of the
High Priest.

Thus the dating of the Triumphal Entry in the autumn,
rather than the spring, makes much more sense of the whole
series of events; this is just the time that someone seriously
putting himself forward as the Messiah would have chosen to
enter Jerusalem. One more important argument has not yet
been mentioned. The prophecy of Zechariah says that the great
battle of the Last Days would take place in the autumn, at the
time of the Feast of Tabernacles. On the anniversary of this
great event, all the nations of the earth would be required to
come to Jerusalem to celebrate the Feast of Tabernacles in
Messianic times, (Zech. xiv. 16). When Jesus entered Jerusalem
riding on an ass's colt, he was committing himself to
Zechariah's concept of the Last Days. Those who knew their
Scripture (and there were many who did) would know from
Jesus's manner of entry what his intentions were—to engage
the Romans in battle before the Feast of Tabernacles came to an
end.

Why then did the Gospel-writers (probably following an

already established Gentile-Church tradition) place the Triumphal Entry in the spring? The most likely reason is that to the Gentile-Christians the important event in Jesus's life was his *death by crucifixion*, which they came to regard as the real point of the story. It seemed more dramatic therefore to telescope events, subordinating them all to the Crucifixion and crowding them all into the last scene of the play. The Crucifixion took place in the spring; this, therefore, became the time of all the culminating events of Jesus's life.

In the resurrection-cults of Adonis, Attis and Osiris, the death and resurrection of the Young God took place in the spring. The Triumphal Entry, therefore, would accord with the feting of the Young God before his sacrifice in these cults; and it would therefore be felt right to move the Triumphal Entry much closer to the Sacrifice to which it was now merely the preliminary. The appeal of Christianity to the ancient world depended a good deal on such affinities.

To Jesus, however, who expected success, not failure, and who would not have understood the romantic apotheosis of failure, the natural time for his arrival in Jerusalem was the autumn, the time of the harvest-rejoicing. Many of Jesus's parables compare the coming of the kingdom of God to the harvest-time. This was the most joyous time of the Jewish year, when the New Year period of purification was over, the harvest was secure, and the time for thanksgiving had arrived. The Feast of Tabernacles is the only one of which Scripture says "And you shall be wholly joyful." Passover, the spring festival, was the time of beginning salvation, the anniversary of the Exodus from Egypt, the beginning of the Jewish story. But the triumphant end of the story could be expected to occur in the autumn; just as King Solomon celebrated in the autumn the end of a long period of tribulation and the inauguration of a Messianic reign.[8]

In the event, Jesus's hopes were tragically falsified, and it was left to the Gentile-Christian Church to turn his failure into a cult. Jesus himself would never have seen more significance in a spring sacrifice than in the fruition of autumn.

13

The Day of the Lord

Jesus's reign as King of the Jews in Jerusalem lasted for less than a week. What happened during that week? According to the Gospels, the only positive action performed by Jesus was his Cleansing of the Temple. After that, apparently, he confined himself to teaching and preaching in the Temple until the time of his arrest. From the argument of the last chapter, we see that Jesus did much more than this. The Cleansing of the Temple was not an isolated incident but a full reform, entailing the occupation of the Temple area by Jesus and his followers. As in so many other insurrections of this kind described by Josephus, Jesus would have made himself master of *part* only of Jerusalem. Most of Jerusalem would still have been held by the Roman troops of Pilate and the Jewish troops of the High Priest. From the point of view of Pilate and Caiaphas, the insurrection was not a great affair. For a few days (as they would have put it) a deluded fanatic with mob support was able to hold a limited area of Jerusalem, including the Temple grounds, thereby interrupting the jurisdiction of the High Priest temporarily. The Temple services were not interrupted, for Jesus allowed the vast majority of the priests to remain at their posts, ejecting only those closely associated with the quisling Caiaphas.

However, for those few days, Jesus reigned supreme in the Temple area. The Gospels make it clear that the High Priest was unwilling to attempt the arrest of Jesus because of the strong popular support given him by the Festival crowd. Caiaphas probably calculated that it would be better to wait until the first wave of enthusiasm was over and then catch Jesus off guard. He did not ask for the aid of Roman troops at this stage because he thought he would be able to handle the matter himself.

Jesus's appearances in the Temple during those few days would have been as a Prophet-King, not as the mere preacher portrayed in the Gospels. His performance of the Tabernacles rites of the King was a political act of great significance, consolidating his claim to the Messiahship. His preaching was no doubt of an apocalyptic character, as the Gospels indeed show, but not prophesying his own death and the doom that would come on the Jews and the Temple; these prophecies were inserted in the Gospels after the defeat of the Jews and the destruction of the Temple by the Romans in 70 A.D.

Jesus did not spend all his time in the Temple area during his few days of kingship. In the evenings he went to the Mount of Olives, on the east of Jerusalem, about a mile outside the city. The prophecy of Zechariah on which Jesus was particularly relying states that the location of the miracle would be the Mount of Olives. This mountain was of great religious significance, especially for a Messiah, for not only was it the location of the expected miracle, it was also the place where King David used to pray. Moreover, it was here that the prophet Ezekiel had seen the appearance of the "glory of God" for which Jesus too was waiting.[1]

It was in Bethany, a small town on the Mount of Olives, that the curious incident of the precious ointment occurred. According to the Gospels, an unnamed woman poured some ointment of spikenard over Jesus's head.[2] This may well be a garbled account of a Coronation ceremony performed on the

Mount of Olives. Jesus's Coronation on Mount Hermon was incomplete, because the holy anointing oil was not available. Having made himself master of the Temple, Jesus would have come into possession of the store of holy oil and taken the opportunity to have the missing rite performed on the holy mountain where he expected his Messiahship to be finally confirmed.[3]

We now come to the incident known as the Last Supper. It follows from the argument of the last chapter that this took place not at Passover time but during the Feast of Tabernacles. In the Gospels the Last Supper has been overlaid with myth serving three purposes: to show that Jesus foresaw and intended his own death on the cross; to show how Judas Iscariot became possessed by Satan and determined to betray Jesus; and to show that Jesus instituted the rite of Communion, with its pagan symbolism of eating the flesh and drinking the blood of the god.

No trace is revealed of any of the special rites of a Passover "Seder," such as the eating of unleavened bread, the eating of the Paschal lamb, the bitter herbs, and the relating of the Exodus from Egypt. The only special rite of Tabernacles, as regards eating, is the taking of meals in the Succah, or booth (from which the festival takes its name). Of this there is some trace in the odd reference to an "upper room," described in Mark as "strewn over" (Greek, "estromenon"). In Jerusalem, the ritual booths or "tabernacles" were often constructed on the flat roofs of houses, so the "upper room" may in fact have been a "tabernacle" which was "strewn over" with tree-branches in the prescribed manner.

The feature of Sanctification ("Kiddush") with wine and bread is common to all Jewish Festivals, and applies to Tabernacles as much as to Passover. There is no mystical symbolism of "flesh" and "blood" in the Jewish use of bread and wine in the ceremony of Kiddush. The wine is used first to pronounce a blessing on the Festival. The bread is then used as a ceremonial beginning to the Festival meal. Jesus would have been appalled to know of the pagan interpretation later put on the simple Kiddush with which he began the Last Supper.

Jesus had no foreknowledge of his failure and crucifixion. The Last Supper was a celebration with his closest disciples of his appearance as King and the imminent overthrow of Roman power. After preparing himself by several nights of meditation and prayer on the Mount of Olives, Jesus was convinced that "the day of the Lord" was close at hand, and he called together his disciples for a final strengthening of the bond between them before their crucial testing-time. The atmosphere must have been extremely tense. They were about to embark on a great venture on which the fate of their country and whole world would depend. But the special poignancy and drama of the Gospel accounts are the product of hindsight and of the myths that grew up later to explain Jesus's failure.

The Last Supper would also have been regarded as a foretaste of the great Supper and Feast which would take place if Jesus were successful. Jewish legend, prophesying Messianic times, contained many details of the great Messianic Feast at which the Leviathan would be eaten and all the great heroes of Jewish history would be present.[4] This is no doubt what Jesus meant when he said at the Last Supper, "Verily, I say unto you, I will drink no more of the fruit of the vine until that day that I drink it new in the kingdom of God." Their next meal would be the Messianic Feast itself, in celebration of victory over God's enemies, the Romans.

After the Last Supper Jesus led his disciples as usual to the Mount of Olives. But this time there was a difference. Jesus was convinced that this was the night on which God would appear in glory and overthrow the foreign invaders of his Holy Land. Accordingly, he required his disciples to equip themselves with swords. Two swords were produced, and Jesus said, "It is enough." The Messiah and his followers, like Gideon and his tiny band, would be required to fight, for the prophecy of Zechariah had said, among its awesome predictions of God's intervention, "And Judah also shall fight at Jerusalem." But two swords would be enough: the miracle would be even greater than in the case of Gideon.

Only Luke, of the Gospel-writers, has retained the incident

of the swords. He could have had no possible motive in inventing it, for it goes against the whole grain of his narrative. The only possible explanation of its inclusion is that it is a survival from the original story which only Luke was not ruthless enough to excise. The Gospel-writers were following the outline of an older Gospel. To twist this Gospel to a new meaning required courage of a kind; sometimes their nerve may have failed them. This would explain why the bones of the old narrative can sometimes be seen jutting out uncomfortably from the body of the new.

Jesus was now determined to put to the test his interpretation of the prophecy of Zechariah. It may be useful, therefore, to have before us this prophecy, which was of such fateful importance for Jesus:

Then shall the Lord go forth, and fight against these nations, as when he fought in the day of battle. And his feet shall stand in that day upon the mount of Olives, which is before Jerusalem in the east, and the mount of Olives shall cleave in the midst thereof toward the east and toward the west, and there shall be a very great valley; and half the mountain shall move toward the north, and half of it toward the south. And ye shall flee to the valley of the mountains; for the valley of the mountains shall reach unto Azal . . . and the Lord my God shall come, and all the saints with thee. And it shall come to pass in that day, that the light shall not be clear nor dark. But it shall be one day which shall be known to the Lord, not day nor night: but it shall come to pass that at evening time it shall be light . . . And the Lord shall be king over all the earth: in that day shall there be one Lord, and his name one . . . And this shall be the plague wherewith the Lord will smite all the people that have fought against Jerusalem. Their flesh shall consume away while they stand upon their feet, and their eyes shall consume away in their holes, and their tongue shall consume away in their mouth . . . And Judah also shall fight at Jerusalem. . . . And it shall come to pass, that everyone that is left of all the nations which came against Jerusalem shall even go up from year to year to worship the King, the Lord of hosts, and to keep the feast of tabernacles . . . and in that day there shall be no more the Canaanite in the house of the Lord of hosts.

The strong influence of the prophecy of Zechariah on Jesus is shown, in particular, by his mode of entrance into Jerusalem riding on an ass's colt. Such deliberate fulfillment of Zechariah ix. 9, suggests that Jesus also had the rest of Zechariah's prophecies in mind.

"The people that have fought against Jerusalem" were none other than the Romans, the heathen barbarians who had united "the nations" in a great empire and had set their faces against God. He himself, Jesus of Nazareth, was the person to whom the prophet was addressing his instructions; the Messiah who would arrive in Jerusalem on an ass's colt, and would stand in "the valley of the mountains" together with a company of "saints" to witness the appearance of the glory of God on the Mount of Olives. He would see the Romans stricken by a plague, and would lead "Judah" in fighting against them. Then, after a great victory, he would reign as the King-Messiah in Jerusalem, where every year on the anniversary of his victory he would welcome representatives of every nation on earth, coming to pay homage to the Lord of Hosts in his Temple.

It may be objected that this account makes Jesus appear insane. Could he really have expected the prophecies of Zechariah to be fulfilled so literally that very night on the Mount of Olives? How could he have been so sure he knew the exact hour of the prophecies, and that it was through him that they would be fulfilled? As a person Jesus was what would today be described as a "manic" character, i.e. one capable of remaining for long periods at a high pitch of enthusiasm and euphoria. This enabled him to perform his miracles of healing, and to impress his associates to such an extent that they could not let his memory die. He was not Judas of Galilee, or Bar Kochba, who were Messiahs of essentially ordinary or normal temperament, men who made their bid for power, failed, and that was that. It was no accident that Jesus gave rise to a new-world religion. Though Christianity was a falsification of everything that Jesus stood for, yet every detail of this falsification was built on something that existed in his temperament and outlook. It was only a step for the Hellenistic Gentiles to transform Jesus's soaring conviction of his universal mission into a dogma of his divinity; or to transform his confidence of victory by the hand of God, rather than by guerrilla methods, into a pacifist other-worldly doctrine which transferred the concept of victory on to a "spiritual" plane. Jesus's "manic" temperament was the mainspring of the early Christian Church, with its ecstatic mood, its universal ambition, and its confidence in ultimate victory.

To modern minds, it would seem insane to expect to overthrow Rome without a proper army and with only two swords, because of some obscure sentences in a book written five hundred years before Jesus's birth. Yet the Christian account of Jesus makes him appear even more insane. According to this account, Jesus regarded himself as one of the Three Persons of the Triune Almighty God, who had descended from the immensities of the World of Light in order to immolate himself on behalf of mankind. Such a combination of megalomania and suicidal fantasy was entirely alien to the society of Judaea and Galilee in Jesus's day. They had their own apocalyptic extravagances, but this kind of Hellenistic schizophrenia was quite outside their experience or understanding. Jesus never regarded himself in this way. His charismatic, profoundly impressive "manic" nature followed the pattern laid down for such temperaments in the Jewish prophetic tradition. His claims would have seemed, to his contemporaries, breathlessly daring but entirely reasonable.

The Jewish Resistance against Rome consisted of various groups, all of which were religious in character. They differed, however, on the question of how much could be left to the intervention of God. The Zealots were prepared for a long, hard fight by realistic military methods. Bar Kochba, successor of the Zealots, is said to have prayed to God, "Master of the Universe, I do not ask that you should fight on my side; only that you should not fight for the Romans, and that will be enough."[5] Some would-be Messiahs, such as Theudas, were at the other extreme, and relied on God even more than Jesus did.[6] The moderate Pharisees were cautious "wait-and-see" people, who like Gamaliel, thought, "If this counsel or this work be of men, it will come to nought; but if it be of God, ye cannot overthrow it." But even they could be carried away by apocalyptic fervour at times, as was Rabbi Akiva in the days of Bar Kochba. Jesus can be placed, in the spectrum of the Jewish Resistance, as an apocalyptic Pharisee whose hopes were similar to those of Theudas, and of the prophet from Egypt, mentioned by Josephus, who also centred his movement round an expected miracle on the Mount of Olives.[7]

Having arrived at the Mount of Olives, Jesus stationed himself with his disciples in the "garden of Gethsemane." This is located traditionally at a spot at the foot of the Mount of Olives, but possibly it is further away from Jerusalem in a low valley between two spurs of the mountain. ("Gethsemane" means "valley of oil."[8]) Zechariah's prophecy says that God's feet would stand on the Mount of Olives, which would split in an earthquake towards the east and west, the mass of the mountain removing towards the north and south. The prophecy goes on, "And ye shall flee to the valley of the mountains." Jesus therefore took his disciples to the spot indicated by the prophet, where he could watch the miracle and not be overwhelmed by it. He was further assured by the prophet, "And my Lord will come, and all the saints with thee." (Alternative translation: ". . . if all with thee are holy.") God Himself would join the Messiah in the valley and fight against the enemy by smiting his ranks with a plague. Other startling miracles would occur: living waters would go out from Jerusalem in two rivers; and "at evening time, it shall be light."[9]

Once in the "valley of decision," Jesus applied himself to prayer and vigil. He told his disciples, "Watch ye and pray, lest ye enter into temptation." Jesus now experienced an Agony of sorrow about his approaching crucifixion. This, at least, is the version of Mark and Matthew. (John omits the whole incident.) Only Luke uses the word "agony," and what he seems to describe is not an agony of sorrow but one of strenuous prayer. "And being in an agony, he prayed more earnestly, and his sweat was as it were great drops of blood falling down to the ground." What was Jesus praying for so earnestly at this time? Why did he instruct his disciples to "watch and pray," an injunction he had used previously to those waiting for the coming of the kingdom of God?[10] Why did he warn them against entering into temptation? If he was resigned to the Crucifixion and was spending the night in Gethsemane waiting for Judas to arrive with the troops to arrest him, there was no particular reason to pray or even to stay awake. And there was no particular temptation which was likely to assail the disciples while they were waiting.

On the theory outlined here, however, there was great reason to pray and to stay awake, and there was great reason to avoid temptation. For Jesus was not waiting passively in the Vale of Gethsemane for his arrest. He was expecting an awesome miracle and the appearance of the glory of God: but he must have felt that this manifestation would depend, to some extent, on his own worthiness and that of his disciples.

Jesus had not merely prophesied the coming of the kingdom of God; he had also prepared for it. He had campaigned among "the lost sheep of Israel," calling them to repentance, because he felt that the coming of God's kingdom was being held back by Israel's sins. Pharisee writings often stress that God's promises to Israel are not automatically fulfilled; they depend on Israel's worthiness and co-operation. Consequently, even though Jesus felt that the time was propitious for the coming of "the day of the Lord," he could not be quite sure. What was needed now was a last great effort of prayer. The belief in the efficacy of prayer was very strong among the Pharisees, especially when the prayer came from a prophet. What might not be accomplished by the powerful prayers of a dedicated Messiah-Prophet, supported by a band of holy men, all concentrating their thoughts toward God, at a time and place appropriate for salvation?

Only the most powerful concerted beam of holy concentration, directed from Gethsemane to God, could obliterate the traces of the sins of Israel, and bring about the hour of redemption. Jesus alone was not sufficient, for Zechariah had said, "And my Lord will come, if all with thee are holy." This explains why Jesus narrowed down his company to the Twelve on that night. He wanted the company of those on whom he could most rely, for the power of sinless prayer would be far more important than the strength of mere numbers.

It is no wonder, then, that Jesus gave the Messianic slogan, "Watch and pray" to his disciples, that he himself went into an agony of prayer, and that he reproved his disciples when he felt a lack of concentration and wholeheartedness in their prayer.

The story of the failure of the disciples in Gethsemane must have developed very early in the history of the Jewish-Christian Church. It was impossible to believe that Jesus himself had failed. His disciples themselves preferred to believe that they had failed him, since by blaming themselves they could go on believing in him. He had temporarily withdrawn from the world, like Elijah when he ascended to heaven, but when they had proved themselves worthy he would return and lead them to victory.

Later, in the Gentile-Christian Church, when Jesus had been turned into a god, the idea that he needed the support of his disciples to accomplish his mission became unthinkable. His mission itself had changed in character, so that any participation or contribution by others became inappropriate. Jesus's injunction to his disciples in Gethsemane to watch and pray, and his own agony of prayer, became pointless and incomprehensible.

It was not difficult for the disciples, after Jesus's arrest and execution, to fall back on guilt-feelings and attach the whole blame to themselves. Jesus must have made them feel guilty on many occasions by his white-hot faith and selflessness, and instances of their unworthiness would have come crowding back into their minds. This may account to some extent for the many stories in the Gospels about the lapses of the disciples.

Jesus, then, stands in the Vale of Gethsemane, with the Mount of Olives looming above him. This, he fervently believes, is the valley of decision, the valley of the Lord's judgment. If he has chosen the moment well, if the hearts of his companions are pure, and if his campaign of reclamation among the "lost sheep of Israel" has been successful, the last battle will be fought. But, as he prays, he feels a great sense of struggle. He wrestles in prayer till his sweat falls like great drops of blood to the ground. The difficulty of his prayer is unpropitious, and he can see that the powers of his chosen companions are flagging. With a great sadness he realises that the long travail of Israel has not yet come to an end.

14

The Arrest and Trial

The miraculous appearance of the Lord God on the Mount of Olives did not occur. Like Theudas and "the prophet from Egypt" and many other messiah-figures of the period, Jesus, despite his great healing powers and tremendous charisma, turned out to be deceived in his apocalyptic hopes. When the Roman troops, reinforced by Jewish police, arrived at Gethsemane they found a handful of rebels equipped with only two swords. A few blows were exchanged, but Jesus was soon captured. The disciples fled in dismay and the troops, who had orders to bring in the ring-leader only, proceeded on their way with their prisoner, congratulating themselves on the ease of his capture.

How did the troops know where to find Jesus? The explanation given in the Gospels is that Jesus was betrayed by his disciple Judas Iscariot, who led the troops to the spot. It seems likely that the troops were given some secret information, for to arrest Jesus in Gethsemane was the ideal way to bring his insurrection to an end. The High Priest was afraid to attempt the arrest in Jerusalem itself because of the mass support for Jesus among the people. Jesus's policy of withdrawing from Jerusalem each evening to the Mount of Olives nullified any plan the High Priest may have had of a surprise attack on him by night. The Mount of Olives, together with its valleys, was such a wide area that special information would be necessary to locate him there, even if his general whereabouts was known.

The story of the treachery of Judas Iscariot, however, is unhistorical.* The Gospel of Peter, of which a fragment was discovered in 1884, does not contain the story of Judas's treachery at all. Its narrator tells how, after the crucifixion, "we, the twelve disciples of the Lord, were weeping and were in sorrow." In this early Gospel there was no defection by any of the twelve disciples; it was written at a time *before* the story of Judas's treachery was invented. Who did betray Jesus, then? Or was he betrayed at all?

In one version of the Judas Iscariot legend (that of John), Jesus *tells* Judas to betray him. "That thou doest, do quickly." The effect of this in the narrative is merely to stress Jesus's foreknowledge. But we may have here a clue to the historical reality, that Jesus actually sent a messenger to bring the enemy troops to Gethsemane. Being sure that he knew the exact hour when the miracle of Zechariah would occur he would want Roman troops to be on hand in "the valley of decision" in order to experience the prophesied defeat.

If the messenger sent by Jesus to bring the Romans was not Judas Iscariot, who was he? There may be a clue to this in the gospel of Mark. An unnamed "young man" is mentioned there, who followed Jesus distractedly after the arrest until he was chased away by the soldiers. This "young man" was not one of the Twelve, nor was he one of the soldiers or the hostile "multitude." He may have been a young follower of Jesus chosen for the task of bringing the Romans to their destruction. Trustingly and confidently he brought them to Gethsemane, expecting Jesus to overwhelm them by a miracle. When the miracle did not occur he was full of confusion and distress and followed the troops in bewilderment until he was chased away.

*See Appendix 3.

The detail that the young man "fled from them naked" may be an attempt to relate the incident to a prophecy of Amos, "And he that is courageous among the mighty shall flee naked in that day, saith the Lord."

As far as the Romans were concerned, Jesus's insurrection was a very minor affair compared with the serious Zealot risings which occurred in the same period. This is why Jesus made very little impact on contemporary historians. Josephus barely mentions him, and authentic references in the Talmud are very few and uninformative. If it were not for the Gospels we would hardly know of Jesus's existence. As far as the majority of the Jews were concerned Jesus was another would-be Messiah or prophet who had raised great hopes for a while, but had finally failed. Such figures were regarded with great sympathy and sorrow; there was no question of blaming or execrating a man for regarding himself as the promised Messiah. If he failed then he had made a mistake, but he was still respected as a brave man and a patriot. But if it were not for the supporters who remained faithful to Jesus's memory and developed a belief in his eventual return he would have been forgotten by the Jewish people.

However, Jesus's capture at Gethsemane had not yet proved him to be a failure. As long as he was still alive his supporters would retain their hopes. God might perform some great miracle to release him and annihilate the Romans after all. The news of Jesus's capture would have plunged the Jerusalem crowd into fear and anxiety, but by no means into despair.

It was Jesus's confidence and faith that had betrayed him to the Romans. He had been convinced that the great miracle would occur on that very night. Why was he so sure? Zechariah had said that the miracle would occur during the Feast of Tabernacles, but the Festival lasted eight days. Which of the eight days was to be the day of deliverance? The obvious answer would have been the seventh day, known in Jesus's time as "the day of Hosanna" (nowadays called by Jews "the Great Hosanna"). On this day the prayers for salvation reached their crescendo in a procession of priests encircling the Altar seven

times carrying willow-branches and calling for salvation. The
night of the expected miracle would be the night *before* the
seventh day, since the Jews reckoned a day from evening to
evening. Jesus would have expected that night and the following day to be occupied in overcoming the Romans; and the next
evening, which ushered in the final day of the Festival, would
be the beginning of a day of victory-rejoicings. The Eighth Day
was always regarded as a separate Festival and was symbolic of
the fulfilment of salvation. This time, Jesus thought, symbolism would turn into reality and the Eighth Day would be
celebrated as the first day of the Messianic Age. (Jesus thought
that the work of salvation would occupy both a night and a day
because of Joel's prophecy that both the sun and the moon
would be darkened in the valley of decision.)

The Eighth Day, however, was the first day of Jesus's
captivity. He himself probably entertained no further hopes.
He had relied so much on the expected miracle at the Mount of
Olives that his whole apocalyptic scheme of salvation was now
shattered. The reports in the Gospels of his silence and
passivity under questioning may well be true; not because of
any resignation to death and desire for crucifixion but because
of sheer dismay and disappointment. The heartrending groan
wrung from him on the cross, "Eloi, Eloi, lama sabachthani?,"
"My God, my God, why hast thou forsaken me?" (unintelligible on the Gentile-Christian theory of his voluntary sacrifice)
reflects the true tragedy of his situation.

The troops who arrested Jesus consisted of a cohort of
Roman soldiers, consisting of 300–600 men. In addition there
were some Jewish officers of the High Priest in attendance.
It was to these Jewish officers that the Roman military tribune
now handed over Jesus for interrogation by the High Priest.
The Romans made it a rule to leave the preliminary examination of suspects to the Jewish collaborating authorities who
were their paid experts on Jewish affairs, and could reach a
reliable decision on whether there was a prima facie case for
prosecution.

Now follows in all the Gospels an account of Jesus's exam-

ination by the High Priest and his officers. The Synoptists
(Mark, Matthew and Luke) add that the High Priest was joined
in this examination by the "elders of the people," in which case
the court would have been none other than the Sanhedrin, the
chief judicial and religious body of the Jews in which the
Pharisees were strongly represented. The *examination* of Jesus is
thus represented by three of the Gospel-writers as a *trial* in
which Jesus was tried and condemned for blasphemy.

It is the fourth Gospel-writer, John, who gives the true
account of the matter. Jesus was never tried before the Sanhedrin for blasphemy.[1] No meeting of the Sanhedrin ever took
place outside the special meeting-place of that august body, the
Chamber of Hewn Stone in the Temple; yet according to the
Synoptists, this trial took place in the High Priest's house to
which the "elders" were summoned in the middle of the night.
It was an express rule of the Sanhedrin that its meetings could
not take place at night. Another rule was that meetings could
not take place in Festival-time. As to the reports that members
of the Sanhedrin spat on Jesus and struck him, this is just as
incredible in the proceedings of that highly-dignified body as if
it were reported of the High Court of England, or the Supreme
Court of the United States.[2]

Clearly the Gospel-writers knew nothing about the Sanhedrin or the Jewish laws relating to blasphemy. Jesus's claim to be
the Messiah, or Christ, or "Son of God," was not blasphemy in
Jewish law. Even if Jesus had claimed to be an angel, as some of
the accounts suggest, this would not have been blasphemy. If
he had claimed to be God Almighty this would have been an
indictable offence (not blasphemy, but idolatry), but not even
the Synoptists put his claim that high.[3]

If the Sanhedrin had been called following Jesus's arrest, the
Pharisees, who held the majority, would have been extremely
sympathetic to him. Any charge of blasphemy against him,
they would have rejected at once. As for charges of sedition
against the High Priest and Rome, they would have regarded
them as evidence of patriotism and religious fidelity. The last
thing, therefore, that the High Priest would have done would

have been to call a meeting of the Sanhedrin. He would have taken good care to keep the Pharisees out of the matter. As the representative of Rome, with his own officers and police court, he had no need to consult the Pharisees in any case relating to sedition. The trial of Peter, reported in Acts, shows that when a High Priest did try to enlist the support of the Pharisees against the Nazarenes he was outvoted and the prisoner released.

The Gospel according to John states plainly that Jesus was interrogated not by "the elders of the people" but by the High Priest Caiaphas alone, after a preliminary interrogation by Annas, Caiaphas's father-in-law. John says nothing about any charge of blasphemy, saying merely, "The high priest then asked Jesus of his disciples and of his doctrine." When Jesus refused to commit himself, Caiaphas decided to hand him over to Pilate, the Roman Governor.

The author of John's Gospel (evidently more intelligent than the Synoptists) also noticed a certain difficulty. Why, if the Jewish authorities were so convinced that Jesus was a blasphemer, did they not execute him themselves, instead of handing him over to Pilate on a trumped-up charge of sedition? John finds an ingenious solution to this difficulty by putting into the mouths of the Jews, "It is not lawful for us to put any men to death." As a matter of historical fact the Jews *did* have the right, at this time, to carry out the death-penalty for religious offences, subject only to the automatic ratification of the Procurator.[4] If Jesus had really been found guilty of blasphemy or idolatry there would have been no need for the Jewish authorities to hand him over to Pilate on a false charge of sedition; they could have executed him themselves. The account of the trial of Peter in Acts shows that the Sanhedrin had the power of life and death in religious matters.[5] This again demonstrates that Jesus was never tried by the Jews on a religious issue. The charge of sedition made by the High Priest when he handed Jesus over to Pilate was the actual, original charge, based on the truth of Jesus's life and actions. For Jesus *was* guilty of sedition; he was a patriot who fought against the Roman domination of his native land.

Jesus was handed over to Pilate by the High Priest according to the normal practice by which political offenders were handed over to the Romans, while religious offenders were dealt with by the Jews themselves. The actual complaint made by the High Priest has been preserved by Luke: "We found this fellow perverting the nation, and forbidding to give tribute to Caesar, saying that he himself is Christ, a King." Every item in this indictment was true. Jesus *was* "perverting the nation," in the sense of turning them away from allegiance to Rome. He *was* "forbidding to give tribute to Caesar." He *was* saying that he himself was "Christ, a King." The charge was subversion and rebellion, not blasphemy.

15

Barabbas

We have now come back, by a long route, to the Barabbas incident with which we began this book. Jesus is lying in Pilate's prison, and in the same prison is Barabbas. He is also the leader of an insurrectionary movement, whose insurrection took place at the same time as that of Jesus, and is facing the same death as Jesus. By a coincidence which caused some difficulty to early Christian writers such as Origen, Barabbas's name was also Jesus. Origen came to the conclusion that this must be a mistake; Barabbas could not have had such a holy name (especially as Christians had come to see significance in the fact that "Jesus" is derived from a Hebrew root "yasha" meaning "to save"). Consequently, the name "Jesus Barabbas" was suppressed in most of the manuscripts of the Gospels. It survived in a few, however, and has been reinstated in modern translations such as the New English Bible.

What kind of man was Barabbas? In the latest Gospel, that of John, he is called a "bandit" (Greek, "lestes"), but as we have seen this is a description often given to the freedom-fighters of the Jewish Resistance, (and indeed to freedom-fighters throughout history). The earlier Gospels make it quite clear that Barabbas was a rebel. Matthew even gives him the respectful description, "a distinguished prisoner," (the Greek, "episemos," wrongly translated as "notorious" in some versions).[1]

Our investigation has narrowed the gap between the two figures, Jesus of Nazareth and Jesus Barabbas. We started with two people who were poles apart: Jesus an unworldly, angelic figure, whose kingdom was not of this world, a Messiah who rejected the concept of success in battle, whose purpose was to die on the cross, and who regarded the Roman occupation of Judaea as a detail beneath his notice; Barabbas, a bandit, a man of soulless violence, determined to fight savagery with savagery.

We are now able to make a juster estimate of the character of Barabbas. As a member of the Jewish Resistance, he was inspired by the internationalist, democratic vision of the Hebrew prophets and by the translation into practice of the prophetic vision by the reformist Pharisee movement, with its long history of resistance to every kind of tyranny. As a leader and a "distinguished" man, Barabbas was probably a Rabbi like the Zealot leaders, Judas the Galilean and Zadok. He was fighting against a cruel and insatiable enemy, who had reduced a proud people to the last degree of humiliation and suffering. He was fighting against a Roman governor, Pontius Pilate, whose policy from the moment he began his term of office was to test how far he could go in offending the religious sensibilities of the Jews.

Our picture of Jesus, too, has had to be drastically revised. We have seen that the "other-worldly" image of him is seriously misleading; that he was far from indifferent to the Roman occupation of the Holy Land; and that his mission to his people was to rescue them from their distress and humiliation under the Romans and so to enable them to continue their own mission as the people of God. He was no ordinary rebel, either, but a Prophet with a lofty vision of the fulfillment of the awesome predictions of Zechariah, and an aspiration to change the course of history, not only for Israel, but for all mankind.

And in addition to being a Prophet he was a King-Messiah determined to rule his earthly kingdom in the spirit of his ancestors David and Solomon. At the same time, he was a Rabbi, whose life and thought were intimately bound up with the progressive religious party of his day, the Pharisees, whose methods and principles he used in his moral and spiritual teaching. He aroused the deadly opposition of the authorities: the Romans, who had the authority of the sword, the Herodians, the pro-Roman party of Romanised Jews, and the Sadducees, with their idolatry of Book, Temple and Priesthood, and their compromise with the power of Rome.

After his death, he fell into the hands of Gentiles who did not understand his aims or his inner life. They cut him off from his roots and turned him into an ineffectual angel and, eventually, an object of worship. This was done in the interests of a world-denying philosophy that he would have hated. It was part of a compromise and accommodation with the power which he had attacked at the cost of his life; for, by a paradox that he would have well understood, a world-denying philosophy is always a surrender to the world, and the only philosophy that engages with and fights the worldly powers is the philosophy that affirms the world.

Jesus and Barabbas, then, have come much closer together. They are both men of the Resistance, both Pharisees, both Rabbis. One wonders, therefore, whether they knew each other? Were their lives connected in any way? Was there any co-operation between their movements? Was it a mere coincidence that their insurrections took place in Jerusalem at the same time and that they were in Pilate's prison together? Or were they in fact two leaders of the *same* movement?

S. G. F. Brandon thought that this must have been the case. "Now the coincidence . . . of Jesus's attack in the Temple with an insurrection also in the city, which Roman forces had quelled with some loss, must surely be regarded as significant. Jerusalem was a small place, and it is difficult to believe that the commotions would not have been related in some way, if only in the minds of the authorities . . . Could the two movements, happening about the same time, have also been linked in both principle and purpose?"[2]

It is puzzling, however, on Brandon's hypothesis, that Barabbas has not been mentioned in the Gospel narratives until this moment. If he was a member of Jesus's movement, important enough to be entrusted with a leading role in the insurrection, why has he not been mentioned before? Why was he given a command, rather than one of the twelve disciples such as Simon Peter? And if Barabbas was a lieutenant of Jesus what sense can we make of the fact that the crowd preferred Barabbas to Jesus? Even if the story is somehow inaccurate, how could the present story have developed out of a situation in which Jesus and a close associate and supporter were in prison together?

Many commentators have felt that there is a clue to the Barabbas mystery in the fact that Barabbas's first name was "Jesus." Can it be that some confusion arose over the fact that two prisoners, both called Jesus, were in Pilate's prison at the same time, and that this confusion gave rise to the story as we have it in the Gospels? The coincidence itself need not stretch our credulity too much, since "Jesus" was a common name, but perhaps the coincidence played some part in the actual formation and development of the story.

A. E. J. Rawlinson has suggested that the origin of the story was a confusion in Pilate's mind about the two Jesuses that he had in custody.[3] When the crowd came and shouted for the release of Barabbas they shouted for him by his first name, Jesus. Pilate mistook them to mean Jesus of Nazareth, and offered to release him. Paul Winter,[4] too, has offered a theory based on a confusion in Pilate's mind. Winter's theory is that Pilate simply asked which was which; and from this incident the story finally developed into the version we find in the Gospels, the motive of the development being to blame the Jews for the execution of Jesus and to exonerate Pilate. One may doubt, however, that so elaborate and dramatic a story could have had such a trivial origin as a mere confusion in Pilate's mind about the identity of two Jesuses.

There is another explanation which also stems from the fact that Barabbas's first name was Jesus and makes use of the idea that the motivation of the development of the story was the desire to shift the blame for the Crucifixion to the Jews, but which makes better sense of the stages by which the story developed into its present form.

Let us first summarise the contradictions which make it difficult to accept the Gospel story at its face value.

The narratives tell how the Roman Procurator, Pilate, was unable to find anything wrong with Jesus, and was anxious to release him. An opportunity to do this arose because of a custom by which the Roman Governor released every year at Passover a prisoner named by the Jewish crowd. Pilate offered to release Jesus, in fulfilment of this custom, but the Jewish crowd rejected this offer and demanded the release of Barabbas instead.

The account is undoubtedly mythical. Careful studies of the evidence from Roman and Jewish sources have shown that there was not, and could not have been, any such Passover custom. That a Roman Governor of an unruly province could release, at the whim of the local crowd and without consultation with Caesar, a prisoner who had been accused of leading the people in rebellion against Rome, is, to say the least, improbable.

Moreover, the character of Pilate, as displayed in the Gospels, is utterly at variance with what is known of him from other sources. Pilate was cruel, head-strong and self-seeking; not, as the Gospels portray him, amiable and politically naïve. The Gospels are clearly trying to divert the blame for Jesus's death from the Romans. The real Pilate (who was finally dismissed from his post by the Syrian legate, Vitellius, for a brutal and pointless massacre) would not have had the slightest hesitation in ordering the crucifixion of anyone who seditiously laid claim to the title "King of the Jews."

Another objection to the story as it stands is the incomprehensible switch of the Jerusalem crowd from strong support of Jesus to hatred of him and desire for his crucifixion. At the time of Jesus's Triumphal Entry the crowd greeted him enthusiastically. Later too, as all the Synoptists record, the "high priests and elders" decided not to arrest Jesus because they were "afraid of the people." It was conceivable that the enthusiasm of the Jewish crowd for Jesus declined, and Barabbas became the popular hero instead; but that would not explain the venom with which they demanded Jesus's crucifixion. Even if they preferred to release Barabbas, the choice would surely have caused them sorrow. They would have preferred to release them both. In any case, if Pilate had really wanted to release Jesus there is no reason why he should not have done so. The release of Barabbas instead of Jesus at the request of the crowd would not have tied his hands with regard to further action. He could have released Jesus immediately afterwards, or a hundred other prisoners, if he had so desired.

The solution to these difficulties and an explanation of the development of the story into its final form is that *Jesus of Nazareth and Jesus Barabbas were the same man.*

All the Evangelists are embarrassed by the emphasis they have given in the earlier part of the story to the popularity of Jesus. This makes an awkward transition inevitable when they want to stress, later in the story, the guilt of the whole Jewish people for Jesus's crucifixion. In the original Gospel Jesus was never rejected at all by the Jewish people or their religious leaders, the Pharisees. His enemies among the Jews were the Sadducees and the Herodians. Later, when the Gentile Christian Church wished to cut its links with its Jewish origins, there was imported into the story, a fictitious opposition between Jesus and the Pharisees and eventually between Jesus and "the Jews." The Barabbas story is an important element in this latter development.

The emergence of a new character, Jesus Barabbas, can now be explained. When Jesus was lying in Pilate's prison the Jewish crowd surrounded the prison and *called for his release*. This was a very natural thing for them to do, and was simply a continuation of their fervent support for him at the time of the Triumphal Entry and later. This incident could not be entirely suppressed since it rested on a strong tradition; but it constituted a great difficulty to the later editors of the Gospels who wanted to show Jesus rejected by the entire Jewish people. They could not deny that the Jewish crowd called for the release of Jesus but they hit on an ingenious solution. The Jewish crowd called for the release of *another* Jesus, who happened to be in prison at the same time as Jesus of Nazareth. This Jesus was Jesus Barabbas. The Jewish crowd did in fact call to Pilate to release "Jesus Barabbas"; but that was because "Jesus Barabbas" was the name of the man also known as "Jesus of Nazareth." Since the tradition that presented such awkward difficulties told how the crowd called for "Jesus Barabbas," it was an easy matter to suggest that this was not another name for Jesus, but another man altogether. Eventually even the fact that Barabbas's first name was "Jesus" was dropped from the text of the Gospels.

A splitting-off had now taken place; a duplication of names was transformed into a duplication of persons. A new separate, fictitious character, Jesus Barabbas, originally identical with Jesus of Nazareth, had now emerged, and the stage was set for new dramatic elaborations of a legend.

If Jesus and Barabbas were the same man, how can the name "Barabbas" be explained? What does it mean, and why should this name have been used of Jesus?

There are several possibilities. The name Barabbas may come from the Hebrew, or rather Aramaic, "Barabba" or from "bar-rabba" (the name is spelt in Greek "Barrabbas," with a double "r," in some manuscripts). The usual explanation is that "bar-abba" simply means "son of Abba," so that Jesus Barabbas would mean "Jesus, son of Abba," "Abba" being quite a common name. But it will not do if Jesus Barabbas was really Jesus of Nazareth, whose father was not Abba but Joseph.

Apart from being a name, "abba" means "father," so "barabbas" could mean "son of the Father." There is a strong tradition that Jesus habitually addressed God in prayer as "Abba" (Mk. xiv. 35, Rom. viii. 15, Gal. iv. 6). There are some examples in the Talmud of other Rabbis who called God "Abba," but Jesus may have made such a distinctive practice of this that he acquired the name "Barabbas" as a nick-name, signifying his intimate relationship with God. Or possibly "Barabbas" may have signified "son of God," not in the Gnostic sense of a divine being, but in the sense of the Davidic king, who according to the Coronation Psalm was the adopted son of God.

If, on the other hand, the correct spelling is "Barrabbas," this would mean "son of a Rabbi." The Aramaic "bar," "son of," was often used very loosely, so that "son of a Rabbi" could mean simply "Rabbi" or "Teacher." But there was also a name for teachers which was spelt with one "r," and which may be the best derivation of Barabbas. This is the title "Berabbi" (literally "house of the Teacher") which was used only of the greatest Rabbis, and came *after* the name as an honorific title. We know that Jesus was actually known as "the Teacher" (see Lk. xxii. 11). So there is no difficulty in supposing that "Barabbas" was the title by which Jesus was generally known, probably equivalent to "Teacher," but possibly a Messianic nick-name.[5]

If Jesus of Nazareth and Jesus Barabbas were the same person, the difficulties of the Barabbas/Pilate story disappear. First of all, we can understand why Barabbas appears so suddenly in the narrative at this point. He is not mentioned before for the simple reason that he did not exist before, having been conjured into existence by the exigencies of the Pilate narrative. As for Barabbas's involvement in a "rising," this is readily explained: it refers to Jesus's own rising when he cleansed the Temple by force. The various unhistorical features of the narrative—the "Passover privilege," Pilate's mildness, Barabbas's deterioration into a "bandit," the Jews' self-pronounced curse—can all be understood as elaborations which were gradually added to the story in order to increase the drama of the "choice," to emphasize the guilt of the Jews in not choosing the right Jesus, and to exonerate the Romans.

After languishing in prison for some weeks or months, Jesus was brought before Pilate for trial, found guilty of the seditious act of claiming the Jewish throne, and condemned to execution by the usual method reserved for rebels: crucifixion. Pilate, with his strong backing of Roman troops, had the greatest contempt for an undisciplined crowd and ignored completely the demands for Jesus's release.

Jesus was arrested towards the end of the eight-day autumn festival of Tabernacles, but he was not executed until just before the spring festival of Passover. This was partly because Roman judicial processes were always slow-moving, and partly because Pilate liked to carry out executions of rebels at a time when they would make the maximum impact on the unruly Jews. Jerusalem was always crowded with pilgrims at festival-time, but there was no pilgrim-festival between Tabernacles and Passover. The Passover-festival, therefore, was the first opportunity to execute Jesus in a really crowded Jerusalem.

Jesus was crucified with two other revolutionaries, possibly members of his own movement. In accordance with Roman custom, the charge on which he had been condemned was inscribed on his cross: that he had claimed to be "the King of the Jews." Enfeebled by his stay in prison and by grief at the disappointment of his hopes, Jesus lasted only six hours on the cross before he died. The Gospel-writers, keeping up their malice towards the Jews to the very end, say that Jesus was reviled by his fellow-Jews as he hung on the cross. They even say that Jesus was reviled by the fellow-sufferers who were crucified together with him. These stories are slanders. The Jews, seeing Jesus on the cross, gave him the same dues of respect and sorrow that they gave to all the other brave men who resisted Roman tyranny and paid the same penalty.

The respect in which Jesus was held by the religious leaders of the people, the Pharisees, is shown by the fact that a Pharisee member of the Sanhedrin, Joseph of Arimathaea, went to Pilate and asked permission to bury the body of Jesus. This permission was granted, and Joseph took down the body and buried it.

Jesus's immediate supporters, the Twelve and a small band of followers, after an initial period of dismay, came to believe that Jesus was still alive. He had been brought back to life, like Elijah, and would soon return to lead a new attack on the Romans which this time would be successful. As we have seen, belief in Jesus's resurrection did *not* mean he was regarded as being divine; the same belief had been held about previous figures in Jewish history without involving any belief in their divinity.

Thus a new Jewish sect arose known as the Nazarenes under the leadership of Jesus's brother James, based on the belief in Jesus's continued Messiahship. The Pharisees did not regard this sect as heretical. Indeed, the Nazarenes were regarded as being *within* the Pharisee party until about 90 A.D. The Nazarenes themselves, however, regarded as heretical the sect of *Gentile*-Christians which, under the influence of Paul, began to worship Jesus as a divine figure.

16

Writing the Gospels

(i) Jewish History after the Death of Jesus

Jesus died in about 30 A.D.[1] and Pontius Pilate continued to be procurator until 36 A.D., when he was dismissed by the Legate of Syria, Vitellius, for a brutal and pointless massacre of Samaritans. The subsequent history of Roman rule in Judaea until the outbreak of the Jewish War in 66 A.D. is a record of such oppression and mis-government by a succession of procurators that historians have wondered why Rome did not interfere more often to keep these procurators in order.

There were strong forces, however, in the Roman Empire which did not want the Jews to flourish. It is hard to believe that the provocative behaviour of successive procurators was without encouragement from Rome—not perhaps from the Emperors but from the powerful civil servants, the self-effacing Greek freedmen who wielded great power behind the scenes. The procurators of Judaea often owed their position to these freedmen. Pontius Pilate, for example, was a creature of Sejanus, who was strongly anti-Semitic. Felix, among the worst of the procurators, was the brother of Pallas, one of the Greek freedman who virtually ruled the Empire during Claudius's dotage.

The rivalry between Greeks and Jews in the Roman Empire
was intense. The Greeks had, in a sense, taken over the Empire,
both by setting the tone of its culture and by providing its civil
service. The Jews were the only threat to Greek cultural
supremacy. Judaism was at this time a missionary faith.
Alexandrian Jews carried on enthusiastic propaganda for
Judaism in the Greek language, and the Pharisees too, especially the Hillelites, were keen proselytizers. The Greeks were
much alarmed at the progress Judaism was making, and an
anti-Semitic literature arose in the Greek language to counteract
the trend towards Jewish conversion. In all the Hellenistic
cities, including those like Caesarea which were situated within
Palestine, anti-Jewish pogroms were frequently instituted by
the Greek inhabitants. The alarm of the Greeks (echoed by
Roman phil-Hellenes like Cicero and Seneca[2]) was not entirely
without cause. The Jews already comprised 10 per cent of the
population of the Empire and were increasing rapidly by their
natural fecundity and by proselytization. There was a definite
possibility that the Empire could eventually become Jewish.
The Greeks fought hard for their cultural supremacy, and one
of their methods may well have been the encouragement of
deliberate misrule in Judaea, in the hope that a war would be
provoked in which the Jews would lose their homeland, the
centre of their religion.

Whatever the reason, the misrule of the procurators was
appalling. Their policy seemed to be directed towards producing chaos, especially in the case of the two last and worst,
Albinus and Florus. They took bribes from everybody, including criminals. Albinus opened the prisons on the comple-
tion of his term of office, in order to "fill the land with robbers."
Florus robbed indiscriminately and plundered whole towns;
his actions seemed aimed at producing anarchy. His final
provocation was to rob the Temple of seventeen talents
($68,000); and when the people demonstrated against this, he
sent the soldiers in to slaughter them and plunder their houses.
In addition, members of the Jerusalem crowd were picked out
at random to be crucified, including some who had been

admitted to the Roman equestrian order. This last action shows a contempt for Roman norms of behaviour which cannot be explained except on the hypothesis that Florus had secret orders from Rome to foment a rebellion.

Having succeeded in causing an open revolt of the Jews, Florus called upon the Legate of Syria, Cestius Gallus, to bring in his legions and crush the rebels. The news of the Jewish revolt was the signal to Greek cities all over the Eastern part of the Empire to massacre their Jewish inhabitants. In Caesarea, the Hellenistic city on the Palestinian coast which was the headquarters for Florus's troops, 20,000 Jews were massacred in one hour and the survivors were taken into slavery. Throughout Syria, massacres of Jews took place; and in Alexandria 50,000 Jews were killed by Roman troops and the Greek inhabitants. The Jews retaliated by attacking the Hellenistic cities and towns that ringed Palestine. The war was a rebellion against the power of Rome; but at an ideological level it was a *kultur-kampf* between the Hellenistic and Jewish civilisations.

The first important event of the war was an astounding success for the Jews. Cestius Gallus, the Legate of Syria, with a formidable army of 30,000, entered Palestine to punish the insurgents. He forced his way through Galilee and Samaria, and after some stronger resistance in Judaea, entered Jerusalem. It looked as if the war would be over after only three months. At this point, for reasons which have never become clear, Gallus broke off hostilities and retreated. On his way back through Judaea he was ambushed by the Zealots and his huge army was routed. By sacrificing his rear-guard Cestius Gallus made his escape with the bulk of his army, but he lost 6,000 troops and great quantities of war material. The place of this great Zealot victory was Beth-horon, the very mountain pass where Judas Maccabaeus had triumphed over the Seleucid Greeks in 165 B.C.

This great victory was so miraculous in character that the whole people became convinced that the Zealots were right and the time for God's salvation had come. They were reminded,

inevitably, of the inexplicable retreat of Sennacherib from
before the gates of Jerusalem in an event crucial in the history of
the Jews as a confirmation of their role as God's people.
Henceforward, all parties, even the Sadducees, were united in
continuing the war.

For the next seven years (66 A.D. to 73 A.D.), the struggle
went on. Outside Palestine the Roman world was convulsed by
crises of its own; the forced suicide of the Emperor Nero was
followed by the "Year of the Four Emperors" (68 A.D.), a
scramble for the succession in which three Emperors, Galba,
Otho and Vitellius died violent deaths before, finally, stable
rule was achieved under Vespasian. Yet throughout these
upheavals the Roman world was aware that the Jews were in
revolt. They became in fact the symbol of the disintegration
that was threatening the Empire, a universal menace, regarded
by the Romans rather as international Communism was regarded by John Foster Dulles and the "China lobby" during the
McCarthy era. The Jews were ubiquitous; their communities
were in every city of the Empire. Seneca had written: "The
customs of that most wicked nation have gained such strength
that they have now been received in all lands. The conquered
have given laws to the conquerors." (Seneca was in charge of
Roman policy in the early days of Nero, when the procurator
Felix filled Judaea with crucified corpses.) And now these Jews
had openly taken up arms against Rome in Palestine.

After the first great Zealot victory at Beth-Horon the Zealots
allowed the conduct of the war to slip back into the hands of the
Hasmonean aristocrats who were the traditional war-leaders
but who had degenerated through the years of collaboration.
One of these aristocrats was Josephus, the historian of the War,
who was given the highly responsible command of Galilee. He
wasted much energy in squabbling with the Galilean Zealot
leader, John of Gischala, failed to build up the defence of
Galilee wholeheartedly, and then defected to the Romans.

The Zealots in Jerusalem, finally realising the half-
heartedness of the aristocrats, took over the direction of the war
themselves. However, even in the early days of the war

dissension had also broken out among the Zealots. Menahem, the son of Judas the Galilean, was killed by an anti-monarchical Zealot group when he claimed the Messiahship. On the death of Menahem his supporters, who had believed him to be the God-sent Messiah, were disheartened and withdrew to the desert fortress of Massada. This group of Zealots, the redoubtable party of the original Zealot leader, played little part in the defence of Jerusalem, though they enacted the finale of the whole tragedy. In Jerusalem two parties of Zealots emerged, the followers of John of Gischala, who had escaped to Jerusalem after the debacle in Galilee, and the followers of Simon bar Giora, the most radical of the Zealots who freed all slaves and cancelled all debts. He was regarded by the Romans as a threat to all established society, another Spartacus. These two parties argued among themselves while Vespasian and his son Titus drew the net ever closer around Jerusalem. Johanan ben Zakkai, the leader of the moderate Pharisees, becoming convinced that Jerusalem was doomed, escaped from the city, despite the vigilance of the Zealots, by being carried out in a coffin. Vespasian granted his request to start an academy in Jamnia; and from this academy came the survival of Judaism.

Vespasian was called to Imperial honours and the siege of Jerusalem was left to his son Titus. The defenders, united at last, fought grimly. Titus surrounded the whole city by a huge rampart of earth, and thus blockaded the city fell into the grip of famine. The traitor Josephus appeared before the walls with an offer of peace from Titus, but was greeted with stones and curses. The Zealots had all taken a vow to fight to the death, but many of those in the city (crowded with festival pilgrims trapped in the siege) wished to escape. If they managed to steal out they were caught by the Romans and crucified in full view of the city walls. The entire plain surrounding the city was full of crosses, the victims writhing and screaming in agony or immobile in exhaustion or death. So many crosses were made that the neighbourhood was denuded of trees. As the Zealots looked out from the city walls at this sight their resolution only hardened. To them the cross was the symbol of Roman imperialism, the filthy torture with which the Romans throughout their occupation had defiled the Holy Land.

A craze developed among the Roman soldiers of slitting open the bellies of escapers in search of gold that they might have swallowed to smuggle out. After 2000 had died in this way Titus put a stop to the practice, deeming it uncivilized. The crucifixions, however, continued.

Inside Jerusalem the streets were full of unburied corpses, victims of the famine. Finally, the Romans, with their huge siege weapons, broke open the walls and poured into the city. After a desperate street-by-street battle Jerusalem was taken. The great Temple, the wonder of the world, was set on fire. While it was burning Titus entered the Holy of Holies and the Roman soldiers made idolatrous sacrifices inside the shrine. Nothing was omitted to demonstrate to the Jews that their God had been thoroughly beaten and humiliated. Yet all this did not destroy the faith of the Jews, who knew that the Temple had been razed before and that Judaism had survived: that their God, the Creator of Heaven and Earth, did not depend on any human habitation; and that the might of Rome would pass away like that of other cruel conquerors. Josephus tries to defend Titus from the charge of deliberately setting fire to the Temple, but another source (Sulpicius Severus, probably basing his account on a lost work of Tacitus) says that Titus made the decision in order to uproot Judaism and Christianity.

Now followed an indiscriminate slaughter in Jerusalem. The Romans, probably the cruellest soldiers in victory that the world has seen, gave themselves up to an orgy of killing, making no distinction between men, women or children. The total number of deaths in Jerusalem during the siege, famine and the final slaughter was over 1,000,000. The siege had lasted five months, and the war, four years, though pockets of resistance still remained in the country.

Following the slaughter came enslavement and, of course, crucifixions. All the surviving people of Jerusalem were herded together in a compound where 17,000 died of starvation and neglect. The Romans searched through the survivors for any remaining Zealots, who were crucified, except for those reserved for the triumph in Rome. Women and youths under sixteen were auctioned as slaves. Other Jewish captives died in the wild beast shows that Titus put on for the entertainment of the crowd during his triumphant tour of the cities of Syria.

A great triumph was held in Rome in 71 A.D. to celebrate the victory against the Jews. Trophies from the Temple, including the sacred golden Menorah, or candlestick, were carried in procession and scenes from the war were enacted. At the climax of the ceremony Simon bar Giora, the radical Zealot leader, was strangled and the news of his death brought, in traditional fashion, to Vespasian and Titus sitting in state. A great roar of triumph filled the whole of Rome. The death of Simon bar Giora, the liberator of the slaves, in the heart of Rome is a scene of symbolic force. He stands for the essence of Judaism; and his name "Bar Giora" means "son of the proselyte." He personifies a universal ideology implacably opposed to tyranny and its companion, idolatry.

In the rest of Judaea resistance still went on in the desert fortresses. Finally, in Massada, the last of the Zealots, led by Eleazar, a descendant of Judas of Galilee, died by their own hands after a heroic resistance. Some of the Zealot groups, having escaped from Jerusalem, went to Egypt and tried to continue the resistance against Rome even there. They were captured and the Romans tried the experiment of torturing them by all possible means, including the application of fire, to make them "acknowledge Caesar as their lord." Under the worst torments, none of them would utter the formula required of them; and even when the Romans had recourse to torturing the Zealot children in the same way they could not make any of them submit.

It can easily be understood how uncomfortable the position of Jews became in all the Greco-Roman cities during the years of the Jewish revolt, and especially in Rome itself. And it was in Rome, towards the end of the Jewish War, or possibly just after it, that the Gospel of Mark, the first of the canonical Gospels, was written; the Gospel in which the lines of policy towards the

Jews were laid down by the Gentile-Christian Church; a policy of condemnation of the Jews as an accursed people.

(ii) THE CHRISTIAN CHURCH AFTER THE DEATH OF JESUS

What had been the history of the Christian Church since the death of Jesus? The book of the New Testament which purports to give this history is *The Acts of the Apostles;* but this is a Gentile-Christian composition written about 100 A.D. by Luke, giving a Gentile-Christian slant to the events of those years. By reading between the lines of *Acts,* by following through the arguments derived from the study of the Gospels, by using supplementary sources such as Josephus, the Talmud and early Christian historians, we can reconstruct the true history of the early Church.

"The first fifteen bishops of Jerusalem were all circumcised Jews; and the congregation over which they presided united the law of Moses with the doctrine of Christ." This sentence of Gibbon[3] sums up the most important fact about the early Church; except that Gibbon does not make clear that "the doctrine of Christ" held by the earliest Christians was very different from that current in later Christianity. The earliest followers of Jesus were not even called "Christians" (that was a name adopted later by followers of Paul in Antioch); they were called "Nazarenes." They believed that Jesus was the "Christ" in the Jewish sense of that term, i.e. the "anointed one," the rightful king of Israel, who would return one day to liberate the Jews from foreign oppression and inaugurate an era of peace for the world. They did *not* believe that Jesus was a divine being, or even that he had become one after his death. They *did* believe that Jesus was still alive; that by a special miracle he had been resurrected by God after his crucifixion and would soon appear to complete his mission of "salvation" (i.e. liberation). But Jesus's resurrection did not mean that he was divine; it only meant that Jesus joined the select band of human beings, including Enoch, Elijah (and in later legend King Arthur, Charlemagne, Frederick Barbarossa and others) whose protective role rendered them superior to death in the eyes of their devoted followers. The constantly re-iterated claim that resurrection and divinity are inseparably connected would make divine beings of all the above-mentioned heroes, not to mention humbler subjects of resurrection-stories such as Lazarus and the widow's son raised by Elijah. The Pharisees believed that *all* deserving humans (whether Jews or Gentiles) would one day be resurrected from the dead. The Nazarene belief was merely that this resurrection had taken place earlier for Jesus than for others.

The Nazarenes, therefore, were not regarded as heretics by the Jewish religious authorities, the Pharisees. Indeed, the Nazarenes were regarded as forming a group *within* the Pharisees, and an ultra-pious group at that. The first leader of the Nazarenes, James the Just, the brother of Jesus, was famous for his devotion to the Temple, his meticulous observance of all the minutiae of Jewish law and for undertaking the Rechabite and Nazirite vows, which were taken only by the most devout of the Pharisees.[4] The Nazarenes observed the Sabbath, the dietary laws, the laws of purity and the laws of tithing, and in doing so they were convinced that they were following the instructions and example of Jesus himself.

The Nazarenes were not only regarded as a variety of Pharisaism, they were even regarded as a variety of Zealotism. Jesus was well-known to have been a rebel against Rome. His followers, therefore, were looked upon by the Sadducee and Herodian collaborators as potential trouble-makers. The Nazarenes were persecuted from time to time by the quisling authorities, especially the High Priest, and on these occasions they looked to the Pharisees for support and protection. When the Nazarene Peter was arrested by the Sadducees he was saved from death by the Pharisee leader Gamaliel.[5] When James himself, the Nazarene leader, was illegally executed by a High Priest, the Pharisees protested vigorously and succeeded in having the High Priest dismissed (62 AD.).[6]

The accusations made in *Acts* that the Pharisees persecuted the Nazarenes are just as untrue as the similar accusations made in the Gospels in connection with Jesus himself. The Pharisees had no reason to persecute the Nazarenes. They were not teaching any doctrine which was opposed to Pharisaic Judaism. There was nothing heretical or blasphemous in believing that the Messiah had come in the person of Jesus, who had been brought back to life by God and would soon return. The majority of the Pharisees did not believe this, but then many different Messianic beliefs were current among them. The Nazarenes attended the same synagogues as the other Pharisees, joined together with them in worship in the Temple, and shared with them without distinction in all the rites of Judaism. This went on for sixty years after the death of Jesus, until finally, as a result of events to be described, a split took place between the Nazarenes and the other Pharisees.

The Nazarenes shared also the missionary activities in which the Pharisees were engaged in this period, and in fact the Nazarenes were one of the most successful missionary groups among the Pharisees. They gained many adherents within the Pharisee party itself, especially among the lower ranks of the priesthood who were opposed to the quisling policies of the High Priest's clique.[7] In the wider field of missionary activity among the Gentiles, the Nazarenes were markedly successful. Nazarene groups were set up in many cities of the Empire, including Rome itself. The message of "good news," that the Messiah had come and would soon return, was attractive to many who might have remained impervious to ordinary Pharisaism. It should be remembered, however, that the whole Pharisee movement, not only the Nazarenes, was in the phase of rapid expansion and keen proselytising. The kingdom of Adiabene in Mesopotamia was converted to Pharisaic Judaism about ten years after Jesus's death. Roman writers testify with alarm to the spread of Judaism in the Roman Empire.

Like the other Pharisees, the Nazarenes recognized two grades of conversion to Judaism: full conversion, which involved circumcision, the acceptance of the Jewish law in its entirety and the adoption of Jewish nationality, and a kind of partial conversion (that of the "God-fearers," or "proselytes of

the gate") which was much less stringent in its requirements
and did not involve either circumcision or transfer of nationality. It was expected that in the coming days of the Messiah only
a minority of the world's population would undertake full
conversion, while the majority would become "God-fearers,"
accepting only the "seven laws of the sons of Noah," while
revering the Jews as a "nation of priests." The Nazarene groups
of converts contained both types of proselyte, and it must be
stressed again that this was the characteristic Pharisaic missionary pattern which the Nazarenes did not vary in any way.
Those Nazarene converts who accepted full conversion were
expected to observe the full Jewish law, as the Nazarenes did
themselves.

We now come to the turning-point in the history of the Jesus
movement; the advent of Paul, who transformed Nazarenism
into Christianity. Paul (originally Saul) began as an opponent of
the Nazarenes, whom he persecuted as an agent of the Sadducee High Priest.[8] However, in about 36 A.D. he became a
convert to Nazarenism as a result of a personal revelation. Soon
he began to propound a new view of Jesus's lifework which was
quite inconsistent with either Nazarenism or Pharisaism. Paul's
views are to be found in his Epistles, written at about 50–55
A.D. These Epistles, most of which are the genuine work of
Paul, are the earliest documents in the New Testament. They
give divine status to Jesus, declare the Jewish law abrogated,
and interpret Jesus's death in terms of Gnostic soteriology
("salvation"-doctrine). The full Gentile-Christian doctrine has
not quite developed in them (for example, Paul says nothing
about the Trinity or about the Virgin Birth), but the theological
basis for later doctrines—dualism, antinomianism, predestination, absolutism, "original sin"—is already consciously
present. Paul, a mystic of the Gnostic type, never knew Jesus
personally, but he claimed to know by special revelation what
Jesus meant. The Gospels as we have them are Paulinist
documents, i.e. reinterpretations of the life and death of Jesus
in the light of Paul's theories, though the three Synoptic
Gospels are attempting to effect this reinterpretation by the

adaptation of existing Nazarene documents rather than by a complete re-writing. The only New Testament document which appears to have survived from the Nazarenes with only slight Paulinist revisions is the Epistle of James, which is the work of the Nazarene leader, Jesus's own brother.[9]

Paul was a missionary of genius and his new version of the Jesus-message made great headway, especially with the "proselytes of the gate" or second-class converts who had already been converted from paganism by the Nazarenes. Paul's abrogation of Jewish law abolished the distinction between first-class converts and second-class converts and rendered unnecessary such difficult requirements as circumcision. The Nazarenes of Jerusalem, however, led by Jesus's brother James, were dismayed by Paul's activities which seemed to them to be a surrender to paganism and idolatry. A great split took place (about 60 A.D.) between the Jewish-Christians (or Nazarenes) and the Gentile-Christians (or Paulinists).[10] The term "Gentile-Christian Church" has been used in this book to refer to the Paulinist community which now arose in rivalry to the "Jewish-Christian Church"; though it should be remembered that Paul also converted Jews, that many of his adherents had previously been converted to some form of Judaism, and that the Nazarenes never at any time called themselves "Christians." The bulk of Paul's adherents certainly had a pagan Hellenistic background which enabled them to respond to the Gnostic aspects of his teaching.

So only thirty years after Jesus's death a great quarrel developed among his followers. There can be no doubt that the Nazarenes could justly claim to be the authentic transmitters of Jesus's own teaching; they were the eye-witnesses of Jesus's deeds, his companions and kinsfolk. Paul, on the other hand, deriving his ideas about Jesus from visions, was really the originator of his own doctrines, the founder of Christianity as a historical phenomenon and as a distinct religion from Judaism.

The struggle between Nazarenes and Paulinists went on for the next 10 years with the Nazarenes holding their own, and perhaps even gaining the upper hand. The Nazarenes, from their base in Jerusalem, sent out missionaries to all the centres of Paulinism to combat Paul's new doctrines and reclaim his converts for Nazarene Judaism.

The event, however, that weakened the Nazarenes fatally and gave the victory to the Paulinists was the siege and capture of Jerusalem by the Romans in 70 A.D. The Nazarenes, as loyal Jews, took part in the defence of the city, and in the ensuing massacre most of them died.[11] A few survived to continue an enfeebled existence, but they were unable to resume missionary activity or to exercise influence outside Palestine. Paulinism flourished unchecked, and the Gentile-Christian Church became the chief form of Christianity. The remnants of the Nazarenes, now sometimes called Ebionites, were regarded as heretics by the main body of Christians. To add to their miseries, they now for the first time came into conflict with their fellow-Jews, the Pharisees, who regarded the development of anti-Semitic Christianity as proof that Jesus could not have been the Messiah, and requested the Nazarenes to give up the Messianic belief that differentiated them from their fellow-Jews. In about 90 A.D. the Nazarenes were finally expelled from the Jewish Synagogue and became a heretical group in Judaism as well as in Christianity. The Nazarenes continued to exist until about 400 A.D. declaring to the last that Jesus was the Messiah, that he would soon return, that he was the Son of God but not himself divine, that the Jewish law had never been abrogated by him, and that Paul was a deceiver who had perverted Jesus's message.*

(iii) THE MAKING OF THE GOSPELS

What were the Christians of Rome thinking as the Jewish War went on, and the faces of Gentiles were turned towards Jews everywhere with hate? What did they think as they watched the procession of chained Jewish prisoners going through the

*See Appendix 8.

streets of Rome in Vespasian's triumph to the exultant execrations of the crowd, and as they heard the roar of savage joy on the news of the death of Simon bar Giora?

We can learn what they were thinking by reading the Gospel of Mark, written about this time, and the other three Gospels which carried further the orientation first laid down in Mark. Here we can see how the Christians, originally an integrally Jewish sect, detached and dissociated themselves from the Jews in the hour of their defeat.

The main Christian community of Rome was founded by Paul (Acts xxviii. 28–30), so the Pauline interpretation of Jesus's death as a divine sacrifice was already current there. Paul himself, by his doctrine of Christology, had detached Jesus from the politics of Judaea and "spiritualized" him to a point at which he was no longer a revolutionary. It would have been possible, one might think, for the Roman Christian community to have based itself entirely on Paul's teaching; to have made Paul's Epistles their Scripture and jettisoned the Gospel which derived from the Jerusalem Church and which portrayed Jesus as a man, teaching and acting in a Jewish environment. This, however, was not possible, because the Jerusalem Church and their Nazarene Gospel still had too much authority to be simply discarded. It was necessary, therefore, to *re-write* the Gospel and to give it a slant consonant with Pauline Christology. This, unfortunately, in the circumstances of the time, involved giving it an anti-Jewish slant. For the Gospel portrayed Jesus as a rebel against Rome; as one who was killed because he defied authority. Since Jesus was now a "spiritual" figure who took no interest in earthly politics it must have been a "spiritual" authority that he defied. The fact that he was a Jew who died on the cross, like so many thousands of Jewish rebels in the Jewish War, was an uncomfortably topical consideration. Having developed a form of Christianity which was divorced from Jewish history and Jewish national aspirations, the Roman Church had no wish to be implicated in the obloquy which the Jewish community had incurred. Their new form of Christianity was non-revolutionary; it was quite possible for them to live at peace with their Roman neighbours since the kingdom of God was no longer situated on earth but in some region beyond the skies. Paul had told them explicitly not to be revolutionaries: "Let every soul be subject unto the higher powers. For there is no power but of God: the powers that be are ordained of God" (Romans xiii. 1). In any case, they did not have the same motive for revolution as did the Jews; though many of them belonged to an oppressed class, they were not living in an occupied country under the heel of invaders. Yet here they were, with their anti-revolutionary attitude, being confused with the seditious Jews simply because the god whom they worshipped was a Jew and had been crucified for sedition. The solution that must have seemed to them so blindingly right as to be God-given was that Jesus had fought not against the Romans but against the Jews. The Gospel which they had received from the Jewish-Christians of Jerusalem must surely have been distorted by a pro-Jewish bias; it was up to them to put it right and to restore the facts as they must have been. In this frame of mind (not necessarily a consciously fraudulent one) Mark sat down to write his "edited" version of the Gospel.

The current school of Gospel study and criticism lays great stress on what is called the "sitz im leben" (environmental function) of the Gospels, as an explanation of their form and development. But, with a few honourable exceptions, the scholars of this school have ignored the main element in the environment, the one that was staring them in the face: the fact that the Gospel of Mark was written in the throes of the great disaster which befell the Jews in 70 A.D., when all Jews, and all connected with them in any way, had to examine their position and assess very carefully where their loyalties lay. The Hellenistic converts to Christianity, people such as Mark himself, came from a background in which anti-Semitism was strong. It was not hard for them to choose their stance. An important function of the Gospels, therefore, was to provide an orientation for the Gentile-Christians in the post-70 A.D. situation; to enable them to say, "We are not Jews. Jesus himself was not really a Jew, except by an accident of birth. Jesus was loyal to Rome, and so are we."

Eventually Jesus ceased altogether to be a Jew in the minds of his Gentile-Christian worshippers. Where the earlier Gospels describe Jesus as being in conflict with the Pharisees, John describes him as being in conflict with "the Jews." The effect of this on the reader is to take Jesus himself out of the category of "the Jews" altogether. Even today, many unsophisticated Christians are unaware of the fact that Jesus was a Jew, and react with shock if told this elementary fact. The deification of Jesus, of course, reinforces this tendency to obliterate his Jewishness; and another function of the Gospels was to urge the doctrine of Jesus's divinity, a doctrine which was never held by the Jewish-Christian Church of Jerusalem.

The development of the Gospels* may be summarised as follows:

(a) THE GOSPEL ACCORDING TO MARK.   This is the earliest of the Canonical Gospels, and was written in Rome in about 70 A.D.[12] The author Mark was a poorly educated Gentile who writes a rough Greek. All scholars now agree, on internal evidence, that Mark's Gospel is earlier than those of Matthew and Luke, with which it has much in common—so much that the three Gospels are called "the Synoptic Gospels." The relationship between these three Gospels is such that Matthew and Luke must have borrowed the common material from Mark, whereas Mark cannot have derived his Gospel from Matthew or Luke.

An anti-Jewish orientation is already very strong in Mark. The Jewish religious leaders are portrayed as Jesus's bitter enemies, and as refusing to acknowledge his divinity. However, certain elements of the earlier story have not yet been thoroughly censored; e.g. the friendly argument between Jesus and the Pharisee scribe (Mk. xii). The process of deification of

---

*For further information on the Gospel manuscripts, see Appendix 2

Jesus has not advanced to the same extent as in the later Gospels. There is no mention of the Virgin Birth or the infancy legends.

(b) THE GOSPEL ACCORDING TO MATTHEW. This was written about 80 A.D., probably in Alexandria, but possibly in Antioch. Matthew incorporates in his Gospel nearly the whole of Mark, and in addition has about 200 verses in common with Luke (these verses are held to be derived from a common source, known as "Q"). Matthew has about 400 verses of his own, not found in any other Gospel. Some scholars consider that Matthew was a Jew because he shows a special interest in evidence that Jesus fulfilled the prophecies of the Hebrew Scriptures. This, however, is hard to believe in view of the virulence of anti-Jewish feeling shown, for example, in Chapter xxiii, and in the story of the alleged curse pronounced by the Jews on themselves in the Barabbas episode (this curse is found only in Matthew). Also, Matthew is very ignorant of Jewish law (e.g. in the Sabbath incidents). It seems much more likely, then, that Matthew was a Gentile who wished to show that the Jewish prophecies themselves foretold the supersession of the Jews by the Gentiles in God's favour. Matthew does include, however, certain verses, evidently survivals from the Jerusalem Church's gospel, which go quite against his general tenor, e.g. Jesus's testimony to the inviolability of the Jewish Law (Mt. v. 18, 19) and Jesus's declarations that his mission was to the Jews only (Mt. x. 5 and xv. 24).

(c) THE GOSPEL ACCORDING TO LUKE. This was written about 85 A.D. in Greece or Syria. All scholars agree that Luke was a Gentile. He includes most of Mark and also has common material with Matthew (see above). It is unlikely, however, that Luke ever saw Matthew's Gospel. Luke has a more cultured style than either Mark or Matthew, and has considerable gifts as a writer. In his elaborate Prologue he shows sensitivity to the cadences of the Old Testament (he read it in the Greek translation, the Septuagint), which he imitates skillfully. Luke was also the author of *The Acts of the Apostles*, the main source for the history of the early Church.

Luke's Gospel continues the anti-Jewish and pro-Roman

tendencies of the previous Gospels. Like the other Gospel-writers, Luke has his lapses of attention and allows certain passages from earlier sources to stand, though they contradict his main theses; e.g. the incident in which the Pharisees warn Jesus of danger from Herod (Lk. xiii. 31), and the incident in which Jesus distributes swords to his disciples (Lk. xxii. 38).

(d) THE GOSPEL ACCORDING TO JOHN. This was written about 100 A.D. probably in Asia Minor. Some scholars consider that John was a Jew on the ground that he shows some knowledge of Jewish law and customs. Again, however, his standpoint is so anti-Jewish that this is hard to believe. He seems to have had the intelligence to enquire more accurately into Jewish law than the other Gospel-writers, and thus corrects some of their more obvious mistakes (e.g. in the Sabbath episodes), but his knowledge is still very superficial.

For a long time it was believed that the Gospel-writer John was one of Jesus's disciples and that therefore his Gospel was an eye-witness account of Jesus's life. Modern scholarship has proved that this cannot be the case, and that this Gospel is the latest of the four. The proofs are many and convincing. Jesus is portrayed as a non-Jew, speaking, for example, of "your law," and "the feasts of the Jews" as if the Jews he is addressing belong to a different race. Whereas the Synoptic Gospels all show a belief in the imminent return of Jesus, John's Gospel has dropped this belief and in fact says nothing about Jesus's Second Coming. This Gospel was written at a later date, when hope of a speedy return of Jesus had been abandoned. The anti-Semitism of John's Gospel has advanced to a point beyond that of the previous Gospels, and the Jews are portrayed as the pre-ordained, Satan-inspired enemies of the Light. Moreover, there is external evidence of the lateness of John's Gospel: certain writers (Polycarp, Papias, Justin) who have knowledge of the other Gospels have no knowledge of John.

Despite this, the doctrine of the earliness of John's Gospel is so attractive to Christian scholars that they are constantly trying to find new reasons to justify an early dating. This Gospel presents the doctrines of the Gentile-Christian Church in their most unmistakeable form, without the slightest adulteration from surviving traces of Jewish-Christian views of Jesus's role. In John's Gospel Jesus proclaims himself to be the Son of God in the true Gnostic style; a divine figure from the World of Light, without human affiliations or connections with his historical background.

Unlike the Synoptic Gospels, the Fourth Gospel is a unified composition springing from the creative urge of a single author who embodies in his work his own personality and outlook. John is not following the outline of a previous Gospel, but re-shaping his material in accordance with an artistic plan of his own. He alters events magisterially to suit his plan, (for example, he shifts the cleansing of the Temple from the end of Jesus's career to the beginning, and he scraps altogether the Synoptists' story of Jesus's gradual disclosure of his Messianic status). In the Synoptists' account Jesus is still a recognizably Jewish figure, sparing in words and human and concrete in approach; in John, Jesus has become a Greek: voluble, full of abstractions, mystical.

Nevertheless, John, with all his creativeness of method, is still using authentic sources as the colours in his palette, and sometimes he retains elements from those sources which the earlier Gospel-writers have suppressed; e.g. the account of Jesus's examination by the High Priest, and the information that the troops who arrested Jesus were Roman.

With the composition of the Gospels, then, a fictitious Jesus was created, suitable for the needs of the Hellenistic Gentile-Christian Church. The Prophet-King, human and Jewish, who was revered but not worshipped by the Jewish-Christian Church was turned into a Divine Sacrifice. Jesus, who was, in reality, an apocalyptic Pharisee rabbi who claimed the titles of Prophet and King, was turned into a pagan god.

17

The Dualism of the New Testament

The reader may reasonably ask, "What degree of certainty, or probability, should be assigned to the theory of the Barabbas incident outlined in Chapter 15?" The answer is that the last step in the argument—the identification of Barabbas as Jesus himself—is offered as the best available solution to a well-known crux or problem in New Testament studies, but the arguments for it do not amount to a demonstration. However, in the preliminary analysis and criticism of the Barabbas story we are on firm ground. The points that may be regarded as reasonably established are:

(a) the Barabbas story is a piece of anti-Jewish propaganda;

(b) certain elements in the story are completely fictitious, viz. the Passover privilege, the mildness of Pilate, the denigration of Barabbas as a "bandit," the demand of the Jewish crowd for Jesus's crucifixion, the acceptance by the Jewish crowd of a curse upon itself;

(c) all the above fictitious elements have one purpose only: to shift the responsibility for the Crucifixion from the Romans to the Jews.

These points (which have been established in this book by

reference to the Roman and Jewish background, to the circumstances in which the Gospels were written, and to the text
of the Gospels themselves) have to be taken into account by
anyone wanting to construct a theory of the relation between
Jesus and Barabbas. The dramatic polarity of the story, the
black-and-white melodrama of the choice between the Son of
God and the bandit, depends on the elements listed above and
vanishes when they were recognised to be fictitious. We are
then left with two rebel leaders of very much the same type and
have to consider what connection there may have been between
them.

The simplest theory, of course, is that Barabbas is just an
invention, like the Passover privilege, and the whole incident
arose from the fertile imagination of Mark or one of his
predecessors. I have no very strong objection to this theory,
except that it does not attempt to account for the origin of the
name "Barabbas," and it makes the Gospel-makers seem too
much like novelists rather than religious believers desperately
trying to make sense of a story which they regarded as
all-important and on which they believed their salvation depended. If we think of the position of someone like Mark,
poised uneasily between the Jews and the Romans, convinced
that the claims of the Jews had been refuted by their defeat and
disgrace, and that, as Paul had said, "the salvation of God is sent
unto the Gentiles" (Acts xxviii. 28), we can understand the
psychological conditions under which the story became
modified and, in time, radically changed. Whereas the Passover
privilege is understandable as a detail which was invented to
increase the drama of choice between the "good" Jesus and the
"bad" Jesus, it is hard to believe that the whole story arose out of
nothing; and a theory which demonstrates how the story could
have arisen out of a substratum of fact, and how it could then
have been gradually elaborated, is much to be preferred.

Whether or not one regards Jesus and Barabbas as the same
historical personage, the chief general characteristic which we
are bound to recognise in the story is its *dualism*. If there was a
separate person called Jesus Barabbas, distinct from Jesus of

Nazareth, then he must have been, as we have seen, a person not very different from Jesus himself; a sincere religious leader unable to avoid a clash with the Romans because of the intensity of his belief in the destiny of Judaism. Yet in the story Jesus has become all "good" and Barabbas all "bad." Everything active, political, physical and earthy has become bad, and is concentrated in the figure of Barabbas; the "good," represented as passivity and unearthliness, is concentrated in the figure of Jesus. This means that a "splitting" process has taken place in the character of Jesus, *even if one regards Barabbas as a separate historical personage;* in that case, Barabbas has been the receptacle into which the unwanted characteristics of Jesus have been dumped.

It was inevitable that the story should develop in this dualistic way in view of the Gnostic, and mystery-religion, background of the Gentile-Christian believers, and in view of the Gnostic interpretation which Paul, the real founder of Gentile-Christianity, had put upon the death of Jesus. In this interpretation, Jesus had died not in the struggle between Judaea and Rome, but in a supernatural, cosmic contest between the Powers of Good (based in Heaven) and the Powers of Evil (based in their captured stronghold, Earth). Salvation was to be achieved now not by any kind of political struggle but by a mystical sharing in the experience of crucifixion, a dying to be born again in another world. The "salvation" offered was not any kind of political liberation, but a "spiritual" liberation which could be experienced even in bondage; which is why Paul advised slaves to be docile and obedient ("Slaves, obey your earthly masters with fear and trembling," Ephesians vi. 5). The exercise of moral effort, the attempt to work out one's own destiny by grappling with the problems of the world and overcoming them, was regarded as a kind of slavery; one could become free from this slavery (which the Jews with their concept of the gradual mastery of the world by the moral law would have called freedom and responsibility) by becoming passive to the world, and by sinking one's individuality into the mystical organism of Christ. In this scheme the real enemies,

the allies of the powers of Darkness, were not those who sought
to enslave the bodies of men (the Romans) but those who sought
to weaken the efficacy of Christ's sacrifice by denying its cosmic
validity, by insisting on the reality and goodness of this world,
and by declaring that salvation was through the liberation of
Man on earth.

It was thus inevitable that the Jews should be cast for the role
of earthly agents of the Powers of Darkness. Many factors came
together to produce this result: political (the Jewish disaster,
pressure on Christian communities as seditious organisations
by Roman authorities), religious (conflict between Pauline and
Jewish Christianity, conflict between Gentile-Christianity and
the Jews themselves) and cultural (the Gnostic heritage of
anti-Semitism and the general Hellenistic-Jewish cultural
conflict).

Nevertheless, when all possible allowances have been made,
the Gentile-Christian Church's decision to assign the responsibility of the Crucifixion to the Jews and to elect the Jews to the
role of the people of the Devil, was deplorable. It could only
happen as a result of a deep moral and psychological flaw; the
flaw which vitiated all the religiosity of the Hellenistic world.
The despair that induces people to give up the hope of the
perfectibility of man, the spiritual lassitude that leads people to
regard man as a failure whose only hope is to escape into the
bosom of the Divine, must always lead to a split in the Universe
and to a split in the mind. The age-long effort of the Jews
towards a unification of the world and of the mind was thrown
aside by those who claimed to be the followers of a Jewish
teacher; and in the ensuing division of life between the powers
of Light and Darkness the Jews were rewarded for their
contribution towards the development of humanity by being
identified with the powers of Darkness.

There is nothing more seductive to the human mind than
dualism. It is romantic and exciting to see the world as the
battleground of cosmic powers of Good and Evil. It is satisfying
to one's natural humility to disavow human capacity for good;
and at the same time it is satisfying to one's omnipotence-

fantasy to see oneself as caught up in the sweep of the Divine Power-for-Good. It is satisfying, too, to one's feelings of sadism and aggression to identify some group of people with the World and the Powers of Evil; and it is usually some helpless group which is thus identified because to condemn a powerful group might lead to real engagement and commitment.

The dualism of the New Testament can be seen at its most obvious in the constant reference to hell, the Devil and to evil spirits.[1] Many people (especially humanists and agnostics, who have ceased to read the Bible) think that doctrines of hell-fire are part of the "bad legacy of Christianity from the Old Testament." In point of fact, the Old Testament contains nothing whatever about hell or the Devil, and hell-fire is never used as a threatened punishment for sin. (The word "hell" appears in some translations, but the Hebrew word "sheol" means "the grave" or perhaps sometimes "the underworld"; it never means "hell.")

The terrible fear of hell which was such a feature of Gentile-Christianity, reaching a level of desperation in the Middle Ages, arises from the terror of the Wrath of God. God Himself is split into two aspects—the God of Love, and the God of Wrath, and the object of religion is to escape from one to the other. This separation of two aspects of God is reflected also in the enormous importance in Gentile-Christianity of the figure of the Devil, or Satan, who is really a second God, the hypostatisation of the wrathful side of God. The wrathful God whose pitiless justice is pictured as the everlasting flames of hell is a *projection* of deep guilt or self-condemnation so despairing that no possibility is envisaged of human self-respect or self legislating conduct. This despair is expressed in the Gentile-Christian doctrine of Original Sin by which the Jewish myth of Adam was perverted to express a Hellenistic self-hatred. (The original story describes the birth of *knowledge* and adult self-awareness, as well as the birth of guilt.) The final dichotomy of Hellenistic Christianity is the split between the human and the divine, a split so profound that the human *loses its right to exist* and the only solution appears to be the swallowing up of the

human by the divine or (otherwise expressed) the escape of the
human soul into the bosom of God. The Jewish feeling that the
human body was made "in the image of God" (Genesis i. 27) is
combined in Judaism with the refusal to conceptualize any
image of God. Humanity takes its sanction from its origin in the
Infinite, which gives it the right to respect itself, to regard itself
as a created Idea of God with purely human potentialities
which it has been set the task to fulfill. This feeling of the divine
origin of the human, the sense that *all* human beings are the
"sons of God," that the whole body-soul continuum is God's
creation, has been lost in Gentile-Christianity; instead there is
the Hellenistic idea of the "divine spark" of the soul *imprisoned* in
the body from which it must be taught a desire to escape.
Christians have stigmatized the Jewish refusal to "surrender" to
God as evidence of a fear of the divine, of belief in an unpassable
barrier between the human and the divine, indeed of a kind of
dualism which finds the fusion of the human and the divine
impossible and fails to appreciate the "mercy" of God which
makes such a fusion possible. The truth is that the Jews do not
conceive religion as an exercise in becoming gods but as an
exercise in becoming truly human. It would be an insult to God
as Creator to spurn his handiwork, humanity, as mere dross
from which the soul must seek to purge itself.

The attempt to argue that there is a sanction for humanism in
the Gentile-Christian doctrine of the Incarnation does not bear
examination. In the Incarnation God does not become flesh in
order to be truly human, to engage in sex, for example, or to
make a living by "soiling his hands" with money; but on the
contrary to give an example of how to mortify the flesh by
undergoing crucifixion, a sado-masochistic torture which all
mankind must vicariously undergo if they wish to be saved.
The Incarnation is not the glorification of the flesh but its
supreme disparagement. God's only son undergoes the ultimate humiliation of entering the world of matter, of soiling
himself with the flesh, in order to rescue a few chosen souls
(chosen not by merit but by the arbitrary mercy of God) from
the contamination of being human. There is in Pharisaic

Judaism a very different doctrine of Incarnation: that the whole of humanity is the incarnation of God, and that the aim of humanity is to work out the possibilities of this incarnation, not to destroy it by self-immolation.

The dualism of the story of Barabbas, then, with its division of the spirit and the flesh, is symptomatic of the dualism of Hellenistic Christianity, its despair of human nature and its inability to retain the ideal of the unification of all human impulses into an integral personality.

Jesus was a good man who fell among Gentiles. That is to say, he fell among those who did not understand that to turn him into a god was to diminish him. He tried to bring about the kingdom of God on earth, and he failed; but the meaning of his life is in the attempt, not in the failure. As a Jew, he fought not against some metaphysical evil but against Rome. Yet the movement which denied his life by deifying him misrepresented him as being opposed to the people whom he most loved and on whose behalf he fought. It was an entirely fitting outcome that this movement, Gentile-Christianity, made a successful accommodation with Rome and became the official religion of the Empire which crucified Jesus.

Appendices

APPENDIX 1.
THE BARABBAS INCIDENT IN THE FOUR GOSPELS

"At the festival season the Governor used to release one prisoner at the people's request. As it happened, the man known as Barabbas was then in custody with the rebels who had committed murder in the rising. When the crowd appeared asking for the usual favour, Pilate replied, 'Do you wish me to release for you the king of the Jews?' For he knew it was out of malice that they had brought Jesus before him. But the chief priests incited the crowd to ask him to release Barabbas rather than Jesus. Pilate spoke to them again: 'Then what shall I do with the man you call king of the Jews?' They shouted back, 'Crucify him!' 'Why, what harm has he done?' Pilate asked; but they shouted all the louder, 'Crucify him!' So Pilate, in his desire to satisfy the mob, released Barabbas to them; and he had Jesus flogged and handed him over to be crucified."

Mark, xv. 6–15. (This is the earliest account of the Barabbas story, written probably about 70 A.D. in Rome.)

"At the festival season it was the Governor's custom to release one prisoner chosen by the people. There was then in custody a man of some notoriety, called Jesus Bar-Abbas. When they were assembled Pilate said to them, 'Which would you like me to release to you—Jesus Bar-Abbas, or Jesus called Messiah?' For he knew that it was out of malice that they had brought Jesus before him.

"While Pilate was sitting in court a message came to him from his wife: 'Have nothing to do with that innocent man; I was much troubled on his account in my dreams last night.'

"Meanwhile the chief priests and elders had persuaded the crowd to ask for the release of Bar-Abbas and to have Jesus put to death. So when the Governor asked, 'Which of the two do you wish me to release to you?' they said, 'Bar-Abbas.' 'Then what am I to do with Jesus called Messiah?' asked Pilate; and with one voice they answered, 'Crucify him!' 'Why, what harm has he done?' Pilate asked; but they shouted all the louder, 'Crucify him!'

"Pilate could see that nothing was being gained, and a riot was starting; so he took water and washed his hands in full view of the people, saying, 'My hands are clean of this man's blood; see to that yourselves.' And with one voice the people cried, 'His blood be on us, and on our children.' He then released Bar-Abbas to them; but he had Jesus flogged, and handed him over to be crucified."

Matthew, xxvii. 15–26. (This is the second account written probably about 80 A.D. in Alexandria.)

"Pilate now called together the chief priests, councillors, and people, and said to them, 'You brought this man before me on a charge of subversion. But, as you see, I have myself examined him in your presence and found nothing in him to support your charges. No more did Herod, for he has referred him back to us. Clearly he has done nothing to deserve death. I therefore propose to let him off with a flogging.' (At festival time he was obliged to release one person for them) and now there was a general outcry, 'Away with him! Give us Barabbas.' (This man had been put in prison for a rising that had taken place in the city, and for murder.) Pilate addressed them again, in his desire to release Jesus, but they shouted back, 'Crucify him, crucify him!' For the third time he spoke to them: 'Why what wrong has he done? I have not found him guilty of any capital offence. I will therefore let him off with a flogging.' But they insisted on their demand, shouting that Jesus should be crucified. Their shouts prevailed and Pilate decided that they should have their way. He released the man they asked for, the man who had been put in prison for insurrection and murder, and gave Jesus up to their will."

Luke, xxiii. 13–25. (This account was written probably about 85 A.D. in Greece or Syria.)

"Pilate said, 'What is truth?,' and with those words went out again to the Jews. 'For my part,' he said, 'I find no case against him. But you have a custom that I release one prisoner for you at Passover. Would you like me to release the king of the Jews?' Again the clamour rose: 'Not him; we want Barabbas!' (Barabbas was a bandit.)

"Pilate now took Jesus and had him flogged; and the soldiers plaited a crown of thorns and placed it on his head, and robed him in a purple cloak. Then time after time they came up to him crying, 'Hail, King of the Jews' and struck him on the face.

"Once more Pilate came out and said to the Jews, 'Here he is; I am bringing him out to let you know that I find no case against him'; and Jesus came out, wearing the crown of thorns and the purple cloak. 'Behold the Man!' said Pilate. The chief priests and their henchmen saw him and shouted, 'Crucify! crucify!' 'Take him and crucify him yourselves,' said Pilate; 'for my part I find no case against him.' The Jews answered 'We have a law; and by that law he ought to die, because he has claimed to be Son of God.'

"When Pilate heard that, he was more afraid than ever, and going back into his headquarters he asked Jesus, 'Where have you come from?' But Jesus gave him no answer. 'Do you refuse to speak to me?' said Pilate. 'Surely you know that I have authority to release you, and I have authority to crucify you?' 'You would have no authority at all over me,' Jesus replied, 'if it had not been granted you from above; and therefore the deeper guilt lies with the man who handed me over to you.'

"From that moment Pilate tried hard to release him; but the Jews kept shouting, 'If you let this man go, you are no friend to Caesar; any man who claims to be a king is defying Caesar.' When Pilate heard what they were saying, he brought Jesus out and took his seat on the tribunal at the place known as 'The Pavement' ('Gabatha' in the language of the Jews). It was the eve of the Passover, about noon. Pilate said to the Jews, 'Here is your king.' They shouted, 'Away with him! Away with him! Crucify him!' 'Crucify your king?' said Pilate. 'We have no king but Caesar,' the Jews replied. Then at last, to satisfy them, he handed Jesus over to be crucified."

John, xviii. 38; xix. 16. (This is the latest account, written probably about 100 A.D. in Asia Minor.)

APPENDIX 2.

THE MANUSCRIPTS OF THE NEW TESTAMENT

The language of the New Testament is Greek (that of the Old Testament is Hebrew, except for a few passages in the related language, Aramaic). There may have been a Hebrew or

Aramaic source for the Synoptic Gospels (this would have been a document of the Jerusalem Church), but no such document has yet been found. There is a Syriac New Testament (Syriac is a kind of Aramaic), but this is a translation from the Greek, and dates from the third century.

The earliest continuous texts (incomplete) of the New Testament date from the third century A.D.; these are the Chester Beatty papyri and the Bodmer papyri. There are also some very important fourth-century complete manuscripts, the Codex Vaticanus and the Codex Sinaiticus. These early texts establish, for example, that the ending of Mark (xvi. 9–20) and the story in John about the woman "taken in adultery" were later additions; they are missing from these texts altogether.

The very earliest New Testament texts are in the form of papyrus fragments, preserved in the dry climate of Egypt. These too are in Greek and their date can be determined fairly accurately from the handwriting styles used in them. The earliest of them have been dated to the second century; the earliest of all is a fragment of John's Gospel, assigned to about 120 A.D. No fragments from the first century have been found.

APPENDIX 3.

JESUS AND HIS BAND OF BROTHERS

The Gospel of John contains the record of a rebuke administered to Jesus by the apostle Judas:

"Judas saith unto him, not Iscariot, Lord how is it that thou wilt manifest thyself to us, but not unto the world?" (Jn. xiv. 22)

This is a very mild rebuke, but it appears rather more serious when one compares it with the very similar rebuke administered to Jesus by his brothers, but in a most hostile fashion (Jn. vii. 4). Perhaps the disagreement or quarrel between Jesus and Judas was in fact a serious one. Perhaps Judas was the leader of those disciples who wanted Jesus to adopt a more actively militaristic policy, like the Zealots. If so, Judas was supported by Simon Peter, who had a disagreement with Jesus, reported by the Synoptics as a serious quarrel (Mk. viii. 31, etc.), on a similar issue.

Now all this relates to Judas the Apostle, not to Judas Iscariot, who is supposed to be a different man. I suggest, however, that there was only one Judas among Jesus's disciples in the original story (Mark's and Matthew's lists of the twelve contain only one Judas, i.e. Judas Iscariot). Later, this Judas was split into two—a good Judas and a bad Judas, and the bad Judas became a devil-figure, representing mainly the alleged treachery of the Jewish people, whose eponymous name Judas bore. So on the basis of the memory of a genuine quarrel between Jesus and his disciple Judas, a legend developed in which this disciple became more and more evil—so evil that he could not be identified any more with the blessed apostle but had to be split off as a separate figure, fated to act the role of the Devil's secret agent.

The name "Iscariot" is usually derived from the Hebrew "ish Keriyoth," i.e. "man of Keriyoth," a place in Judaea. This etymology is very shaky, and a much more convincing etymology is from the Latin word "sicarius" or "knife-man," which was a name for the Zealots. Thus Judas, like Simon the Zealot, and like Simon Peter himself (known as "Barjonah," or "rebel"), was originally a member of the Zealot party, which would explain his impatience with Jesus's apocalyptism.

One may push this speculation a little further. There is a *third* Judas involved in Jesus's story, namely his brother Judas who is supposed to have become converted to Christianity only after Jesus's death, like another of Jesus's brothers, James. However, a surviving fragment of the early Gospel known as "the Gospel of the Hebrews" declares that James the brother of Jesus was present at the Last Supper. This suggests that James was in fact one of the twelve disciples, and is identical with the apostle known as "James the less" (who coincidentally had a mother called Mary and a brother called Joses, who are *supposed* to be quite different people from Jesus's mother Mary and Jesus's brother Joses). Now if James the brother of Jesus was one of the twelve after all (which in any case seems very likely from the fact that after Jesus's death he became the leader of the Jerusalem Church), then it may well be the case that Judas the brother of Jesus was one of the twelve too. This conflicts with the Gospel accounts that Jesus's brothers were hostile to him during his lifetime; but these accounts are very hard to reconcile with the fact that two of his brothers were so active in the Jerusalem Church immediately after his death. No doubt the Gospel-writers exaggerated the picture of Jesus at odds with his family in order to make him seem an other-worldly figure, superior to family ties.

If Judas the apostle was in fact Jesus's brother, it becomes quite understandable that his rebuke to Jesus (Jn. xiv. 22) is almost identical with that of Jesus's "brethren" (Jn. vii. 4). It is interesting, by the way, that John represents Jesus's brothers as taking great interest in Jesus's career and advising him to extend his mission to Judaea; in contrast to the other Evangelists, who portray Jesus's brothers as dismissing him as a madman (Mk. iii. 21). John does add that his brothers did not believe in him, but he gives a picture of much closer relations between Jesus and his brothers than we find elsewhere.

If the above speculations are well-founded, we come to the conclusion that Judas Iscariot was none other than Jesus's brother; that he was identical with Judas the Apostle; and that though he had a strong disagreement with Jesus at one point, he did not betray him but remained faithful to the end. Judas Iscariot was thus not a Judaean, but a Galilean like all the other apostles. And we now have a picture of Jesus not as a lonely other-worldly figure without family ties, but as the leader of a band of brothers, like Judas Maccabaeus and Athronges.

APPENDIX 4.

JESUS AS PHARISEE

A. *Sayings of Jesus represented as original, but actually Pharisaic or Scriptural.*

"Therefore all things what ever ye would that men should do to you, do ye even so to them for this is the law and the Prophets." (Mt. vii. 12).

This is similar to Hillel's saying: "What is hateful to you, do not do to your fellow-man: this the whole law, and the rest is commentary." Hillel was born in 75 B.C. Hillel's formulation is negative, while Jesus's is positive. Both Hillel's and Jesus's formulations are based on the Old Testament precept, "Thou shalt love thy neighbour as thyself."

"The Sabbath was made for man, not man for the Sabbath." (Mk. ii. 27).

This is similar to the Talmudic saying: "The Sabbath was handed over to you, and you were not handed over to the Sabbath." (Babylonian Talmud, Yoma 85b and elsewhere.) This saying is used in the Talmud to justify leniency in interpreting the Sabbath law.

"If a man on the Sabbath day receive circumcision, that the law of Moses should not be broken; are ye angry at me, because I have made a man every whit whole on the Sabbath day?" (John vii. 22).

This particular argument is also found in the Talmud. "If circumcision, which concerns one of the 248 members of the body, overrides the Sabbath, shall not a man's whole body override the Sabbath?" (B. Yoma 85b).

"Love your enemies . . . do good to them that hate you."

Based on the Old Testament saying: "If thou meet thine enemy's ox or his ass going astray, thou shalt surely bring it back to him again." (Exodus xxiii). Also "Thou shalt not avenge, nor bear a grudge against the children of thy people, but thou shalt love thy neighbour as thyself: I am the Lord." (Leviticus xix. 18).

"For if ye forgive not men their trespasses, neither will your Father forgive your trespasses." (Mt. vi. 15).

Similarly, "Forgive the wrong done by thy neighbour, and then when thou dost ask it thy sins will be remitted." Or, "When thou hast mercy on thy fellow, thou hast One to have mercy on thee; but if thou hast not mercy on thy fellow, thou hast none to have mercy on thee." (Tanhuma).

This applies to a neighbour's sins against *oneself*. But there is no Pharisaic sanction for forgiving a neighbour's sins committed against *other people*. The story that Jesus said to the sick man, "Son, thy sins be forgiven thee," does not ring true. In Pharisee doctrine, not even God could forgive sins unless reparation had been made to the injured party. This story is part of the "absolutionist" attitude of the Gentile-Christian Church, by which all sins could be forgiven because the difference between good and bad people was illusory, no one could ever acquire merit by any kind of good deeds, and "justification" could come about only by a gratuitous act of Divine mercy.

God's love and the love of God.

It is often represented that the Old Testament and Pharisee doctrine held God to be a stern God of Justice, as opposed to the New Testament God of Mercy and Love. Alternatively, that the Pharisee was required to *fear* God, while the Christian was required to love Him. In fact, the Old Testament is full of the topic of God's mercy and love: "the Lord is long-suffering and of great mercy" (Numbers xiv. 18), "his mercy endureth for ever" (passim), "the earth is full of the mercy of the Lord" (Psalms xxxiii. 5), "unto thee, O Lord, belongeth mercy" (Psalms lxvii. 12), etc. etc. "I have loved thee with an everlasting love" (Jeremiah, xxxi. 3), "How excellent is thy loving-kindness, O God! therefore the children of men put their trust under the shadow of thy wings" (Psalms xxxvi. 7), etc. etc. The chief expression of man's love for God in N.T. is quoted from O.T.: "Thou shalt love the Lord thy God with all thy heart, and with all thy soul, and with all thy might" (Deuteronomy vi. 5). Jesus's form of address to God, "Our Father" is taken from the Pharisee liturgy. The Pharisee doctrine of God's Attributes (taken over by Christian theologians) gave the two chief attributes as Justice and Mercy. The Pharisees would not have accepted, however, the idea of God's Justice being entirely swamped by his Mercy, because this concept implies that man has really no merit in God's eyes. In Pharisaism, man need not necessarily be overwhelmed by God's Attribute of Justice, because adherence to the Law would enable man to satisfy God in his aspect of Judge. Gentile-Christianity's picture of God as a God of Mercy only, really implies a terrifying picture of God's Attribute of Justice as entirely unsatisfied by anything in man; this explains why the fear of hell is so strong in Gentile-Christianity, despite the doctrine of Mercy (or rather, because of it).

B. *Sabbath-healing.*

A good summary of the Talmudic laws on the question of healing on the Sabbath is that of Rabbi David Feldman, in his commentary on the "Kizzur Shulhan Aruch" (The Abbreviated *Shulhan Aruch*). This summary is the more valuable in that it was made with no thought to its implications for New Testament exegesis, but as a practical guide for rabbis and teachers. I translate from the Hebrew (my italics):

> The Rabbis' prohibition against the use of medicines on the Sabbath was a precaution in case people should think wrongly that it is permitted to *grind* medicines on the Sabbath.
>
> Therefore, any kind of healing *which does not involve the use of medicines* is permitted, even for a slight ailment. . . .
>
> In a cure by the use of medicines, the Rabbis made certain distinctions.
>
> (a) In the case of one who has a *dangerous* illness, they permitted treatment entirely, and it is a very meritorious

action to disregard the Sabbath laws, in such a case, and the more actively one does so, the more praiseworthy it is.

(b)   In the case of an invalid who is in bed but not in danger, they permitted treatment by a non-Jew, when treatment involves a major infringement of Sabbath laws, and by a Jew if treatment involves minor (Rabbinical) Sabbath laws. The patient is permitted to take any kind of medicine.

(c)   Someone who is in great pain, even if he can walk, is regarded as if he is in bed (e.g. severe toothache).

(d)   Where there is danger to one limb, but not to life (except in the case of the eyes, danger to which is equivalent to danger to life), the rule is as in (b).

(e)   The prohibition against the use of medicines applies to someone with a slight ailment . . . Such a person must not take *as medicine* even food normally permitted to a healthy person, if it is unusual food for a healthy person.

The person who decides whether the sick man is dangerously ill is the doctor, and also the patient himself, who knows best how he feels. In the absence of a doctor, the decision may be made by anyone present who knows the disease, or who even says that he thinks it is dangerous. In the case of an *internal* complaint, the Sabbath law is annulled by any suspicion that treatment may be urgent, even if no doctor is present and the patient says nothing.

Illnesses mentioned in the Talmud as dangerous should be regarded as dangerous even if the doctor and patient say there is no danger. Illnesses which the Talmud describes as non-dangerous should be regarded as dangerous if the doctor says so.

Every teacher should be perfectly familiar with all the above laws, so that no delay may be caused by consulting books.

Note that there is no mention of *healing itself* being a forbidden Sabbath activity. Problems arise only when the *method* of healing involves some forbidden activity.

The Talmudic source is mainly B Shabb. 147.

C. *Sabbath-healing incidents in the Gospel of John.*

There is one curious story, in the Fourth Gospel (Jn. v), which involves Sabbath-breaking and healing but in which the Sabbath-breaking is separate from the healing. This is the incident in which Jesus cured a man "which had an infirmity thirty and eight years," and then told him "Rise, take up thy bed and walk." In the Synoptic Gospels, a similar incident occurs, but not on the Sabbath; the incident arises out of Jesus's alleged claim to forgive sins (Mk. ii. 11, etc.). Evidently, John has imported the Sabbath-breaking aspect into this story where orginally it did not exist. John, in many details throughout the Fourth Gospel, shows more knowledge of the Pharisaic laws than the Synoptists show. He must have known that the Synoptists were wrong in representing the Pharisees as objecting to Sabbath-healing. However, he finds a way to produce a clash between Jesus and the Pharisees on another aspect of Sabbath-breaking. He knows (as the Synoptists do not) that carrying objects was forbidden on the Sabbath (this is a prohibition included in the list of 39). So he takes the story in which Jesus told a man to carry his bed and shifts this story to the Sabbath. The Pharisees can now be represented as objecting not to the healing but to the subsequent flouting of the Sabbath law about "carrying." The only trouble is that while in the original story Jesus had good reason to perform the healing, (i.e. a humane desire to remove suffering) he has no reason, in John's story, to flout the Sabbath law of "carrying" except an arbitrary whim. The artificial conflation of stories produces a very unconvincing narrative. Moreover, John's knowledge of Pharisaic law, while superior to that of the Synoptists, is not perfect. For the law of "carrying" lays down that no major infringement of the law has taken place unless someone carries an object from a public domain into a private domain (or vice versa). Merely to carry an object along the street in a walled city such as Jerusalem, as in this case, would be no infringement of the "Scriptural" law against "carrying," but only of a minor Rabbinical bye-law or "fence round the Law." That the

Pharisees or "Jews" (as John calls them) wished to execute Jesus for this alleged minor offence is quite impossible.

This cooked-up scissors-and-paste story of John's is instructive because it shows that John's superior knowledge of Pharisee law affords no reason to suppose him a reliable witness to the events of Jesus's time (as some have argued). He merely uses his knowledge to tamper with the Synoptists' stories (themselves the end-result of a process of tampering) in order to remove from these stories some of their more obvious blunders. The final result in John is even less reliable than in the Synoptists' versions. This particular story is an excellent example of John's methods, and provides useful evidence that John knew the Synoptic Gospels.

Another excellent example in a later Chapter of John also concerns Sabbath-healing, and again John is careful not to allege that the healing itself was forbidden by Pharisee law. He tries to show that another Sabbath law was infringed, and again his knowledge, while superior to that of the Synoptists, is imperfect. The detail in which Jesus is supposed to have infringed the Sabbath is taken from an incident in the Synoptic Gospels which did not occur on the Sabbath. The method used by John in building up his story is exactly parallel in both cases (Jn. ix).

This story concerns the healing of a blind man, by a method involving the application of clay, formed from Jesus's spittle mixed with dust from the ground. The story is told in Mark 8, where, however, Jesus simply uses his spit, without making clay. (He also uses spit alone when curing a deaf man in Mark 7.) In Mark the story does not take place on the Sabbath, and no altercation with the Pharisees follows. John shifts the story to the Sabbath (by a very artificial aside) and also brings in the clay-making because he knows that clay-making would be an infringement of the Sabbath law. What he neglects, or does not know, is that any disease of the eyes threatening blindness was regarded in Pharisee law as a matter of extreme urgency for which any Sabbath-law, however important, could be infringed, and *had* to be infringed.

These two cases are in fact the only incidents adduced by John which connect healing with Sabbath-breaking. They show John as conscious of inaccuracies in the Synoptic Gospels which he is anxious to patch up. He aimed to produce stories which, while connecting healing with Sabbath-breaking, did not make the mistake of representing Pharisee law as forbidding Sabbath-healing itself.

The possibility must, of course, be considered that John's version of the Sabbath-healing incidents is the earlier one. The superior knowledge of Pharisee law shown in John's version might be held to lead to this conclusion. However, this possibility only has to be considered to be rejected. For John's version of the stories has a quality of heterogeneity about it that betrays its patched-up nature. The stories begin as if they are to be about Sabbath-healing and then turn out to be about something else. The simplest explanation of the development of the Sabbath-healing stories in John is as follows:

(a)   They were originally about clashes between Jesus and the *Sadducees*, in which Jesus advocated the more humane Pharisee point of view.

(b)   The Synoptists changed "Sadducees" to read "Pharisees," thus absurdly representing the Pharisees as having a Saducee point of view.

(c)   John, aware of this absurdity, changed the story (incorporating elements not originally related to the Sabbath-question) to be more in accordance with Pharisee law, but destroying the logic of the stories.

We conclude, then, that examination of these Sabbath-episodes reinforces the view that Jesus was not an anti-Pharisee and was in fact himself a Pharisee.

APPENDIX 5.

PHARISEE REFORMS

1. They made many reforms in the Law in order to make it more humane, especially in the penal code. They interpreted

the Biblical "lex talionis," "an eye for an eye, a tooth for a tooth," to mean that compensation should be paid in money for an injury. (Compensation had to include payment for medical expenses, for loss of employment, for the pain suffered and for the "indignity," as well as for the actual injury.) As for capital punishment, the Pharisees did not actually abolish it, but they hedged it round with so many conditions and qualifications that it was hardly ever carried out in practice. The evidence of the crime had to be clear to an improbable extent before a capital sentence could be carried out: there had to be two actual eye-witnesses to the crime (circumstantial evidence or even a confession was not admissible), and evidence of premeditated action was strictly required. A Court which carried out a capital sentence once in seven years (some say, once in seventy years) was called "a Court of blood."

The punishment of scourging had been fixed in the Torah at a maximum of forty stripes (Deut. xxv. 3). This itself was humane compared with contemporary codes, but the Pharisees further enacted a) that the maximum should be 39 instead of 40, b) that the person being punished should be medically examined beforehand and should undergo no more lashes than the doctor declared him capable of bearing, c) that if in the course of punishment he befouled himself with excrement or urine, the punishment should stop at once.

The Torah (Deut. xxi. 18) contains a law about the stoning of a "stubborn and rebellious son." The Pharisees turned this law into a dead letter by giving such a strict definition to the term "a stubborn and rebellious son" that the sentence could never be carried out (Mishnah, Makkoth iii). This is an instructive example of how the Pharisees carried out reforms without impugning the inspiration of the Bible. It also shows how the Pharisee love of hair-splitting definitions, condemned in the New Testament and by all anti-Pharisee writers, could sometimes be a humane device.

The Torah prescribes a Trial by Ordeal for a woman suspected of adultery (Numbers v). This is much less objectionable than most such trials in the ancient and medieval world, since if the woman drank the "bitter waters" without ill effect she was presumed innocent. However, the Pharisee Rabbi Johanan ben Zakkai, a contemporary of Jesus, abolished the ordeal on the grounds that women were expected to undergo it only when their men-folk were pure, which was no longer the case (Mishnah, Sotah ix. 9). This ironic argument is really part of a general tendency among the Pharisees to improve the condition of women.

Josephus too bears witness to the humanity of the Pharisees in penal matters. He says that the Pharisees "tend to be lenient in punishments" (Antiquities xiii. 10,6). The Sadducees, on the other hand, accepted the penal code of the Bible in its harshest literal sense. The day, during the reign of the pro-Pharisee Queen Alexandra, when the harsh decrees of the Sadducees were rescinded, was celebrated thereafter by the Pharisees and the people as a public holiday. We can see now how false is the charge in the Gospels that the Pharisees wished to execute Jesus for a minor infringement of the Sabbath laws—especially as, in the Pharisee view it was not an infringement of the Sabbath laws at all.

It hardly needs to be said that the Pharisee code did not contain such abominations as crucifixion, torture to obtain confession (confession being invalid as evidence anyway even if not induced by torture), the death penalty for trivial offences, or other such features which were absent from the Biblical code too, and were as repugnant to the Sadducees as to the Pharisees.

2.   Quite apart from the question of legal punishments, the Pharisees reformed many out-of-date Biblical laws which bore too hardly on individuals or groups in the population. The most celebrated of these enactments is Hillel's abolition of the law of the Seventh Year, by which all debts became void every seventh year (Deut. xv). This piece of primitive socialism had proved unworkable, and Hillel annulled it by devising a legal instrument called the "Prozbol" by which the law could be evaded. Again, the inspiration of Scripture had not been impugned, but a much-needed reform had been effected. Another important piece of Pharisee legislation was the deci-

sion that a married woman's property belonged to her and had to be returned to her in the event of divorce, an important protection for women which did not enter English law until 1882. The law that Ammonite and Moabite converts to Judaism were not allowed to marry within the Jewish community (Deut. xxiii. 3) was repealed on the ground that Sennacherib, King of Assyria, had mixed up the nations so much that there were no true Ammonites or Moabites left. These are just a few of the Pharisee reforms of Biblical law, about which a whole book could be written. Many writers argue that not one of these are true reforms because they do not involve the repeal or abolition, in the strictest sense, of Scriptural law. But a frontal assault on Scripture was unthinkable at this time and would have resulted in cultural collapse. The Pharisee method was dictated by compassion and common sense, and it provided relief to the oppressed just as effectively as the more direct method. The few examples given above are enough to show that the Pharisee "traditions" which the New Testament describes as "burdens too grievous to be borne" were in many cases not burdensome additions to Biblical law but welcome alleviations of it.

3. It is true, of course, that the Pharisees worked out elaborate laws about the kinds of "work" that were forbidden on the Sabbath. The Pharisees had a passion for precise definitions, and they found the Biblical laws of the Sabbath too vague for practical purposes. But it is a mistake to confuse precision with severity; the Sadducee Sabbath laws, though fewer and simpler, were far more severe. The Pharisees defined thirty-nine kinds of work that were forbidden on the Sabbath; but such exact definitions also made it quite clear what kinds of activity were *not* forbidden on the Sabbath. Many people think that the Pharisee Sabbath was like the Calvinist Sunday; a day when any kind of enjoyment or light-heartedness was frowned on. This was not so. The Pharisee Sabbath was intended to be, in the most literal sense, a day of rest, i.e. of leisure and recreation. The work forbidden on it was the week-day work of

agriculture and industry. All attempts to make the day enjoyable, or to make it a day of intellectual refreshment, were encouraged. It was a day of rest for animals and slaves too. It was associated so much with joy and peace that the World to Come was called "the time that is all Sabbath."

4. Even more important than the reforms which they introduced into religious law were the new attitudes and institutions by which the Pharisees breathed new life into Judaism. The institution of the *synagogue* was due to them. In other words, they were the creators of congregationalism, one of the most important developments in the whole history of religion, and one without which the development of Christianity and of Western civilisation would have been very different. This development, with its accompaniments of public prayer, the sermon, the readings from Scripture, and the religious study-circle, went along with a new attitude towards sacerdotalism, by which the Temple and the Priesthood were demoted in importance and the dignity of the layman was enhanced. Since the Law was considered to be an open-ended process, rather than a closed oracle, an atmosphere of democratic discussion was encouraged. Among the lay experts, the Rabbis, it became the practice to settle disagreements on religious questions by voting—this alone was one of the most significant religious developments in history. There was no doctrine of infallibility in connection with such decisions; it was recognised that they might be mistaken, and might have to be reversed at a later date.

5. In the course of their discussions, the Pharisees certainly brought a new intellectual rigour into religious thought, for which they have been much criticised by those who consider that the use of one's mind is incompatible with emotion and sincerity. On the other hand, however, the Pharisees had a strong vein of poetry. The Haggada (found mainly in the Midrash) is the poetical side of Pharisaism, and comprises folktales, parables, quaint fancies and metaphysical speculations. In particular, the *parable*, which was used so

much by Jesus, was the creation of the Pharisees. Some of the finest of the Psalms included in the Biblical canon were composed by Pharisee poets, and the Pharisee liturgy is unsurpassed in poetic feeling in the literature of religion. The charge of hypocrisy and dry-as-dust legalism cannot be sustained in the face of this evidence, though no doubt the movement, like every other religious movement, contained some hypocrites.

6. The Pharisees, in accordance with their new appreciation of the importance of the layman, instituted a system of universal education, by which schools were set up in every town and village in Jewry for all who wished to attend.

7. The Pharisees added new Festivals (Chanukah and Purim) to the Jewish religious year; they added to the canon of Scripture by including books not recognised by the Sadducees (e.g. Ecclesiastes and the Song of Solomon); they added new doctrines to Judaism (e.g. belief in angels, and belief in the resurrection of the dead); they added new rites to the Temple worship (e.g. the joyful ceremony of the Water-drawing on the Feast of Tabernacles); as well as being continual creators of new prayers and ceremonies in the synagogue.

Yet, despite everything, the Pharisees are still portrayed as stick-in-the-mud traditionalists who added nothing to Judaism except burdensome and unnecessary restrictions! They did in fact add some restrictions to the Law by their policy of "making a fence for the Torah," e.g. they enacted that not only was digging forbidden on the Sabbath, but a man should not even touch a spade to move it, lest this should lead to digging. But in Jesus's day, these additions had not accumulated to the extent that they did in late Talmudic times; and in any case, these "Rabbinical" precautionary enactments were never given the same status as the more fundamental commandments, and could be relaxed in cases of hardship. It would be quite out of proportion to place more emphasis on such precautions than on the manifold liberal innovations and reforms instituted by the Pharisees.

APPENDIX 6.

JESUS AS MIRACLE HEALER

There is no need to doubt the historicity of Jesus's miracle-healing. We are aware nowadays of the astonishing power of suggestion in curing disease, and the number of diseases which have proved to be amenable to such treatment is constantly increasing. There is no difficulty in believing that a person of great charismatic power, capable of working up a crowd into a state of mass-hypnosis, could have performed the cures with which Jesus is credited in the Gospels. This is the only part of Jesus's work which remained in the folk-memory of the Jewish people, as is shown by passages in the Talmud referring to cures performed long after Jesus's death by means of charms inscribed with his name.* The Talmud shows also that the ascription of disease to "evil spirits" was especially common among the Galilean Pharisee rabbis; as opposed to the Judean rabbis, who tended to adopt a more physicalist theory of medicine.† This division of opinion corresponds quite closely with the modern division between psycho-therapeutic and physical means of treatment in a certain range of diseases.

Jesus, then, by the power and attractiveness of his personality and the miracle-cures which this made possible, achieved a success far beyond that of the gaunt, forbidding John the Baptist. It should be noted that Jesus's miracle-cures were not without their political aspect. The re-appearance of an age of miracles would be regarded as a sign of approaching deliverance, as in the case of the deliverance from Egypt. Also, miracles of healing in particular would help the people to believe in Jesus as an authentic Prophet, and specially to identify him as the prophet Elijah whose name was associated with miracles of healing. In fact, many of Jesus's miracle-cures

---

*Tosephta, Hullin, II, 22; B. Av. Zar. 27b; Y. Av. Zar. II, 40d; Y. Sabb. XIV, 14d.

†Article 'Demons and Spirits (Jewish)', Herbert Loewe, *Enc. of Rel. and Ethics.*

are similar to those recorded of Elijah in the Hebrew Scriptures. The Gospels make it quite clear that Jesus was for some time regarded as the reincarnation of Elijah who, it was popularly believed, had never died. "Elijah" was a name of great political power, because it was thought that his return would immediately precede the coming of the Messiah. The more strongly Jesus was identified with him, the more resolute the people would be in defying the Romans. An Elijah figure was hardly less obnoxious to the Romans and pro-Roman Jews than was a popular Messiah-figure. So Jesus's miracle-cures were not a mere manifestation of religious fervour, as in a modern "evangelical" meeting; they were political acts, confirming the approach of the great day when the Romans would be thrown out of the Holy Land.

It must be emphasized again that Jesus's miracles would have no tendency to make the Jews worship him as divine. The miracles recorded of Jesus in the Gospels are no greater than those recorded of the prophets in the Hebrew Scriptures.

APPENDIX 7.

PHARISEE PARABLES

Body and Soul

Antoninus (a Roman Emperor) said to Rabbi (Judah the Prince), "On the Day of Judgment, the body and the soul can both plead innocence. The body can plead, 'Without the soul, I am blind and dumb.' The soul can plead, 'Without the body, I can commit no deed.' "

He replied, "I will tell thee a parable. A king owned a beautiful orchard which contained fine figs. He appointed two watchmen therein, one lame and one blind. One day, the lame man said to the blind, 'I see beautiful figs in the orchard. Come and take me upon thy shoulder, that we may procure and eat them.' So the lame bestrode the blind, procured and ate them. Some time after, the owner of the orchard came and asked, 'Where are those beautiful figs?' The lame man replied, 'Have I then feet to walk with?' The blind man replied, 'Have I then eyes to see with?' What did the king do? He placed the lame upon the blind and judged them together. So will the Holy One, blessed be He, bring the soul, replace it in the body, and judge them together."

B. Sanhedrin, 91a-91b.

There could be no better illustration than this of the Jewish doctrine of the unity of the body-soul continuum.

Repentance.

A king's son was at a distance of a hundred-days' journey from his father. Said his friends to him, "Return to your father." He said to them, "I cannot. The way is too far." His father sent to him and said, "Go as far as you are able and I shall come the rest of the way to you." Thus the Holy One, blessed be He, said to Israel, "Return unto Me, and I will return unto you" (Mal. iii, 7). Midrash.

Pharisee parables are often tied to the exegesis of a Biblical text. It is probable that, as Graves and Podro have argued, many of Jesus's sayings and parables were originally tied to texts in the same way.

APPENDIX 8.

JEWISH-CHRISTIANS (NAZARENES) AND GENTILE-CHRISTIANS

There are many references to the Nazarenes in early Christian literature, but they are treated as a heretical Judaizing sect, not as representatives of the original beliefs of the Jerusalem Church. That the first Christians were called Nazarenes can be shown from the New Testament itself (Acts xxiv. 5) and from Jewish sources (Hebrew, Nozrim). References to the Nazarenes and their beliefs (human status of Jesus, opposition to Paul) can be found in the writings of Justin Martyr, Epiphanius, Jerome, Irenaeus, Hippolytus and Origen. The Nazarene Gospel(s) were suppressed, but fragments of them survive (Gospel according to the Hebrew, Gospel of Peter). It has been argued by Hugh Schonfield (*According to the Hebrews*, Duckworth, London, 1937) that the medieval Jewish anti-Christian work *Toldoth Yeshu* is an adaptation of a Jewish-Christian Gospel.

The Nazarenes were later called Ebionites, and an important Ebionite or part-Ebionite work that has survived is the "pseudo-Clementine literature" (Clementine Homilies and Clementine Recognitions).

F. C. Baur was the first scholar to identify the Nazarenes with the primitive Jewish-Christians and to see the history of the early Church as a struggle between Nazarenes and Paulinists (*Kirchengeschichte*, 1853). For a scholarly modern treatment of this thesis, see S. G. F. Brandon, *The Fall of Jerusalem and the Christian Church* (1957), also the same author's *Jesus and the Zealots* (1967). An imaginative attempt to reconstruct the content of Nazarenism is *The Nazarene Gospel Restored* by Robert Graves and Joshua Podro (1953).

Many scholars still resist the view that the earliest Christians did not believe in the divinity of Jesus, and accordingly adhere to the official Catholic position that the Nazarenes were a later heresy.

Notes

1   Luke alone suggests that the crowd of Palm Sunday was a
    different crowd from that of the Barabbas incident (Lk. xix.
    37, where the crowd of Palm Sunday consists of "disci-
    ples"). The other Gospels stress that both crowds con-
    sisted of the Jewish masses; and Luke, like the rest,
    stresses the representative character of the crowd who
    condemned Jesus. John *at first* says that it was only the
    "chief priests and their henchmen" who shouted "Crucify
    him!" but soon alters this designation to his usual blanket
    expression "the Jews." Modern scholars (e.g. Eduard
    Meyer) have suggested that the crowd before Pilate
    consisted only of Barabbas's supporters, but there is no
    ground for this theory in the texts. Whatever may have
    been the historical facts, the intention of the texts is to
    incriminate the Jews as a whole for Jesus's crucifixion.*

    *Matthew and Luke use the Greek word "laos" (people,
    nation) instead of Mark's word "ochlos" (crowd); see Mt. xxvii.
    25, and Lk. xxiii. 13.

    A more "liberal" interpretation (such as that of Vatican
    Council II), while intended to exonerate the majority of
    the Jews, has the incidental effect of whitewashing the
    Gospels.

2   Early Christian writings of the 1st and 2nd centuries regard Pilate as a saintly man who was entirely guiltless in the matter of the Crucifixion. Pilate was actually canonised as a saint in the Ethiopian Church. The first note of criticism of Pilate's conduct is found in the writings of Eusebius (about 300 A.D.), and it was from this time that the familiar view of Pilate as well-meaning but weak and ineffectual—a moral coward—became current. This impression arises from inconsistencies in the Gospel story, not from any intention of the Gospel writers. Their aim was to show that Pilate was forced by the malevolence of the Jews to acquiesce in the murder of Jesus; but since the story gives no real reason for this acquiescence, Pilate's character began to be interpreted as weak.

3   Only John specifies Passover as the time when the crowd was entitled to release a prisoner. The other Gospels say "at the festival season"; and there were three pilgrim-festivals, Passover, Pentecost and Tabernacles.

4   See Paul Winter, *On the Trial of Jesus*, p. 94; S. G. F. Brandon, *Jesus and the Zealots*, p. 259; Haim Cohn, *The Trial and Death of Jesus*, pp. 166–167.

5   Another centurion is mentioned in Matthew and Luke (Mt. viii, Lk. vii) as showing great faith in Jesus in the matter of a sick servant. Luke's account is not in any way derogatory to the Jews; but Matthew alters the story. He omits the fact that Jesus performed the cure at the request of the Jews to whom the centurion had applied for help; and adds the moral that the Jews would be "cast out into outer darkness." He thus puts this story into line with the story of the other centurion by contrasting Gentile faith with Jewish unfaith.

NOTES ON CHAPTER 2.   HOW THE ROMANS CAME

1   Josephus, *Antiq.* XIV. x. 6.

2   Joseph Klausner, *From Jesus to Paul*, Ch. 3.

3   Stewart Perowne, *The Life and Times of Herod the Great*, p. 138.

NOTES ON CHAPTER 3.   THE ROMAN ADMINISTRATION

1   A recently discovered inscription (1961) gives the title of Pontius Pilate, the fifth-appointed governor, as "praefectus," not "procurator." This may represent a promotion or an additional title. The governor of Egypt was called both "praefectus" and "procurator." Josephus refers to the governors of Judaea as procurators.

2   See Joseph Klausner, *Jesus of Nazareth*, pp. 187–188.

3   Suetonius, *Tiberius*, xxxii. 2.

4   Cicero, *In Verrem*, II. iii. 12, and ii. 7.

5   Tacitus, *Histories*, iv. 74. 1.

6   See E. Schürer, *History of the Jewish People in the Time of Jesus Christ*, Div. I, Vol. 2, p. 51.

7   Philo, *De Legatione ad Caium*, sec. 38.

8   Moses Aberbach, *The Roman-Jewish War (66–70 A.D.)*, p. 55, quoting Eusebius, *Hist. Eccl.* II, 5, 7 and other sources.

NOTES ON CHAPTER 4.   ROMANS AND JEWS

1   Genesis Rabbah s. 36.

2   For an important corrective to the usual picture of the "benefits" of Roman rule, see Karl Kautsky, *Foundations of Christianity*, Part Two. Kautsky shows that the Empire even in its so-called best days produced, by its slave-holding system, a decrease in population, exhaustion of the soil, and finally economic collapse; while, politically, it destroyed all forms of true political life.

Notes on Chapter 5. Religion and Revolt: The Pharisees

1   Some scholars (S. Zeitlin, A. Richardson, Morton Smith) argue that the party founded by Judas was not identical with the Zealots. But the unbroken dynastic succession leading from Judas to the later Zealot leaders tells against this view.

2   Y. Yadin, "Finding Bar Kochba's Despatches," *The Illustrated London News*, 4 November, 1961.

3   The literature of the Pharisees consists of the Talmud and the Midrash, each of which consists of many separate works compiled over a long period from materials of varying dates. The Mishnah, the main basis of the Talmud, was compiled by Rabbi Judah the Prince about 200 A.D. Some scholars would argue, therefore, that the humane standpoint of the Mishnah represents the views of a later time, and cannot be held to represent the views of the Pharisees of Jesus's time. It is now generally recognised, however, that much of the Mishnah stems from Jesus's time and earlier. By the time the Mishnah was compiled, the name "Pharisees" had fallen largely into disuse, because all rival sects had ceased to exist among the Jews, and a sectarian name was no longer necessary. There is thus no real need to distinguish between Pharisaism and a "rabbinical movement" succeeding it. For the continuity of Pharisaism and the so-called "rabbinical movement" see E. P. Sanders, *Paul and Palestinian Judaism* (1977). George Foot Moore's *Judaism in the First Centuries of the Christian Era* should also be consulted.

4   B. Kiddushin, 66a.

5   B. B. Metz, 59b.

6   Josephus, *Antiq*. XIII. x. 6. Philo, ed. Mangey, II, 629 (preserved in Eusebius, *Praeparatio Evangelica*, VIII. 7. 6).

7   Josephus, *Antiq.* XIII.x.6.

8   Josephus, *Antiq.* XIII.x.5.

9   It is sometimes suggested that the "scribes" mentioned in the Gospels were Sadducee, not Pharisee, scribes. This is hardly plausible, since the "scribes" are nearly always associated closely in the text with the Pharisees. The suggestion is motivated by the desire to defend the Gospels from the charge of misrepresentation. Similar motivation lies behind the equally baseless suggestion that the scribes were Shammaiites, not Hillelites.

10   Josephus, *Antiq.* XVII.ii.4.

11   See Appendix 4B.

12   But see Appendix 4C, on John's variations on the Sabbath-healing stories.

13   A very plain example of the substitution of "Pharisees" for "Sadducees" is the argument about respect for parents, reported in Mark vii and Matthew xv. Here Jesus reproves the "Pharisees" for holding that a man might legally prevent his parents from benefiting from certain goods, by the device of dedicating the goods to the Temple. The actual ruling of the Pharisees on this point is the exact opposite (Mishnah, Nedarim iii. 2). The Pharisees placed respect for parents much higher than respect for the Temple. The Sadducees, on the other hand, with their exaggerated respect for the Temple, may have had the ruling described. Jesus is here undoubtedly urging a Pharisaic viewpoint; yet he is represented as urging it *against* the Pharisees.

NOTES ON CHAPTER 6.   THE JEWISH SECTS

1   B. Avodah Zarah, 17b.

2   The New Testament itself reports a case when the High

Priest was overruled by the Sanhedrin (Acts v, the case of Peter).

3   Adolf Büchler, *Das Synedrion in Jerusalem und das grosse Beth Din in der Quader-Kammer*, Vienna 1902. Hugo Mantel, *Studies in the History of the Sanhedrin*, Harvard University Press, 1961, p. 92 ff. Solomon Zeitlin, "The Crucifixion of Jesus Re-examined" in *Studies in the Early History of Judaism*, Ktav, New York, 1975, Vol. III, p. 263 ff.

4   In particular, the following features may be mentioned:
        (a) The sect was centred round the Priesthood, to which it gave extraordinary reverence. Even the Messianic hopes of the sect were coloured by this attitude, for they looked forward to a Messiah descended from Aaron, equal in status, if not superior, to the Davidic Messiah.
        (b) The sect followed a version of the Jewish Law which was stricter, less humane and less flexible than that of the Pharisees; e.g. their code forbade going to the relief of an animal which had fallen into a pit on the Sabbath. Their religious calendar differed considerably from that of the Pharisees; so the theory, held by many scholars before the discovery of the Dead Sea scrolls, that the Essenes formed part of the Pharisee movement has been proved to be incorrect.
        (c) Their Messianic expectations were very militaristic in character. The "War Rule" scroll describes in great detail the military formations of the Messianic army which would destroy the Gentiles in a holy forty years' war. These ideas remained largely in the realm of vain dreaming; but that the Essenes were not averse to war was already known from the fact, recorded by Josephus, that one of the Jewish generals in the first War against Rome was John the Essene.

NOTES ON CHAPTER 7.   THE MESSIAH

1   Exodus, xxiii.20–22.

2   In recent years, many efforts have been made to show that

the leading ideas of Gentile-Christianity are rooted in Judaism. Indeed, as much effort has gone into this line of argument as used to be put into the opposite view that Christianity represents an entirely new departure from Judaism. Many ingenious, though strained, arguments have been proffered to show that doctrines such as the Virgin Birth, Predestination, vicarious atonement, etc. had their origin in Judaism. Naturally, among these efforts are to be found attempts to show that the idea of a Divine Messiah is also to be found in Judaism (this line of argument is to be found in medieval Christian-Jewish disputations, such as that between Pablo Christiani and Nachmanides in 1263). Even W. D. Davies, however, a leading exponent of the "Jewish origin" line, had to reject the attempts of H. Windisch and others to find a doctrine of the Divine Messiah in Judaism (see W. D. Davies, *Paul and Rabbinic Judaism*, p. 162: "We have now examined those passages brought forward by Windisch to prove that the Messiah had been interpreted as the Wisdom of God in Judaism, and in all cases we have found the evidence unconvincing.")

3   Josephus, *Jewish War*, II, xvii.8.

4   See Strack-Billerbeck, *Kommentar sum Neuen Testament aus Talmud und Midrasch*, vol. ii, p. 282.

5   See Joseph Klausner, *The Messianic Idea in Israel*, trans. W. F. Stinespring, 1955, p. 469.

6   Ezekiel, xi.19; Isaiah, xi.9.

NOTES ON CHAPTER 8. REALISM AND MYSTICISM

1   See J. Leipoldt, *Sterbende und auferstende Götter*, Leipzig 1923, pp. 77–78; and *Von den Mysterien zur Kirche*, Hamburg 1962, p. 201.

2   The discovery of a library of Gnostic texts at Nag Hammadi in Upper Egypt in 1945 has much increased our

knowledge of Gnosticism. Much work remains to be done on these texts, but it seems very probable that some of them are non-Christian and are translations or adaptations of pre-Christian texts. See the works by G. Macrae and R. M. Wilson cited in the Bibliography.

3 Gilbert Murray, *Five Stages in Greek Religion*, Chapter IV.

4 Jude, 14–15. See also Hebrews, xi.5.

5 Genesis Rabbah, xxv.

NOTES ON CHAPTER 9.   WHAT REALLY HAPPENED

1 Certain writers (Plummer, Schürer) have elaborated a theory that the Pharisees warned Jesus as a trap, hoping to entice him out of Galilee into Judaea, where he could be arrested by the Sanhedrin. This highly imaginative theory is based on nothing whatever in the text.

2 An interesting indication of the hunted existence that Jesus and his disciples led is provided by a little-understood passage dealing with corn-plucking on the Sabbath. Jesus defends his disciples for plucking ears of corn by quoting an incident from Scripture. David, when fleeing for his life from Saul, broke the law forbidding the eating of sacred food by non-priests. The emergency and danger of starvation over-rode such laws. In a similar emergency the Pharisees permitted breaches of the Sabbath laws, and Jesus even cites the Pharisee maxim which covers such cases, "The Sabbath was made for man, not man for the Sabbath." But Jesus's citation of the case of David is apposite only if his own case was similar, i.e. he too was fleeing for his life. The Gospels suppress the fact that Jesus was on the run from Herod or the Romans, and represent Jews as *attacking* Pharisee attitudes towards the Sabbath when he was in fact applying them.

NOTES ON CHAPTER 10.   JESUS, RABBI AND PROPHET

1   See Emil Schürer, *A History of the Jewish People in the Time of Jesus Christ*, Div. 1, Vol. 2, 105–143.

2   It may well be that Jesus reproved certain elements in the Pharisaic party for ostentation and hypocrisy; for the Pharisee writings themselves contain such reproofs. The question of hypocrisy was one of which the Pharisees were strongly aware. For example, Rabban Gamaliel II issued the warning, "Let no disciple who is not inwardly as he is outwardly enter the lecture hall" (B. Berachoth, 28a). The Mishnah (Sotah, iii. 4) refers to hypocrisy as "the plague of the Pharisees," and the Talmud, commenting on this phrase, enumerates various types of hypocritical Pharisee, the descriptions of some of which are reminiscent of phrases attributed to Jesus (e.g. the Talmud's "shoulder Pharisee" may have some connection with Jesus's "they bind heavy burdens and grievous to be borne, and lay them on men's shoulders"). Self-criticism was a Pharisee tradition, and Jesus no doubt engaged in criticism of the movement to which he himself belonged; but later redactors of the Gospels twisted this healthy self-criticism into a condemnation of the Pharisee movement *as a whole*. The Old Testament too is full of self-criticism; no nation has exposed its own failings so unsparingly as the Jews. Anti-Semites have always taken advantage of this openness and have used the Jewish records against the Jews. An example of anti-Semitic use of Old Testament self-criticism is Matthew xxiii. 32–37. Such use of frank records ignores the good side of the picture, gives no credit for honesty, and fails to understand that self-criticism is possible only to those who are basically of good conscience. See Graves and Podro, *The Nazarene Gospel Restored*, Ch. XIII, "Feigned Pharisees."

3   It has been argued, mainly by D. Flusser and G. Vermes, that Jesus shows an affinity to a particular group of the Pharisees called the Hasidim, who were charismatic figures and miracle-workers (e.g. Hanina ben Dosa). There is much to be said for this view, but there is no

ground for Vermes's contention that the Hasidim were at
loggerheads with the rest of the Pharisees. The Pharisaic
movement was flexible enough to contain many trends,
which had mutual respect for each other (e.g. the schools
of Hillel and of Shammai).

4   At the Baptism, Jesus is unmistakeably marked out as the
Son of God by the descent of the Holy Ghost (Lk. iii. 22);
yet later John sends an inquiry to Jesus, "Art thou he that
should come? or look we for another?" Evidently John's
subjection to Jesus was previously exaggerated. Mk. ii. 18
shows rivalry between John and Jesus, but this is disguised in the later accounts (Mt. ix. 14 and Lk. v. 33). In
Acts (xviii. 25) we read of a certain Apollos, who "spake
and taught diligently the things of the Lord, knowing only
the baptism of John." This shows that the Johannites
continued as an independent movement even after Jesus's
death. For a time after John's death, Jesus was regarded by
many people as John's reincarnation, which shows that
the idea of John as subordinate to Jesus was not current.
(Mk. viii. 28, Mt. xiv. 2). Even today, there remains a sect
of 15,000 people in Iraq, called the Mandaeans, who
regard John the Baptist as their chief prophet and regard
Jesus as a false Messiah. This sect can be traced back to the
2nd century and possibly earlier, though there is some
doubt about when the traditions about John entered their
teachings and from what source. (See E. Yamauchi,
Gnostic Ethics and Mandaean Origins, 1970.) According to
Mt. xi. 14, Jesus assigned the role of Elijah to John at an
early stage; yet after the Transfiguration, we find Jesus
explaining John's Elijah-status to his disciples as if this is a
new idea (Mt. xvii. 10). Evidently, the earlier announcement never really happened. An interesting detail, preserved by Luke only (Lk. xi. 1), is that Jesus introduced
the Lord's Prayer in imitation of John the Baptist.

5   *Antiquities*, xviii, v. 2.

NOTES TO CHAPTER 11.   THE KINGDOM OF GOD

1 See, e.g. Mk. viii. 28, and ix. 11, showing the disciples' perplexity.

2 Jn. xiv. 22.

3 B. Ber. 34b.

4 B. Av. Zar. 17b and elsewhere.

5 It should be noted that there is no support in the parables mentioned for the view that repentance is the *only* avenue to God's grace. The loyal son in the Prodigal Son parable is not a complacent prig; nor is it asserted that there cannot be "ninety and nine just persons." Some of the parables attributed to Jesus can be interpreted to mean that merit does not exist at all, and grace can be obtained only by surrender to God's mercy. In the parable of the Two Sons (Mt. xxi) the contrast is not between a righteous son and an erring but repentant son; it is between two sons one of whom is repentant and the other a hypocrite. This parable may in fact be a later version of the Prodigal Son parable itself, altered to be in line with the Gentile-Christian doctrine of Original Sin, by which there cannot be any "just persons." In the Prodigal Son parable, the loyal son symbolises the Pharisees, of whom Jesus said, "they that are whole have no need of a physician" (the idea that this was meant sarcastically is a later manifestation).

6 *Zealot nicknames of the Disciples.* Simon's nickname, "the Zealot" (Greek, "zelotes") is given plainly by Luke (vi. 15), but is disguised by Mark and Matthew as "the Canaanite." The Canaanites no longer existed at this time, but the Hebrew word for Zealot is "kanai," which Mark and Matthew misread as "kena'ani" (Canaanite).

For the derivation of Judas's nickname "Iscariot," see p. 202.

Simon Peter's nickname, "Bar-jona" (Mt. xvi. 17) is

evidently derived from "baryona," an Aramaic word meaning "outlaw," often applied to the Zealots.

The nickname "Boanerges" of James and John is glossed "The sons of thunder" in Mk. iii. 17, probably equivalent to the Hebrew "benei ra'ash." The nickname has a martial ring appropriate to Zealots. This probably explains the omission of the name from the other Gospels.

7   Two Pharisee Rabbis, Hillel and Hanina ben Dosa, were considered to be of near-prophetic status. Hillel was regarded as "worthy to be a prophet." Hanina b. Dosa was asked, "Are you a prophet?" but he disclaimed the title. (B. Bk, 50a).

NOTES TO CHAPTER 12.   KING OF THE JEWS

1   See Midrash Deuteronomy Rabbah, where God is represented as promising Moses, "Moses, I swear to you . . . in the time to come when I bring Elijah, the prophet, unto them, the two of you shall come together" (III. 17).

2   The idea that the Gospels contain a disguised account of Jesus's coronation was put forward by Robert Graves and Joshua Podro, in their *The Nazarene Gospel Restored* (1953). These authors drew on the work of Raphael Patai *(Hebrew Installation Rites)*, who made important deductions about Near Eastern coronation rites by relating them to African rites described by Tor Irstam *(The King of Ganda: Studies in the Institution of Sacred Kingship in Africa*, Stockholm, 1944). Graves and Podro, however, failed to see the significance of the Transfiguration in this connection, and regarded Jesus's Baptism by John the Baptist as the occasion of the Coronation. The Baptism contains few of the features of a coronation, and is in any case an apocryphal event, designed to demonstrate an unhistorical submission on John's part to Jesus (see note 4, Chapter 10). Graves and Podro were obliged therefore to regard most of the coronation data as displaced from the Baptism scene. If the Transfiguration was in fact the Coronation, very little

displacement has occurred. The miracle of the loaves, for example, rightly regarded by Graves and Podro as a disguised form of the coronation rite in which the King distributed bread to the people, occurs just before the Transfiguration. The incident in which Jesus, dressed in a purple robe, was mocked by Herod and his "men of war" (Lk. xxiii. 11) may be a genuine case of displacement, since a ritual mocking and the donning of a purple robe were both features of a coronation.

3 For various theories on the date of the Triumphal Entry, see F. C. Burkitt, "Studies in the Western Text of St. Mark (Hosanna)," *J.T.S.* o.s. XVII (1916), 139–152; W. R. Farmer, "The Palm Branches in John 12, 13," *J.T.S.* n.s. III (1952), 62–66; T. W. Manson, "The Cleansing of the Temple," *Bulletin of the John Rylands Library*, XXXIII (1950–1951), 271–282; B. A. Mastin, "The Date of the Triumphal Entry," *New Test. Stud.*, 16, pp. 76–82.

4 The alternative form "Hoshiya-na" occurs, not prominently, in the Hallel of every Festival. Scholars, however, have failed to note the difference between the two forms, and have thus underestimated the uniqueness of "Hosanna" in relation to Tabernacles.

5 It should be mentioned that the appearance of the King in the Temple Court was not an occasion for royal self-glorification. It was a ceremony of re-dedication of the King, and a demonstration of his obedience to the rule of Law. Part of the passage which he had to read was as follows:

> And it shall be with him (the king), and he shall read therein all the days of his life: that he may learn to fear the Lord his God, to keep all the words of this law and these statutes, to do them. That his heart be not lifted up above his brethren, and that he turn not aside to the right hand or to the left: to the end that he may prolong his days in his kingdom, he, and his children, in the midst of Israel.

This was the ideal of kingship to which Jesus dedicated himself; a far cry from the Gentile ideal of the god-king above the rule of Law to which the Gentile-Christian Church succumbed under the impression that they were embracing a more "spiritual" conception than that of Judaism.

6   See I Kings viii, and II Chronicles vii. 10 (for the dating).

7   According to John's story (Jn. vii), which is contained in no other Gospel, Jesus was urged to go up to Jerusalem by his brothers at the time of "the feast of the Tabernacles." Jesus refused to go, saying, "My time is not yet come." Yet he did go after all, "not openly, but as it were in secret." Despite this intention of secrecy, a disturbance arose among the people about him; and "about the midst of the feast," Jesus appeared openly in the Temple, preaching boldly. Some of the people declared him to be "the very Christ." When the rulers tried to arrest him, he disappeared, "because his hour was not yet come." The story appears to be an intermediate version of the Triumphal Entry: it is here admitted that Jesus went to Jerusalem at Tabernacles, but not in a Triumphal Entry—that came later, at Passover. The Tabernacles visit is represented as merely preliminary; and in the other Gospels, it drops out altogether.

8   In the Talmud, however, Rabbi Eliezer and Rabbi Joshua (2nd century) disagree about whether the final salvation will take place in spring or autumn. Rabbi Eliezer, supporting the older tradition as usual, advocates the autumn date (B. Rosh Hashana, 11a). R. Le Déaut ("Pâque Juive et Nouveau Testament," *Studies on the Jewish Background of the New Testament*, 1969) has argued one-sidedly that Passover was the accepted date for final deliverance. He quotes Rabbi Joshua and even later authorities, but ignores Rabbi Eliezer and the Biblical authority for Tabernacles.

NOTES ON CHAPTER 13.   THE DAY OF THE LORD

1   See II Samuel, xv. 32; and Ezekiel xi. 23.

2   Mk. xiv. 3; Mt. xxvi. 7. Luke and John vary the story;
    Luke making the anointer into a "sinner," and John
    identifying her as Mary, the sister of Martha, and both
    making the anointer apply the ointment to Jesus's *feet*
    instead of his head.

3   The Mount of Olives was known as "the Mount of
    Anointing" (Mishna, R. Hash, ii. 4).

4   Pesik. R. s. 41; Lev. R. s. 13.

5   Lam. R. to ii. 2. See H. Graetz, *History of the Jews*, Vol.
    II, p. 414.

6   Josephus, *Antiq.* XX. 5. 1.

7   Josephus, *Antiq.* XX. 8. 6.

8   The derivation from Hebrew "gath-shemen" cannot pro-
    duce the translation "oil-press," as often stated, since
    "gath" means "wine-press." Much preferable is the deri-
    vation from "geshemen" ("valley of oil").

9   Another prophet, Joel, also located the Last Judgment of
    God on the nations in a valley, which he called the Valley
    of Jehoshaphat ("God's judgment"), and also "the valley of
    decision." Because of the similarity of Joel's vision to that
    of Zechariah, the valley of Jehoshaphat was early
    identified with the valley of the Kidron, part of which is
    the Vale of Gethsemane. It is very probable that Jesus
    made this identification too, so that the prophecies of Joel,
    as well as those of Zechariah, were in his mind as he
    stationed himself in Gethsemane.

10 Mk. xiii. 33: "Take ye heed, watch and pray: for ye know
    not when the time is." The whole passage shows that

"watch and pray" had a Messianic connotation, and was not merely an injunction to ordinary prayer.

NOTES ON CHAPTER 14. THE ARREST AND TRIAL

1   See Paul Winter, *On the Trial of Jesus*, pp. 24–25; S. G. F. Brandon, *The Trial of Jesus of Nazareth*, pp. 87–92; M. Goguel, *Jesus and the Origins of Christianity*, Vol. II, p. 512; Haim Cohn, *The Trial and Death of Jesus*, pp. 97 ff.; and many other writers.

2   One argument often urged against the authenticity of the trial, however, must be rejected. This is that Jesus was convicted of blasphemy by his own confession, whereas confession was not admissible as evidence in Jewish law. Jesus is represented not as *confessing* blasphemy, but as actually perpetrating it in court, so that the members of the Sanhedrin themselves were the witnesses.

3   Actually there is no instance in the entire Jewish literature of any person being indicted for declaring himself to be God, and it is probable that such an individual would have been regarded as a harmless lunatic. Some Talmudic passages, based on Christian sources of information, refer to Jesus as one who "incited others to idolatry" (Sanhedrin 43a), but do not mention that the object of such idolatry was himself, this detail evidently being regarded as too bizarre for credence. "Blasphemy" (Hebrew, *"gidduf"*) was the offence of cursing God, of which Jesus was certainly never accused.

4   See Haim Cohn, *op. cit.*, pp. 346–350; Paul Winter, *op. cit.*, p. 10 and p. 154; S. G. F. Brandon, *op. cit.*, p. 92; H. Mantel, *Studies in the History of the Sanhedrin*, pp. 254–265.

5   The execution of James, the brother of Jesus (Josephus, *Antiq.* XX. ix. 1), and the trial of Paul, also show that the Sanhedrin had the power of capital punishment. The "trial" of Stephen seems to have been nothing more than a mob-lynching.

NOTES ON CHAPTER 15. BARABBAS

1 Mk.: ". . . the man known as Barabbas was then in custody with the rebels who had committed murder in the rising."
Mt.: "There was then in custody a notable man called Jesus Bar-Abbas."
Lk.: "This man had been put into prison for a rising that had taken place in the city, and for murder."

2 S. G. F. Brandon, *The Trial of Jesus of Nazareth*, p. 102.

3 A. E. J. Rawlinson, *The Gospel According to St Mark* (London, 1925), pp. 227 f. See also Joel Carmichael, *The Death of Jesus*, (London, 1963) p. 146.

4 Paul Winter, *On the Trial of Jesus* (Berlin, 1961), pp. 91–99.

5 See H. Z. Maccoby, "Jesus and Barabbas," *New Test. Stud.*, 16, pp. 55–60.

NOTES ON CHAPTER 16. WRITING THE GOSPELS

1 For various reasons, the dates 29, 30 or 33 are thought the most probable for Jesus's arrest and death. If the argument of this book is correct, 33 is the most probable for his arrest, as this was a Seventh Year. If Jesus was in fact kept in prison for six months after his arrest, as argued on p. 132 ff., he was executed in the spring of 34 A.D. (That 33 was a Seventh Year can be calculated from Josephus's statement in *Antiquities*, 14. 475, that 37 B.C. was one.)

2 Cicero, *Pro Flacco*, 69; Seneca, *Epist.*, 95, 47.

3 *Decline and Fall of the Roman Empire*, Chapter xv.

4 Hegesippus, preserved in Eusebius, *Hist. eccl.* 23. 11–18.

5 *Acts* v. 37. Gamaliel likens the case of the Nazarenes to that of Judas the Galilean and Theudas, both insurrec-

tionist leaders. The whole passage makes sense only on
the basis that the Nazarenes were regarded as a threat to
Roman power.

6   Josephus, *Antiq.* XX. ix. 1. The Pharisees are not
    explicitly named, but "those who seemed the equitable of
    the citizens, and such as were the most uneasy at the
    breach of the laws" cannot be other than the Pharisees,
    especially when acting in opposition to a High Priest
    explicitly described by Josephus as a Sadducee.

7   *Acts*, iv. 7.

8   *Acts*, ix. 1. It is doubtful that Paul was ever a Pharisee. If
    he had been, he would have had the same tolerant attitude
    towards the Nazarenes as was shown by his alleged
    teacher, Gamaliel.

9   This Epistle calls the community a "synagogue" instead of
    using the Gentile-Christian term "ecclesia." It combats
    fiercely the Pauline doctrine of justification by faith,
    saying "faith without works is dead." It attacks the vices of
    the rich, thus aligning itself with the radical anti-rich
    policies of the Zealots. It is purely monotheistic and
    contains no Pauline Christology or Gnosticism. Luther
    excluded this Epistle from the canon on doctrinal
    grounds.

10 One of the objects of *Acts* is to minimise the conflict
    between Paul and the Nazarenes of Jerusalem. We see,
    however, from Galatians ii. 11 ff. that Paul quarrelled
    seriously with the elders of the Jerusalem Church. *Acts*
    gives an idealised version of this conflict (xv), and claims
    that it was decided in Paul's favour, and that Paul's
    mission to the Gentiles was given the blessing of the
    Jerusalem elders. That this was not so is shown by the
    Ebionite (Nazarene) hostility to Paul, and by the much-
    disguised version of the final break between Paul and
    James in *Acts* xvi.

11 The story that the Jewish Christians left Jerusalem in a

body for Pella in the middle of the siege has been convincingly refuted by S. G. F. Brandon (*Jesus and the Zealots*, pp. 208–216), and shown to be a late legend, designed to provide continuity for the Jerusalem (Gentile-Christian) Church which settled in the ruins of the city, re-named Aelia Capitolina, after the Hadrianic disaster in 135 A.D.

12   The 2nd century Christian writer Irenaeus testifies that Mark's Gospel was written after the Neronian persecution of 64 A.D. It could not have been written later than about 75 A.D. since the Gospels of Matthew and Luke, attested for about 80 A.D., were based on it, and time must be allowed for its dissemination. The only real question is whether *Mark* was written during the Jewish War or after it had ended. Relevant here is the interpretation of ch. xiii, which may or may not presuppose knowledge of the destruction of the Temple in 70 A.D. For the purposes of the enquiry of this book, it does not matter whether *Mark* was written during the War or after it; Jewish obloquy began as soon as the War started. The balance of argument seems to be for the later date.

NOTES ON CHAPTER 17.   THE DUALISM OF THE NEW TESTAMENT

1   The emphasis in the Gospels on evil spirits is probably derived, as suggested earlier, from the belief in evil spirits characteristic of Galilean rabbis and healers. However, the paranoiac scheme by which the demons are organised in a Kingdom of Satan or Beelzebub (see, e.g. Mt. xii. 24) is un-Jewish and is a later Gnostic development of the story. In the Old Testament there is no mention of evil spirits as independent entities. On a rare occasion when an evil spirit is mentioned (I Samuel, xvii. 23), it is called "the evil spirit from God." In the Mishnah, Satan is not even mentioned; and in the Talmud, he is a minor angel, who does nothing without orders from God—he is a kind of prosecuting counsel, whose task is to urge the case against sinful humanity (though traces of a more dualistic doctrine do appear from time to time).

Selected Bibliography

The Authorized Daily Prayer Book. Edited by S. Singer. Many editions.

The Babylonian Talmud in English. Vols. I-XXXVI. Edited by I. Epstein. London: Soncino Press, 1935-53.

Documents of the Christian Church. 2d ed. Edited by Henry Bettenson. London: Oxford University Press, 1968.

The Mishnah. Translated by Herbert Danby. London: Oxford University Press, 1933.

The Works of Josephus. Translated by William Whiston. Edited by D. S. Margoliouth. London: Myers and Co., 1906.

Aberbach, Moses. *The Roman-Jewish War (66-70 A.D.): Its Origin and Consequences* (Jewish Quarterly publ.). London: Golub, 1966.

Abrahams, Israel. *Studies in Pharisaism and the Gospels*. Rev. ed. Library of Biblical Studies. New York: Ktav Publishing House, Inc., 1968.

Baeck, Leo. *The Essence of Judaism*. Rev. ed. New York: Schocken Books, Inc., 1961.

Bevan, Edwyn. *Jerusalem under the High-Priests*. London: Arnold, 1912.

Bevan, E. R., and Singer, C. *The Legacy of Israel*. London: Oxford University Press, 1927.

Brandon, S. G. F. *Jesus and the Zealots*. New York: Charles Scribner's Sons, 1968.

———. *The Trial of Jesus of Nazareth*. Briarcliff Manor, N.Y.: Stein & Day, 1968.

Bultmann, Rudolf. *Primitive Christianity*. Translated by R. H. Fuller. New York: Merriam World, 1956.

Cohn, Haim. *The Trial and Death of Jesus*. New York: Harper & Row, 1971.

Davies, W. D. *Paul and Rabbinic Judaism*. London: The Society for Promoting Christian Knowledge, 1965.

Finkelstein, L. *The Pharisees*. Rev. ed. Philadelphia: Jewish Publication Society of America, 1961.

Goguel, M. *Jesus and the Origins of Christianity*. London: George Allen & Unwin Ltd., 1960.

Graetz, H. *History of the Jews*. Philadelphia: Jewish Publication Society of America, 1933.

Grant, F. C. *The Gospels: Their Origin and Their Growth*. London: Faber and Faber Ltd., 1959.

Grant, Robert. *A Historical Introduction to the New Testament*. New York: Harper & Row, 1963.

Graves, Robert, and Podro, Joshua. *The Nazarene Gospel Restored*. London: Cassell Ltd., 1953.

Herford, R. Travers. *The Pharisees*. Boston: Beacon Press, 1962.

Idelsohn, A. Z. *The Jewish Liturgy and Its Development*. New York: Schocken Books, Inc., 1967.

Irstam, Tor. *The King of Ganda: Studies in the Institution of Sacred Kingship of Africa*. 1944. Reprint. Westport, Conn.: Negro Universities Press.

Kautsky, Karl. *Foundations of Christianity*. Translated by Henry F. Mins. New York: Russell & Russell, 1953.

Klausner, Joseph. *Jesus of Nazareth*. Translated by Herbert Danby. London: George Allen & Unwin Ltd., 1929.

Lightfoot, R. H. *St. John's Gospel: a Commentary*. London: Oxford University Press, 1956.

Maccoby, Hyam. "Jesus and Barabbas." *New Testament Studies* 16:55-60.

———. "Is the Political Jesus Dead?" *Encounter*, February 1976.

Macrae, G. "Nag Hammadi." In *The Interpreter's Dictionary of the Bible*, Supplementary Volume. Nashville: Abingdon Press, 1976.

Montefiore, C. G., and Loewe, H. J. *A Rabbinic Anthology*. London: Macmillan, 1938.

Moore, George Foot. *Judaism in the First Centuries of the Christian Era*. Cambridge, Mass.: Harvard University Press, 1927.

Murray, Gilbert. *Five Stages of Greek Religion*. New York: Doubleday & Co., Anchor Books, 1955.

Parkes, James. *The Foundations of Judaism and Christianity*. London: Vallentine Mitchell & Co. Ltd., 1960.

Patai, Raphael. "Hebrew Installation Rites." *Hebrew Union College Annual* 20 (1947).

Perowne, Stewart. *The Life and Times of Herod the Great*. Nashville: Abingdon Press, 1959.

Pfeiffer, Robert H. *History of New Testament Times*. 1949. Reprint. Westport, Conn.: Greenwood Press, Inc., 1972.

Radin, M. *The Jews among the Greeks and Romans*. 1915. Reprint. The Jewish People: History, Religion, Literature Series. New York: Arno Press.

Rawlinson, A. E. J. *The Gospel according to St. Mark*. London: Methuen & Co. Ltd., 1925.

Roth, C. *A Short History of the Jewish People*. 1969. Reprint. Bridgeport, Conn.: Hartmore House, 1970.

Sanders, E. P. *Paul and Palestinian Judaism*. Philadelphia: Fortress Press, 1977.

Schechter, S. *Studies in Judaism*. New York: Atheneum Publishers, Temple Books, 1970.

Schurer, Emil. *History of the Jewish People in the Time of Jesus*. Edited by Nahum N. Glatzer. New York: Schocken Books, 1961.

Schweitzer, A. *The Quest of the Historical Jesus*. New York: Macmillan, 1968. The work that first stressed the importance of apocalypticism in Jesus's teaching.

Strack, Herman L. *Introduction to the Talmud and Midrash*. New York: Atheneum Publishers, Temple Books, 1969.

Vermes, G. *The Dead Sea Scrolls in English*. New York: Penguin Books, Inc., Pelican Book, 1962.

Wells, G. A. *The Jesus of the Early Christians*. Buffalo: Prometheus Books, 1971.

Wilson, R. M. *Gnosis and the New Testament*. Philadelphia: Fortress Press, 1968.

Winter, Paul. *On the Trial of Jesus*. 2d ed. Edited by T. A. Burkill and G. Vermes. Studia Judaica, Vol. 1. Hawthorne, N.Y.: Walter De Gruyter, Inc., 1973.

Wright, Ernest G. *God Who Acts* (Old Testament) London: S.C.M. Press Ltd., 1952.

Zeitlin, S. *The History of the Second Jewish Commonwealth*. Philadelphia: Jewish Publication Society of America, 1933.

Index of Quotations

General Index

Hosanna, day of, 153
Humanism, 193–4
Human sacrifice, 87
Hyrcanus, 26, 27, 29

Incarnation, 194–5
India, 48
Irenaeus, 218, 239
Irstam, Tor, 232
Isaiah, 78, 79
"Iscariot," 202, 231
Isis, 87

James, brother of Jesus, 122, 168,
    177, 180, 202–3, 232, 236
James, Epistle of, 180, 238
James, son of Zebedee, 121, 128
James the Less, 122
Jamnia, 173
Jehoshaphat, valley of, 235
Jehovah (in Gnosticism), 88
Jerome, 218
Jerusalem
    besieged by Pompey, 27
    pilgrimages to, 29
    attacked by Sabinus, 33–4
    Roman garrison, 42
    standards brought in by Pilate,
        46
    visit of Queen Helen of Adia-
        bene, 86
    captured by Titus, 173–4
Jerusalem Church, 182, 203
Jesus
    overturns tables of money-
        changers, 15
    Triumphal Entry, 14–16, 125,
        131–7, 233
    rejected by crowd, 16

    ignores Roman Occupation,
        23
    basic elements of career, 93
    alleged blasphemy, 97, 155–7,
        236
    alleged clashes with Pharisees,
        97–8
    as Pharisee, 98, 105–9, 117,
        203–6
    an activist, 99–101, 113
    and the tribute, 100
    death not voluntary, 103, 154
    childhood, 104–5
    descent from David, 105
    highly educated, 105–6
    as carpenter, 104, 106
    alleged pacifism, 109–10
    as Prophet, 111, 113–14,
        116 ff.
    as miracle-healer, 115, 216–17
    on reprentance, 118–19
    vision of Last Days, 119–20
    not a Zealot, 120
    alleged isolation from the
        Jews, 121–22
    as King, 122 ff.
    resurrection, 124
    Coronation, 126–9, 140–1, 232
    Transfiguration, 126–9, 230,
        232–3
    and the fig tree, 133
    Cleansing of Temple, 135,
        139–40
    threat to destroy Temple,
        135–6
    Last Supper, 141–2
    precious ointment, 140
    "manic" character, 144–5
    agony in the garden, 146–9
    arrest, 151 ff.
    trial, 155 ff.